The Best Home Study Guide

CDL

Commercial Driver License Examination

Staff of Research & Education Association

Research & Education Association
61 Ethel Road West
Piscataway, New Jersey 08854

The Best Home Study Guide for the
CDL — *Commercial Driver License Examination*

Printed in the United States of America

Library of Congress Control Number 2005903122

International Standard Book Number 0-87891-109-X

Research & Education Association, Inc.
61 Ethel Road West
Piscataway, New Jersey 08854

CONTENTS

PART III — CDL SKILLS TEST REVIEW

PART IV — PRACTICE KNOWLEDGE TESTS

ABOUT RESEARCH & EDUCATION ASSOCIATION

Founded in 1959, Research & Education Association is dedicated to publishing the finest and most effective educational materials—including software, study guides, and test preps—for students in middle school, high school, college, graduate school, and beyond.

REA's Test Preparation series includes books and software for all academic levels in almost all disciplines. Research & Education Association publishes test preps for students who have not yet completed high school, as well as high school students preparing to enter college. Students from countries around the world seeking to attend college in the United States will find the assistance they need in REA's publications. For college students seeking advanced degrees, REA publishes test preps for many major graduate school admission examinations in a wide variety of disciplines, including engineering, law, and medicine. Students at every level, in every field, with every ambition can find what they are looking for among REA's publications.

REA's practice tests are always based upon the most recently administered exams, and include every type of question that you can expect on the actual exams.

REA's publications and educational materials are highly regarded and continually receive an unprecedented amount of praise from professionals, instructors, librarians, parents, and students. Our authors are as diverse as the fields represented in the books we publish. They are well known in their respective disciplines and serve on the faculties of prestigious high schools, colleges, and universities throughout the United States and Canada.

Today, REA's wide-ranging catalog is a leading resource for teachers, students, and professionals. We invite you to visit us at *www.rea.com* to find out how "REA is making the world smarter."

ACKNOWLEDGMENTS

We would like to thank REA's Larry B. Kling, VP, Editorial, for supervising development; Pam Weston, VP, Publishing, for setting the quality standards for production integrity and managing the publication to completion; Cristina Kollet for coordinating development; Jeanne Audino, Senior Editor, for preflight editorial review; Diane Goldschmidt, Associate Editor, for post-production quality assurance; and Christine Saul, Senior Graphic Artist, for cover design. We also extend thanks to the U.S. Department of Transportation, the motor vehicle agencies of the 50 states and the District of Columbia, along with the Canadian Ministry of Transportation. Network Typesetting, Inc., typeset the manuscript.

The Commercial Driver License Exam

Preparing for the CDL

PART I: INTRODUCTION

Chapter 1 – ABOUT THIS BOOK

Since April 1, 1992, all drivers of Commercial Motor Vehicles (CMV's) in the United States have been required to have a Commercial Driver License. In order to get this special license, you must first take and pass the required knowledge and skills tests. Using this book correctly will prepare you to take and pass these tests.

This book is made up of four parts. The first part introduces the Commercial Driver Licensing Tests and helps you figure out which tests you will have to take. The second part reviews the material that will be on the Commercial Driver Licensing Knowledge Tests. The third part reviews the material that will be on the Commercial Driver Licensing Skills Tests. Finally, the fourth part contains one General Knowledge practice test, one practice test for each of the five Endorsement Tests, and one Air Brakes Test. All of these tests are representative of the actual Commercial Driver Licensing Knowledge Tests in both content and format.

Each practice test is followed by an answer key, and each correct answer is explained in detail. We provide detailed explanations so you can see not only why one answer is right, but also why the other answer choices are wrong. By reviewing the material for both the Knowledge Tests and the Skills Test, taking the General Knowledge practice test and any other practice Endorsement Tests that apply to your vehicle type, and studying the explanations of the correct answers for the practice tests, you can find out how well you are prepared for the actual Commercial Driver Licensing tests and what material you need to review again.

THE COMMERCIAL MOTOR VEHICLE SAFETY ACT OF 1986 AND THE COMMERCIAL DRIVER LICENSE

On October 26, 1986, Congress passed the Commercial Motor Vehicle Safety Act of 1986. The purpose of the Safety Act is to help reduce or prevent truck and bus accidents, deaths, and injuries. This will be done by requiring all truck and bus drivers to have a single Commercial Motor Vehicle Driver License and by disqualifying drivers who operate commercial motor vehicles in an unsafe manner.

By law, each state must now meet the same minimum standards for commercial driver licensing. The standards require every person who operates a Commercial Motor Vehicle in interstate, foreign, or intrastate commerce to get a Commercial

Driver License. Once you get a Commercial Driver License you are obligated to return to the state any and all non-CDL driver licenses that you hold.

Classes of License:

The Federal standard requires States to issue a CDL to drivers according to the following license classifications:

Class A – Any combination of vehicles with a GVWR of 26,001 or more pounds provided the GVWR of the vehicle(s) being towed is in excess of 10,000 pounds.

Class B – Any single vehicle with a GVWR of 26,001 or more pounds, or any such vehicle towing a vehicle not in excess of 10,000 pounds GVWR.

Class C – Any single vehicle, or combination of vehicles, that does not meet the definition of Class A or Class B, but is either designed to transport 16 or more passengers, including the driver, or is placarded for hazardous materials.

(Your state may have additional definitions of CMV's.)

CDL EXEMPTIONS

Drivers of the following vehicles which otherwise meet the definition of a CMV are exempt from the CDL requirement:

– A vehicle with a GVWR of more than 26,000 pounds, owned and controlled by a farmer and used to transport agricultural products, farm machinery, or farm products within 150 miles of the farm.

– A vehicle primarily designed for purposes other than the transportation of persons or property, such as certain construction vehicles.

– Fire and police vehicles, operated by authorized personnel.

– Military vehicles when operated by members of the armed forces on active duty.

– Personal vehicles (including rental vehicles up to 26,000 pounds) when operated strictly and exclusively to transport personal possessions or family members for noncommercial purposes.

– A tow truck with a GVWR of 26,000 pounds or less which tows disabled Commercial Motor Vehicles with a GVWR of more than 10,000 pounds for a distance of less than 10 miles.

Other important Safety Act rules that resulted from the Commercial Motor Vehicle Safety Act of 1986 are listed on Pages 11, 12 and 13.

THE CDL TESTS

To get a CDL you must take and pass two kinds of tests:

(1) **Knowledge Tests** and

(2) **Skills Test**.

The Knowledge Tests are written tests that must be taken in your home state. You should contact your nearest Motor Vehicle Department for information regarding location, cost, time allotment, and date of each Knowledge Test that you need to take, as these details differ from state to state.

Once you pass the required Knowledge Tests, you may take the Skills Test. This is an "on the road," or driving, test which must be taken in your home state and in the type of vehicle you wish to be licensed to drive. The Skills Test is usually given by appointment only, as an examiner must be scheduled to ride with you over an approved course. Once again, contact the nearest Motor Vehicle Department in your state of residency for information regarding location, cost, time allotment, and appointment set-up for the Skills Test.

THE KNOWLEDGE TESTS

There are a total of seven Knowledge Tests: one General Knowledge test, five Endorsement Tests, and one Air Brakes Test. This may seem like a lot, but don't worry. Most drivers will only have to take three or four tests. Each of the seven Knowledge Tests will be scored separately.

Which tests should I take?

THE GENERAL KNOWLEDGE TEST

All applicants for a CDL must take the GENERAL KNOWLEDGE TEST. This test assesses your knowledge of the general safety rules that must be followed while driving Commercial Motor Vehicles and while transporting cargo of all types.

In addition to the General Knowledge Test, you may have to take one or more Endorsement Tests and/or the Air Brakes Test depending on what type of vehicle you wish to be licensed to drive.

THE ENDORSEMENT TESTS

There are five Endorsement Tests. Each one tests your knowledge of a particular type of Commercial Motor Vehicle. If you drive or plan to drive one of the specialized vehicles listed, you must take the corresponding test:

If you want to drive...	*you must take the...*
a bus	PASSENGER TRANSPORT TEST
a combination or Class A vehicle	COMBINATION VEHICLES TEST
any vehicle that hauls hazardous materials or waste	HAZARDOUS MATERIALS TEST
any vehicle designed to haul liquids in bulk	TANKER TEST
a tractor pulling double or triple trailers	DOUBLES/TRIPLES TEST

For each Endorsement Test that you take and pass, a special marking, or endorsement, will be placed on your CDL. This marking will indicate to others that you are qualified, or authorized, to drive that particular type of commercial motor vehicle.

THE AIR BRAKES TEST

The Air Brakes Test must be taken if you drive or plan to drive any Commercial Motor Vehicle equipped with air brakes. Unlike the five Endorsement Tests, however, the Air Brakes Test works as a restriction rather than an endorsement. If you fail the Air Brakes Test or take the Skills Test in a vehicle not equipped with air brakes, your CDL will bear a mark of restriction. This restriction mark will indicate to others that you are not qualified, or are unauthorized, to drive a Commercial Motor Vehicle with air brakes.

(For more information on how Endorsements and the Air Brakes Restriction will appear on your CDL, see "What will my Commercial Driver License look like?" on page 9.)

NOTE: For additional assistance in determining which tests you need to take and which sections of this book you need to study, see "How to Use This Book" on page 13.

Which class of vehicles will I be licensed to drive?

The class of vehicle (A, B, or C) that your CDL permits you to drive depends on two factors: (1) the Endorsement Tests that you take, and (2) the class of vehicle in which you take your Skills Test. If, once you have obtained a CDL, you wish to drive a commercial motor vehicle from a different vehicle class than the one indicated on your CDL, you will be required to retake and pass all related tests, except in the following situations:

A)   If you have passed the Knowledge and Skills tests for a combination vehicle (Class A), you may operate a heavy, straight vehicle (Class B) or a small vehicle (Class C) as long as you already have the appropriate endorsements on your CDL and your license is not restricted for Air Brakes.

B)   If you have passed the Knowledge and Skills tests for a heavy, straight vehicle (Class B), you may operate any small vehicle (Class C) as long as you already have the appropriate endorsements on your CDL and your license is not restricted for Air Brakes.

NOTE: To drive a motorcycle or Class A limited use motorcycle, you must have a motorcycle license.

What will the CDL Knowledge Tests be like?

All Knowledge Tests are multiple-choice, and each question has four answer choices. For the majority of the questions on each test, you will be required to do one of the following:

a) complete a sentence,

EXAMPLE: When looking ahead of your vehicle while driving you should look

(A)   to the left side of the road.

(B)   back and forth, near and far.

(C)   straight ahead at all times.

(D)   to the right side of the road.

ANSWER: (B)

b) answer a simple question,

EXAMPLE: What should you do when your vehicle hydroplanes?

(A)   Accelerate slightly   (C)   Release the accelerator

(B)   Counter-steer hard   (D)   Start stab braking

ANSWER: (C)

c) or answer the question "Which of the following...?"

EXAMPLE: Which of the following is a good thing to remember when crossing traffic in a heavy vehicle?

(A)   Because heavy vehicles are easy to see, you can count on other drivers to move out of your way or slow down for you

(B)   Heavy vehicles need larger gaps in traffic than cars

(C)   The best way to cross traffic is to pull the vehicle partway across the road and block one lane while waiting for the other to clear

(D)   The heavier your load, the smaller the gap needed to cross traffic

ANSWER: (B)

A smaller number of the questions on each test require you to:

a) fill in the blank,

EXAMPLE: The driver must be able to see a warning before air pressure, in the service air tanks, falls below _____ psi.

(A)   40   (C)   60

(B)   50   (D)   80

ANSWER: (C)

b) or use a diagram or illustration to answer.

EXAMPLE: When you are driving a truck/bus that cannot make a right turn without swinging into another lane, which diagram shows the correct path you should follow?

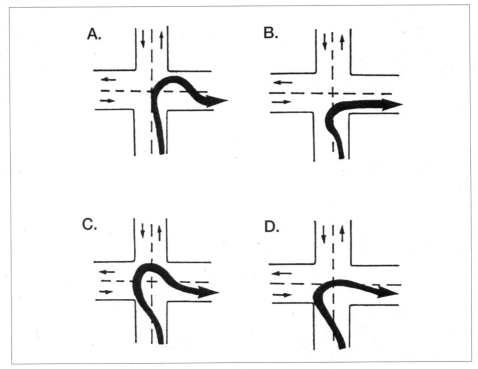

ANSWER: (A)

No matter what the question type, each question will only have one correct answer. You may, however, find questions that include "all of the above" or "none of the above" as answer choices.

You will probably be asked to mark your answer choices for each test on an answer sheet that is separate from the test itself. The answer sheet will most likely require you to darken the circle or oval of the correct answer choice. This preparation guide uses such answer sheets. Be aware, however, that each state is allowed to format its own answer sheet. The CDL test(s) you actually take may have a slightly different design from the practice tests included in this book.

How many questions will be on the test and how can I score a passing grade?

The seven Knowledge Tests do vary in the number of questions asked. No matter what test you are taking, you must answer 80% of the questions correctly to receive a passing grade. If you do not get 80% of the questions correct, you will fail the test and you will have to take it again. Below is a chart listing the number of questions on each test according to the Motor Vehicle Administrator's MODEL Test. The chart also lists the number of questions you must answer correctly in order to pass.

KNOWLEDGE TEST	# OF QUESTIONS	80% CORRECT
GENERAL KNOWLEDGE TEST	50	40
PASSENGER TRANSPORT TEST	20	16
COMBINATION VEHICLES TEST	20	16
HAZARDOUS MATERIALS TEST	30	24
TANKER TEST	20	16
DOUBLES/TRIPLES TEST	20	16
AIR BRAKES TEST	25	20

The same number of questions can be expected on the knowledge tests in your home state. However, the United States Department of Transportation does allow states to modify the CDL Test. Therefore, the General Knowledge Test may ask as few as 30 questions, and the five Endorsement Tests and the Air Brakes Test can contain from 20 to 30 questions each.

All the practice tests in this preparation guide—except Hazardous Materials—have *more* than the required number of questions in order to give you extra practice. The explanations that follow the answer key of each test clearly show you why one answer choice is right, and why the other answer choices are incorrect. Additionally, at the end of each Knowledge Test we include a chart, similar to the one you see below, to help you determine whether you would have been in the passing, borderline, or failing range had the practice test been an actual CDL test. The chart below lists the number of questions on each of REA's practice tests as well as the number of questions you would need to answer correctly in order to receive a passing grade:

KNOWLEDGE TEST	# OF QUESTIONS	80% CORRECT
GENERAL KNOWLEDGE TEST	100	80
PASSENGER TRANSPORT TEST	30	24
COMBINATION VEHICLE TEST	30	24
HAZARDOUS MATERIALS TEST	30	24
TANKER TEST	30	24
DOUBLES/TRIPLES TEST	30	24
AIR BRAKES TEST	30	24

Will guessing help me?

Since both incorrect answers and answer spaces left blank are counted as wrong, it is in your best interest to guess when you are unsure. Even if you really have no idea what the correct answer is, there is more of a chance of answering correctly if you guess than if you leave an answer space blank. In general, you won't be any worse off by guessing since it is likely that you will answer some of the questions you are unsure of correctly.

In order to improve your chances of guessing correctly, try to immediately eliminate the answer choices you recognize as wrong and focus only on the choices that remain. Ruling out two or three choices in a question will increase your chances of choosing the correct answer and will, therefore, help to raise your score.

You should answer every question on each test even if you have to guess the answer. Remember, however, that guessing is your last resort. Even though guessing can help to improve your score, it cannot take the place of being well prepared.

Is there any other way to take the Commercial Driver License Knowledge Tests?

The American Association of Motor Vehicle Administrators is currently developing oral versions of the CDL Knowledge Tests. However, these oral tests will be offered only to functionally illiterate drivers.

What will my Commercial Driver License look like ?

Your Commercial Driver License will be a document bearing the following information:

(1) A statement that it is a "Commercial Driver License" or "CDL."

(2) Your full name, signature, and mailing address.

(3) Information, physical and otherwise, to identify and describe you, including date of birth (month, day, year), sex, and height.

(4) A color photograph of you.

(5) Your state license number.

(6) The name of the state that issued your license.

(7) The dates of issuance and expiration.

(8) The class or classes of CMV(s) that you are authorized to operate, indicated as follows:

A for combination vehicle.
B for heavy straight vehicle.
C for small vehicle.

(9)   Drivers who operate special types of CMVs also need to pass additional tests to obtain any of the following endorsements on their CDL:

T – Double/Triple Trailers (Knowledge Test only)
P – Passenger (Knowledge and Skills Tests)
N – Tank Vehicle (Knowledge Test only)
H – Hazardous Materials (Knowledge Test only)
X – Combination of Tank Vehicle and Hazardous Materials

If a driver either fails the air brake component of the general knowledge test or performs the skills test in a vehicle not equipped with air brakes, the driver is issued an air brake restriction, restricting the driver from operating a CMV equipped with air brakes.

Your state may use additional codes for additional groupings of endorsements as long as the codes are explained on the front or back of the CDL.

(10)   If the CDL is a Nonresident CDL, "Nonresident CDL" must be stated on the CDL.

THE SKILLS TEST

Once you have taken and passed the required Knowledge Tests, you may take the Commercial Driver Licensing Skills Test, which is divided into three parts. The Skills Test is an "on the road," or driving test. The purpose of this test is for you to show the examiner that you have the necessary skills to inspect, maneuver, and drive the Commercial Motor Vehicle for which you wish to obtain a license.

The three different parts of the CDL Skills Test are briefly described below. A more detailed description of the Skills Test can be found in PART III—CDL Skills Test Review, which begins on page 173. Keep in mind that you must take all three tests in the type of vehicle you want to be licensed to drive.

Part I—PRE-TRIP INSPECTION

Purpose: To see if you know whether the vehicle is safe to drive.

Test Procedure: You will be asked to do a pre-trip inspection of your vehicle or to explain to the examiner what you would inspect and why. The examiner will mark on a scoring form each item that you correctly inspect or explain. (If the vehicle fails the Pre-trip Inspection because it is unsafe, your test will not be completed, and you will have to schedule a new test with a safe vehicle.)

Part II—BASIC CONTROL SKILLS

Purpose: To evaluate your basic skills in controlling the vehicle.

Test Procedure: The test set-up consists of various exercises marked out by lines, traffic cones, or something similar. The exercises will include moving the vehicle forward, backing, parallel parking, and performing turning maneuvers. The examiner will explain to you how each exercise is to be done. You will be scored on how well you stay within the exercise boundaries and on how many pull-ups or corrections you make.

Part III—THE ROAD TEST

Purpose: To evaluate your ability to drive safely in a variety of on-the-road situations.

Test Procedure: The test drive is taken over a route specified by the examiner. It will include left and right turns, intersections, railway crossings, curves, up and down grades, rural or semi-rural roads, city multi-lane streets, and expressway driving. You will drive the test route following instructions given by the examiner. The examiner will score specific tasks such as turns, merging into traffic, lane changes, and speed control, at specific places along the route. The examiner will also score whether you correctly do tasks such as signalling, searching for hazards, controlling speed, and lane positioning.

You will be told whether or not you passed at the end of the Road Test. You will automatically fail the Skills Test if you have an accident, commit a serious traffic violation, or take a dangerous action during the Road Test.

OTHER SAFETY ACT RULES

There are other new Commercial Motor Vehicle Safety Act rules which affect drivers.

- You cannot have more than one license. If you break this rule, a court may fine you up to $5,000 or put you in jail. Keep your home state license and return any others.

- If you are an experienced commercial driver and have a safe driving record, you may not need to take the Skills Test to transfer your CDL to another state. Check with your driver licensing authorities.

- You must notify your employer within 30 days of a conviction for any traffic violation (except parking). This is true regardless of the type of vehicle you were driving when the violation occurred.

- You must notify your motor vehicle licensing agency within 30 days if you are convicted in any other state of any traffic violation (except parking). This is true regardless of the type of vehicle you were driving when the violation occurred.

- You must notify your employer if your license is suspended, revoked, or cancelled, or if you are disqualified from driving.

- When applying for any commercial driving job, you must give your employer information on all driving jobs you have held for the past 10 years.

- As of April 1, 1992, no one may drive a Commercial Motor Vehicle without a CDL. A court may fine you up to $5,000 or put you in jail for breaking this rule.

- Your employer cannot let you drive any Commercial Motor Vehicle if you have more than one license or if your CDL is suspended or revoked. A court may fine the employer up to $5,000 or put him/her in jail for breaking this rule.

- All states will be connected to one computerized system to share information about CDL drivers. The states will check on drivers' accident records and be sure that drivers do not get more than one CDL.

Disqualifications:

- For conviction while driving a CMV, drivers must be disqualified and lose their privilege to drive for 60 to 120 days.

- Two or more serious traffic violations within a 3-year period. These include excessive speeding, reckless driving, improper or erratic lane changes, following the vehicle ahead too closely, and traffic offenses in connection with fatal traffic accidents: 90 days to 5 years.

- One or more violations of an out-of-service order within a 10-year period: 1 year.

- Driving under the influence of a controlled substance or alcohol; or Leaving the scene of an accident; or Using a CMV to commit a felony: 3 years.

- Any of the 1-year offenses while operating a CMV that is placarded for hazardous materials: Life.

- Second offense of any of the 1-year or 3-year offenses; or Using a CMV to commit a felony involving manufacturing, distributing, or dispensing controlled substances.

- States have the option to reduce certain lifetime disqualifications to a minimum disqualification period of 10 years if the driver completes a driver rehabilitation program approved by the State.

- If a CDL holder is disqualified from operating a CMV, the State may issue him/her a license to operate non-CMVs. Drivers who are disqualified from operating a CMV can not be issued a "conditional" or "hardship" CDL or any other type of limited driving privileges to continue driving a CMV.

- For disqualifications purposes, convictions for out-of-state violations will be treated the same as convictions for violations that are committed in the home State. The CDLIS will ensure that convictions a driver receives outside his or her home State are transmitted to the home State so that the disqualifications can be applied.

- If you are driving when your blood alcohol concentration is 0.04 percent or more, you are driving under the influence of alcohol. You will lose your CDL for one year for your first offense. You will lose it for life for your second offense. If your blood alcohol concentration is less than 0.04, and you have any detectable amount of alcohol in your bloodstream, you will be put out-of-service for 24 hours.

These rules will improve highway safety for you and for all highway users.

Your state may have additional rules which you must also obey.

HOW TO USE THIS BOOK

Refer to the following pages to determine your vehicle class and vehicle type. Then, read below those descriptions to determine which sections of this book to study and which of REA's practice tests to take.

NOTE: All drivers should also study Part III—CDL Skills Test Review.

CLASS A:

If you drive...

- a tractor trailer; or,

- a truck and trailer with a gross combination weight rating (GCWR) of 26,001 or more pounds, provided the GCWR of the vehicle being towed is more than 10,000 pounds...you need to have a Class A license. You also qualify to operate vehicles in Class B and Class C, provided you have the proper extra endorsements.

Read the INTRODUCTION and study these sections of PART II— CDL Knowledge Tests Review

Driving Safely
Transporting Cargo Safely
Air Brakes
Combination Vehicles
Doubles and Triples (if needed)
Tank Vehicles (if needed)
Hazardous Materials (if needed)

Take these practice tests in PART IV—Practice Knowledge Tests

General Knowledge
Air Brakes
Combination Vehicles
Doubles/Triples (if needed)
Tanker (if needed)
Hazardous Materials (if needed)

Endorsements

Most commercial motor vehicle operators will need to obtain at least one special endorsement. Each requires a separate test.

- **Double and Triple Trailer Endorsement:** Needed for operators of vehicles pulling two or three trailers. A Class A license is required to operate this type of vehicle.

- **Passenger Endorsement:** Needed for operators of all motor vehicles, including buses and limos, designed to transport 8 or more passengers for hire. Requires a road test. (Check with your state for special regulations.)

- **Tank Vehicle Endorsement:** Needed for operators of vehicles that transport liquids or gas in bulk.

- **Hazardous Materials Endorsement:** Needed for operators of vehicles transporting hazardous materials. Must be trained and retested every two years.

- **Air Brakes:** Needed for any vehicle equipped with air brakes. (Road test required.)

CLASS B:

If you drive...

- any vehicle with a gross vehicle weight rating (GVWR) of 26,001 or more pounds; or
- a vehicle with a gross vehicle weight rating of 26,001 or more pounds towing a trailer with a gross vehicle weight rating of less than 10,000 pounds; or
- a bus with a GVWR or 26,001 pounds or more designed to transport 16 or more passengers, including the driver...you need to have a Class B license. You also qualify to operate vehicles in Class C, provided you have the proper extra endorsements.

Read the INTRODUCTION and study these sections of PART II— CDL Knowledge Tests Review

Driving Safely
Transporting Cargo Safely
Air Brakes (if needed)
Transporting Passengers (if needed)*
Hazardous Materials (if needed)
Tank Vehicles (if needed)

Take these practice tests in PART IV—Practice Knowledge Tests

General Knowledge
Air Brakes (if needed)
Passengers Transport (if needed)
Hazardous Materials (if needed)
Tanker (if needed)

* Applicants for passenger endorsements must meet more exacting requirements than most commercial drivers. Check with your state's Department of Motor Vehicles for information on the specific requirements.

CLASS C:

If you drive...

- any vehicle with a GVWR of less than 26,001 pounds used and placarded to transport hazardous materials; or,
- any bus, including school buses, designed to carry 16 or more passengers, including the driver, **and** with a GVWR of less than 26,001 pounds and all school buses designed for 15 or less passengers, including the driver,
- any bus, limo or van which is used for hire, designed to transport 8 to 15 passengers, including the driver...you need to have a Class C license.

Read the INTRODUCTION and study these sections of PART II— CDL Knowledge Tests Review

Driving Safely
Transporting Cargo Safely
Transporting Passengers (if needed)
Hazardous Materials (if needed)
Tank Vehicles (if needed)

Take these practice tests in PART IV—Practice Knowledge Tests

General Knowledge
Passenger Transport (if needed)
Hazardous Materials (if needed)
Tanker (if needed)

PART II: CDL KNOWLEDGE TESTS REVIEW

Chapter 2 – Driving Safely

THIS CHAPTER COVERS

- ❏ Vehicle Inspection
- ❏ Vehicle Control
- ❏ Shifting Gears
- ❏ Seeing
- ❏ Communicating
- ❏ Speed & Space Management
- ❏ Night Driving
- ❏ Bad Weather Driving
- ❏ Mountain Driving
- ❏ Emergencies
- ❏ Staying Alert

This chapter contains general knowledge and safe driving practices which all commercial drivers should know. You must take a test on this information to get a commercial driver license.

This section does **not** contain information on air brakes, combination vehicles (tractor-semitrailer, doubles, triples, truck pulling heavy trailer) or buses. You must read other sections to get such information if it applies to the type of vehicle you wish to drive.

This section does have some information on hazardous materials. It is included so that you will know when you require a Hazardous Materials Endorsement. You will find the information you need to get this endorsement in Chapter 9.

2.1 VEHICLE INSPECTION

Why Inspect?

Safety. Safety is the most important and obvious reason. Inspecting your vehicle helps you to know your vehicle is safe.

Legal Requirements. Federal and state laws require inspection by the driver. Federal and state inspectors also inspect commercial vehicles. An unsafe vehicle can be put "out of service" until the driver or owner fixes it.

Types of Vehicle Inspection

Pre-trip Inspection. You should do a pre-trip inspection before each trip to find problems that could cause a crash or breakdown.

During a Trip. For safety you should:
- Watch gauges for signs of trouble.
- Use your senses to check for problems (look, listen, smell, feel).
- Check critical items when you stop:
    - Tires, wheels and rims.
    - Brakes.
    - Lights and reflectors.
    - Brake and electrical connections to trailer.
    - Trailer coupling devices.
    - Cargo securement devices.

After-Trip Inspection and Report. You do an after-trip inspection at the end of the trip, day, or tour of duty on each vehicle you operated. It may include filling out a **vehicle condition report** listing any problems you find. The inspection report helps the vehicle owner know when to fix something.

What to Look for

Tire Problems. It is dangerous to drive with bad tires. Look for problems such as:
- Too much or too little air pressure.
- Bad wear. You need at least 4/32 inch tread depth in every major groove on front wheels. You need 2/32 inch on other wheels. No fabric should show through the tread or sidewall.
- Cuts or other damage.
- Tread separation.
- Dual tires that come in contact with each other or parts of the vehicle.
- Mismatched sizes.
- Radial and bias-ply tires used together.
- Cut or cracked valve stems.
- Regrooved, recapped, or retreaded tires on the front wheels of a bus. These are prohibited.

Wheel and Rim Problems. Look for:

- Bad wheels or rims. These could cause an accident.
- Damaged rims. These can cause the tire to lose pressure or come off.
- Rust around wheel nuts may mean the nuts are loose—check tightness. After a tire has been changed, stop a short while later and recheck the tightness of the nuts.
- Missing clamps, spacers, studs, lugs means danger.
- Mismatched, bent, or cracked lock rings are dangerous.
- Wheels or rims that have had welding repairs are not safe.

Bad Brake Drums or Shoes. Look for:

- Cracked drums.
- Shoes or pads with oil, grease, brake fluid on them.
- Shoes worn dangerously thin, or missing or broken.

Steering System Defects. (See Figure 2-1) Check for:

- Missing nuts, bolts, cotter keys or other parts.
- Bent, loose, or broken parts, such as steering column, steering gear box, or tie rods.
- If power steering-equipped — hoses, pumps, and fluid level; check for leaks.
- Steering wheel play of more than 10 degrees (approximately 2 inches' movement at the rim of a 20-inch steering wheel). This can make it hard to steer.

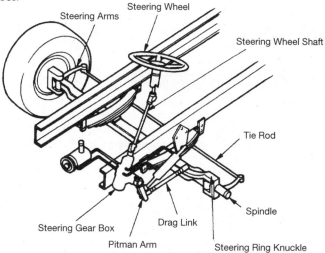

Figure 2-1 Examples of Steering System Key Parts

Suspension System Defects. The suspension system holds up the vehicle and its load. It keeps the axles in place. Therefore, broken suspension parts can be extremely dangerous. You should check for:

- Spring hangers (Figure 2-2) that allow movement of axle from proper position.
- Cracked or broken spring hangers.
- Missing or broken leaves in any leaf spring. If one-fourth or more are missing, it will put the vehicle "out of service," but any defect could be dangerous (Figure 2-3).
- Broken leaves in a multi-leaf spring or leaves that have shifted so they might hit a tire or other part.
- Leaking shock absorbers (Figure 2-4).
- Torque rod or arm, U-bolts, spring hangers, or other axle positioning parts that are cracked, damaged, or missing (Figures 2-2 and 2-4).
- Air suspension systems that are damaged and/or leaking.
- Any loose, cracked, broken, or missing frame members.

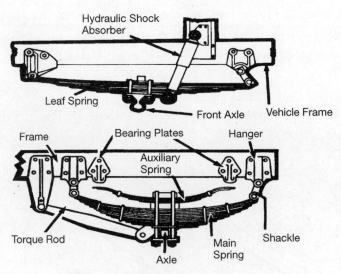

Figure 2-2 Key Suspension Parts

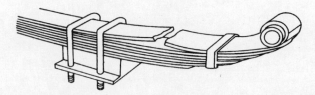

Figure 2-3 Safety Defect: Broken Leaf in Leaf Spring

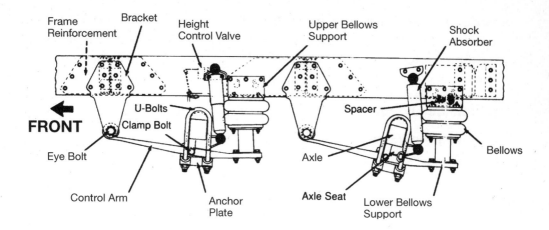

Figure 2-4 Air Suspension Parts

Exhaust System Defects. A broken exhaust system can let poisonous fumes into the cab or sleeper berth. You should check for:

- Loose, broken, or missing exhaust pipes, mufflers, tailpipes, or vertical stacks.
- Loose, broken, or missing mounting brackets, clamps, bolts, or nuts.
- Exhaust system parts rubbing against fuel system parts, tires, or other moving parts of vehicle.
- Exhaust system parts that are leaking.

Emergency Equipment. Vehicles should be equipped with emergency equipment:

- Fire extinguisher(s).
- Spare electrical fuses (unless equipped with circuit breakers).
- Warning devices for parked vehicles (for example, three reflective warning triangles).

Cargo (Trucks). You must inspect for cargo overloading and correct balance and securement before each trip. If the cargo contains hazardous materials, you must inspect for proper papers and placarding.

A Seven-Step Pre-Trip Inspection Method

Method of Inspecting. You should do a pre-trip inspection the same way each time so you will learn all the steps and be less likely to forget something. The following seven-step procedure should be a useful guide. Memory aids are shown in Figures 2-5, 2-6, and 2-7. They may help you remember important things to inspect. You can cut them out and bring them with you when you take your CDL test. When you take your test you must explain to the examiner what parts of the vehicle you are inspecting. Describe the possible defects you are looking for. It will help you pass the test if you practice this with a friend beforehand. You will be marked down for important items on your vehicle that you fail to inspect.

1. Vehicle Overview

Approach the Vehicle. Notice general condition. Look for damage or vehicle leaning to one side. Look under the vehicle for fresh oil, coolant, grease, or fuel leaks. Check the area around the vehicle for hazards to vehicle movement (people, other vehicles, objects, low-hanging wires, or tree limbs, etc.).

Review Last Vehicle Inspection Report. Drivers may have to make a vehicle inspection report in writing each day. The vehicle owner should repair any items in the report that affect safety. You should look at the last report to find out what was the matter, if anything. Inspect the vehicle to see if problems have been fixed.

Vehicle Inspection Memory Aids

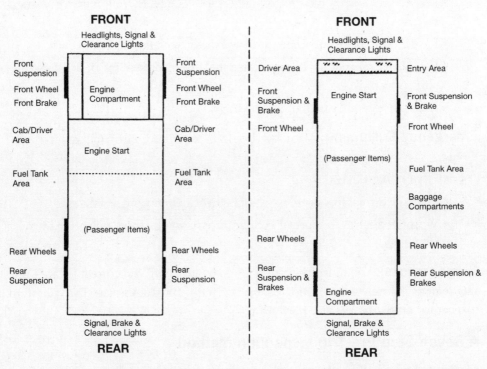

Figure 2-5 Straight Truck/
School Bus

Figure 2-6 Coach/Transit Bus

Vehicle Inspection Memory Aids

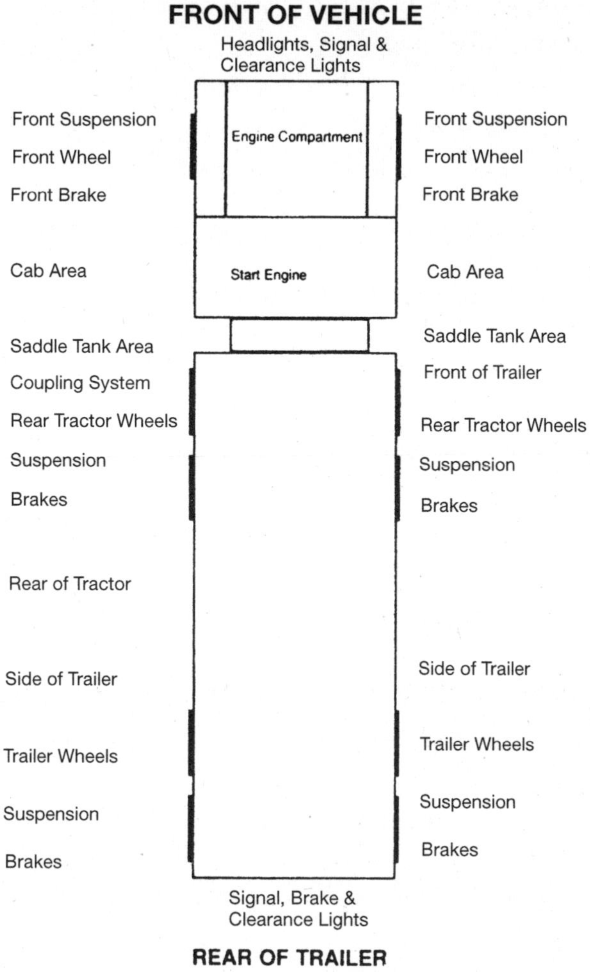

FRONT OF VEHICLE

Headlights, Signal &
Clearance Lights

Front Suspension	Front Suspension
	Engine Compartment	
Front Wheel	Front Wheel
Front Brake	Front Brake
Cab Area	Start Engine	Cab Area
Saddle Tank Area	Saddle Tank Area
Coupling System	Front of Trailer
Rear Tractor Wheels	Rear Tractor Wheels
Suspension	Suspension
Brakes	Brakes
Rear of Tractor	
Side of Trailer	Side of Trailer
Trailer Wheels	Trailer Wheels
Suspension	Suspension
Brakes	Brakes

Signal, Brake &
Clearance Lights

REAR OF TRAILER

Figure 2-7 Tractor-Trailer

2. Check Engine Compartment

Check that the Parking Brakes Are On and/or Wheels Chocked. You may have to raise the hood, tilt the cab (secure loose things so they don't fall and break something), or open the engine compartment door. Check the following:

- Engine oil level.
- Coolant level in radiator; condition of hoses.
- Power steering fluid level; hose condition (if so equipped).
- Windshield washer fluid level.
- Battery fluid level, connections, and tiedowns (battery may be located elsewhere).
- Automatic transmission fluid level (may require engine to be running).

- Check belts for tightness and excessive wear (alternator, water pump, air compressor) — learn how much "give" the belts should have when adjusted properly, and check each one.
- Leaks in the engine compartment (fuel, coolant, oil, power steering fluid, hydraulic fluid, battery fluid).
- Cracked, worn electrical wiring insulation.

Lower and secure hood, cab, or engine compartment door.

3. Start Engine and Inspect Inside the Cab

Get in and Start Engine

- Make sure parking brake is on.
- Put gearshift in neutral (or "park" if automatic).
- Start engine; listen for unusual noises.

Look at the Gauges. (Figure 2-7.1)

- **Oil pressure.** Should come up to normal within seconds after engine is started.
- **Ammeter** and/or **voltmeter.** Should be in normal range(s).
- **Coolant temperature.** Should begin gradual rise to normal operating range.
- **Engine oil temperature.** Should begin gradual rise to normal operating range.
- **Warning lights and buzzers.** Oil, coolant, charging circuit warning lights should turn off right away.

Check Condition of Controls. Check all of the following for looseness, sticking, damage, or improper setting:

- Steering wheel.
- Clutch.
- Accelerator ("gas pedal").
- Brake controls:
  - Foot brake.
  - Trailer brake (if vehicle has one).
  - Parking brake.
  - Retarder controls (if vehicle has them).
- Transmission controls.
- Interaxle differential lock (if vehicle has one).

Identification of Vehicle Instruments

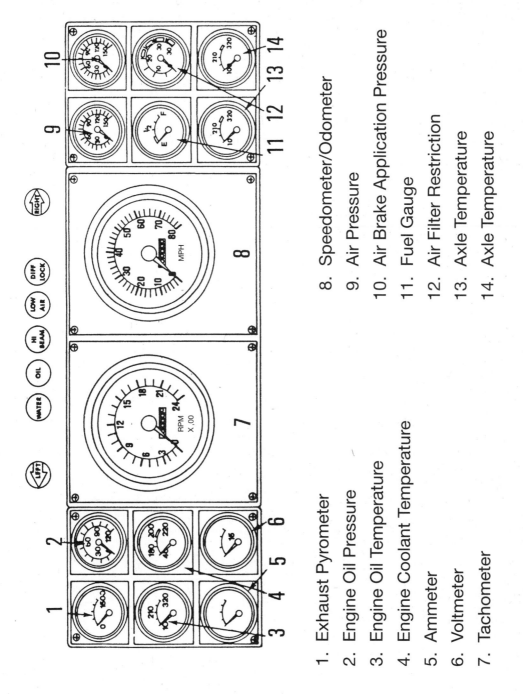

1. Exhaust Pyrometer
2. Engine Oil Pressure
3. Engine Oil Temperature
4. Engine Coolant Temperature
5. Ammeter
6. Voltmeter
7. Tachometer

8. Speedometer/Odometer
9. Air Pressure
10. Air Brake Application Pressure
11. Fuel Gauge
12. Air Filter Restriction
13. Axle Temperature
14. Axle Temperature

Figure 2-7.1

- Horn(s).
- Windshield wiper/washer.
- Lights:
    - Headlights.
    - Dimmer switch.
    - Turn signal.
    - Four-way flashers.
    - Clearance, identification, marker light switch(es).

Check Mirrors and Windshield. Inspect mirrors and windshield for cracks, dirt, illegal stickers, or other obstructions to your vision. Clean and adjust as necessary.

Check Emergency Equipment

- Check for safety equipment:
    - Spare electrical fuses (unless vehicle has circuit breakers).
    - Three red reflective triangles.
    - Properly charged and rated fire extinguisher.
- Check for optional items such as:
    - Tire chains (where winter conditions require them).
    - Tire changing equipment.
    - List of emergency phone numbers.
    - Accident reporting kit (packet).

4. Turn Off Engine and Check Lights

Make sure the parking brake is set, turn off the engine, and remove the key. Turn on headlights (low beams) and four-way flashers and get out, taking the key with you.

- Go to front of vehicle and check that low beams are on and both of the four-way flashers are working.
- Get back into vehicle, push dimmer switch. Get out and check that high beams work.

5. Do Walkaround Inspection

Get in and Change Lights

- Turn off headlights and four-way hazard warning flashers.
- Turn on parking, clearance, side-marker, and identification lights.
- Turn on right turn signal. Get out and start walkaround inspection.

General

- Walk around and inspect.
- Clean all lights, reflectors, and glass as you go along.

Left Front Side

- Driver's door glass should be clean.
- Door latches or lock should work properly.
- Left front wheel:
    - Condition of wheel and rim—no missing, bent, or broken studs, clamps, or lugs; no signs of misalignment.
    - Condition of tires—properly inflated, valve stem and cap OK, no serious cuts, bulges, or tread wear.
    - Use wrench to test rust-streaked lug nuts, indicating looseness.
    - Hub oil level OK, no leaks.
- Left front suspension:
    - Condition of spring, spring hangers, shackles, U-bolts.
    - Shock absorber condition.
- Left front brake:
    - Condition of brake drum.
    - Condition of hoses.

Front

- Condition of front axle.
- Condition of steering system:
    - Check to see there are no loose, worn, bent, damaged, or missing parts.
    - Grab steering mechanism to test for looseness.
- Condition of windshield:
    - Check for damage and clean if dirty.
    - Check windshield wiper arms for proper spring tension.
    - Check wiper blades for damage, "stiff" rubber, and securement.
- Lights and reflectors:
    - Parking, clearance, and identification lights must be clean, operating, and proper color (amber at front).
    - Reflectors must be clean and proper color (amber at front).
- Right front turn signal light must be clean, operating, and proper color (amber or white on signals facing forward).

Right Side

- Right front: check all items as for left front.
- Primary and safety cab locks engaged (if cab-over-engine design).
- Right fuel tank(s):
    - Securely mounted, not damaged or leaking.
    - Fuel crossover line secure.
    - Tank(s) contain enough fuel.
    - Cap(s) on and secure.
- Condition of visible parts:
    - Rear of engine—not leaking.
    - Transmission—not leaking.
    - Exhaust system—secure, not leaking, not touching wires, fuel, or air lines.
    - Frame and cross members—no bends or cracks.
    - Air lines and electrical wiring—secured against snagging, rubbing, and/or wearing.
    - Spare tire carrier or rack not damaged (if so equipped).
    - Spare tire and/or wheel securely mounted in rack.
    - Spare tire and wheel adequate (proper size, properly inflated).
- Cargo securement (trucks):
    - Cargo properly blocked, braced, tied, and chained, etc.
    - Header board adequate, secure (if required).
    - Side boards, stakes strong enough, free of damage, and properly set in place (if so equipped).
    - Canvas or tarp (if required) properly secured to prevent tearing, billowing or blocking of mirrors.
    - If oversize, all required signs must be safely and properly mounted and all required permits in driver's possession.
    - Curbside cargo compartment doors securely closed, and latched/locked required security seals in place.

Right Rear

- Condition of wheels and rims—no missing, bent, or broken spacers, studs, clamps, or lugs.
- Condition of tires—properly inflated, valve stems and caps OK; no serious cuts, bulges, or tread wear; tires not rubbing each other, and nothing stuck between them.

- Tires same type, not mixed radial and bias types.
- Tires evenly matched (same sizes).
- Wheel bearing/seals not leaking.
- Suspension:
    - Condition of spring(s), spring hangers, shackles and U-bolts.
    - Axle secure.
    - Powered axle(s) not leaking lube (gear oil).
    - Condition of torque rod arms and bushings.
    - Condition of shock absorber(s).
    - If retractable-axle equipped, check condition of lift mechanism; if air powered, check for leaks.
- Brakes:
    - Condition of brake drum(s).
    - Condition of hoses—look for any wear due to rubbing.
- Lights and reflectors:
    - Side-marker lights clean, operating, and proper color (red at rear, others amber).
    - Side-marker reflectors clean and proper color (red at rear, others amber).

Rear

- Lights and reflectors:
    - Rear clearance and identification lights clean, operating, and proper color (red at rear).
    - Reflectors clean and proper color (red at rear).
    - Taillights clean, operating, and proper color (red at rear).
    - Right rear turn signal operating and proper color (red, yellow, or amber at rear).
- License plate(s) present, clean, and secured.
- Splash guards present, not damaged, properly fastened, not dragging on ground or rubbing tires.
- Cargo secure (trucks):
    - Cargo properly blocked, braced, tied, and chained, etc.
    - Tailboards up and properly secured.
    - End gates free of damage and properly secured in stake sockets.
    - Canvas or tarp (if required) properly secured to prevent tearing, billowing to block either the rearview mirrors, or to cover rear lights.

– If over-length, or over-width, make sure all signs and/or additional lights/flags are safely and properly mounted and all required permits are in driver's possession.

– Rear doors securely closed and latched/locked.

Left Side

• Check all items as done on right side, plus:

– Battery(ies) (if not mounted in engine compartment).

– Battery box securely mounted to vehicle.

– Box has secure cover.

– Battery(ies) secured against movement.

– Battery(ies) not broken or leaking.

– Fluid in battery(ies) at proper level (except maintenance-free type).

– Cell caps present and securely tightened (except maintenance-free type).

– Vents in cell caps free of foreign material (except maintenance-free type).

6. Check Signal Lights

Get In and Turn Off Lights

• Turn off all lights.

• Turn on stop lights (apply trailer hand brake, or have a helper put on the brake pedal).

• Turn on left turn signal lights.

Get Out and Check Lights

• Left front turn signal light clean, operating, and proper color (amber or white on signals facing the front).

• Left rear turn signal light and both stop lights clean, operating, and proper color (red, yellow, or amber).

7. Start the Engine and Check Brake System

Get In Vehicle

• Turn off lights not needed for driving.

• Check for all required papers, trip manifests, permits, etc.

• Secure all loose articles in cab (they might interfere with operation of the controls, or hit you in a crash).

• Start the engine.

Test for Hydraulic Leaks. If the vehicle has hydraulic brakes, pump the brake pedal three times. Then apply firm pressure to the pedal and hold for five seconds. The pedal should not move. If it does, there may be a leak or other problem. Get it fixed before driving.

NOTE: If the vehicle has air brakes, do the checks described in Chapters 5 and 6 of this book.

Test Parking Brake

- Fasten seat belt.
- Allow vehicle to move forward slowly.
- Apply parking brake.
- If the brake doesn't stop the vehicle, it is faulty; get it fixed.

Test Service Brake Stopping Action

- Go about five miles per hour.
- Push brake pedal firmly.
- "Pulling" to one side or the other can mean brake trouble.
- Any unusual brake pedal "feel" or delayed stopping action can mean trouble.

This completes the pre-trip inspection.

> **If you find anything unsafe during the pre-trip inspection, get it fixed. Federal and state laws forbid operating an unsafe vehicle.**

Inspection During a Trip

Check Vehicle Operation Regularly

While driving, check:

- Instruments.
- Air pressure gauge (if you have air brakes).
- Temperature gauges.
- Pressure gauges.
- Ammeter/voltmeter.
- Mirrors.
- Tires.
- Cargo, cargo covers.

If you see, hear, smell, or feel anything that might mean trouble, check it out.

Safety Inspection

- Drivers of trucks and truck tractors must inspect within the first 25 miles of a trip and every 150 miles or every three hours (whichever comes first) afterward.
- Check these things:
    - Cargo doors and/or cargo securement.
    - Tires—enough air pressure; not overheated.
    - Brakes—not overheated (put back of hand near brake drums to test).
    - Coupling devices.

After-Trip Inspection and Report

You may have to make a written report each day on the condition of the vehicle(s) you drove. Report anything affecting safety or possibly leading to mechanical breakdown.

The vehicle inspection report tells the vehicle owner about problems that may need fixing. Keep a copy of your report in the vehicle for one day. That way, the next driver can learn about any problems you have found.

2.2 BASIC CONTROL OF YOUR VEHICLE

To drive a vehicle safely, you must be able to control its speed and direction. Safe operation of a commercial vehicle requires skill in:

- Accelerating.
- Steering.
- Shifting gears.
- Braking.

Fasten your seatbelt when on the road. Apply the parking brake when you leave your vehicle.

Accelerating

Don't roll back when you start. You may hit someone behind you. Partly engage the clutch before you take your right foot off the brake. Put on the parking brake whenever necessary to keep from rolling back. Release the parking brake only when you have applied enough engine power to keep from rolling back. **On a tractor-trailer equipped with a trailer brake hand valve, the hand valve can be applied to keep from rolling back.**

Speed up smoothly and gradually so the vehicle does not jerk. Rough acceleration can cause mechanical damage. When pulling a trailer, rough acceleration can damage the coupling.

Speed up very gradually when traction is poor, as in rain or snow. If you use too much power, the drive wheels may spin. You could lose control. If the drive wheels begin to spin, take your foot off the accelerator.

Steering

Hold the Wheel Correctly. Hold the steering wheel firmly with both hands. Your hands should be on opposite sides of the wheel. If you hit a curb or a pothole (chuckhole), the wheel could pull away from your hands unless you have a firm hold.

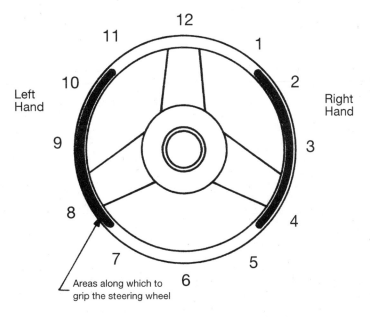

Grip the wheel with your left hand between the 8 and 10 o'clock positions, and place your right hand between the 2 and 4 o'clock positions. With both hands on the wheel in this manner, you have control of your vehicle.

Figure 2-7.2 How to Grip the Steering Wheel

Backing with a Trailer

When backing a car, straight truck or bus, you turn the top of the steering wheel toward the direction you want to go. When backing a trailer, you turn the steering wheel in the opposite direction. Once the trailer starts to turn, you must turn the wheel the other way to follow the trailer.

Whenever you back with a trailer, try to position your vehicle so you can back in a straight line. If you must back on a curved path, back to the driver's side so you can see.

Back slowly. This will let you make corrections before you get too far off course.

Use the mirrors. The mirrors will help you see whether the trailer is drifting to one side or the other.

Correct drift immediately. As soon as you see the trailer getting off the proper path, correct it by turning the top of the steering wheel in the direction of the drift.

Pull forward. When backing a trailer, make pull-ups to reposition your vehicle as needed.

Backing Safely

Because you cannot see everything behind your vehicle, **backing is always dangerous**. Avoid backing whenever you can. When you park, try to park so you will be able to pull forward when you leave. When you have to back, here are a few simple safety rules:

- Look at your path.
- Back slowly.
- Back and turn toward the driver's side whenever possible.
- Use a helper whenever possible.

These rules are discussed in turn below.

Look at Your Path. Look at your line of travel **before** you begin. Get out and walk around the vehicle. Check your clearance to the sides and overhead in and near the path your vehicle will take.

Back Slowly. Always back as slowly as possible. Use the lowest reverse gear. That way you can more easily correct any steering errors. You also can stop quickly if necessary.

Back and Turn Toward the Driver's Side. Back to the driver's side so you can see better. Backing toward the right side is very dangerous because you can't see as well. If you back and turn toward the driver's side, you can watch the rear of your vehicle by looking out the side window. Use driver-side backing—even if it means going around the block to put your vehicle in this position. The added safety is worth it. (See Figure 2-7.3)

Use a Helper. Use a helper when you can. There are blind spots you can't see. That's why a helper is important.

The helper should stand near the back of your vehicle where you can see him or her. Before you begin backing, work out a set of hand signals that you both understand. **Agree on a signal for "stop."**

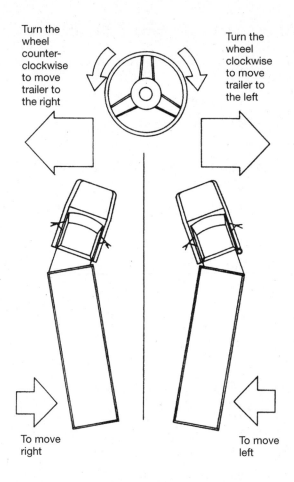

Turn the wheel counter-clockwise to move trailer to the right

Turn the wheel clockwise to move trailer to the left

To move right

To move left

Figure 2-7.3 How to Back Up a Trailer

2.3 SHIFTING GEARS

Correct shifting of gears is important. If you can't get your vehicle into the right gear while driving, you will have less control.

Manual Transmissions

Basic Method for Shifting Up. Most heavy vehicles with manual transmissions require double clutching to change gears. This is the basic method:

1. Release accelerator, push in clutch, and shift to neutral at the same time.
2. Release clutch.
3. Let engine and gears **slow down** to the RPM required for the next gear (this takes practice).
4. Push in clutch and shift to the higher gear at the same time.

5. Release clutch and press accelerator at the same time.

Shifting gears using double clutching requires practice. If you remain in neutral too long, you may have difficulty putting the vehicle into the next gear. If so, don't try to force it. Return to neutral, release clutch, increase engine speed to match road speed, and try again.

Knowing When to Shift Up. There are two ways of knowing when to shift:

- **Use engine speed (RPM).** Study the driver's manual for your vehicle and learn the operating RPM range. Watch your tachometer, and shift up when your engine reaches the top of the range. (Some newer vehicles use "progressive" shifting: the RPM at which you shift becomes higher as you move up in the gears. Find out what's right for the vehicle you will operate.)

- **Use road speed (mph).** Learn what speeds each gear is good for. Then, by using the speedometer, you'll know when to shift up.

With either method, you may learn to use engine sounds to know when to shift.

Basic Procedures for Shifting Down

1. Release accelerator. Push in clutch and shift to neutral at the same time.

2. Release clutch.

3. Press accelerator, **increase** engine and gear speed to the RPM required in the lower gear.

4. Push in clutch and shift to lower gear at the same time.

5. Release clutch and press accelerator at the same time.

Downshifting, like upshifting, requires knowing when to shift. Use either the tachometer or the speedometer and downshift at the right RPM or road speed.

Special conditions where you should downshift

- **Before starting down a hill.** Slow down and shift down to a speed that you can control without using the brakes hard. Otherwise, the brakes can overheat and lose their braking power. Downshift **before** starting down the hill. Make sure you are in a low enough gear, usually lower than the gear required to climb the same hill.

- **Before entering a curve.** Slow down to a safe speed, and downshift to the right gear before entering the curve. This lets you use some power through the curve to help the vehicle be more stable while turning. It also lets you speed up as soon as you are out of the curve.

Multi-speed Rear Axles and Auxiliary Transmissions

Multi-speed rear axles and auxiliary transmissions are used on many vehicles to provide extra gears. You usually control them by a selector knob or switch on the gearshift lever of the main transmission. There are many different shift patterns. Learn the right way to shift gears in the vehicle you will drive.

Automatic Transmissions

Some vehicles have automatic transmissions. You can select a low range to get greater engine braking when going down grades. The lower ranges prevent the transmission from shifting up beyond the selected gear (unless the governor RPM is exceeded). It is very important to use this braking effect when going down grades.

Retarders

Some vehicles have "retarders." Retarders help slow a vehicle, reducing the need for using your brakes. They reduce brake wear and give you another way to slow down. There are many types of retarders (exhaust, engine, hydraulic, and electric). All retarders can be turned on or off by the driver. On some the retarding power can be adjusted. When turned "on," retarders apply their braking power (to the drive wheels only) whenever you let up on the accelerator pedal all the way.

> **CAUTION:** When your drive wheels have poor traction, the retarder may cause them to skid. Therefore, you should turn the retarder off whenever the road is wet, icy, or snow covered.

2.4 SEEING

To be a safe driver you need to know what's going on all around your vehicle. Not looking properly is a major cause of accidents.

Seeing Ahead

All drivers look ahead; but many don't look **far enough** ahead.

Importance of Looking Far Enough Ahead. Because stopping or changing lanes can take a lot of distance, knowing what the traffic is doing on all sides of you is very important. You need to look ahead to make sure you have room to make these moves safely.

How Far Ahead to Look. Most good drivers look 12 to 15 seconds ahead. That means looking ahead the distance you will travel in 12 to 15 seconds. At lower speeds, that's about one block. At highway speeds, it's about a quarter of a mile. If you're not looking that far ahead, you may have to stop too quickly or make quick lane changes. Looking 12 to 15 seconds ahead doesn't mean not paying attention to things that are closer. Good drivers shift their attention back and forth, near and far.

Look for Traffic. Look for vehicles coming onto the highway or into your lane or turning. Watch for brakelights from slowing vehicles. By seeing these things far enough ahead, you can change your speed or change lanes, if necessary, to avoid a problem.

Look for Road Conditions. Look for hills and curves—anything for which you'll have to slow down or change lanes. Pay attention to traffic signals and signs. If a light has been green for a long time, it will probably change before you get there. Start slowing down and be ready to stop. Traffic signs may alert you to road conditions where you may have to change speed.

Seeing to the Sides and Rear

It's important to know what's going on behind and to the sides. Check your mirrors regularly. Check more often in special situations.

Regular Checks. You need to make regular checks of your mirrors to be aware of traffic and to check your vehicle.

Mirror Adjustment. Mirror adjustment should be checked prior to the start of any trip and can only be checked accurately when the trailer(s) is straight. You should check and adjust each mirror as needed.

Traffic. Check the mirrors for vehicles on either side and in back of you. In an emergency, you may need to know whether you can make a quick lane change. Use your mirrors to spot overtaking vehicles. There are "blind spots" that your mirrors cannot show you. Check your mirrors regularly to know where other vehicles are around you and to see if they move into your blind spots.

Check Your Vehicle. Use the mirrors to keep an eye on your tires. It's one way to spot a tire fire. If you're carrying open cargo, you can use the mirrors to check it. Look for loose straps, ropes, or chains. Watch for a flapping or ballooning tarp.

Special Situations

Special situations require more than regular mirror checks. These are lane changes, turns, merges, and tight maneuvers.

Lane Changes. You need to check your mirrors to make sure no one is alongside you or about to pass you. Check your mirrors:

- Before you change lanes to make sure there is enough room.
- After you have signaled, to check that no one has moved out of your blind spot.
- Right after you start the lane change to double-check that your path is clear.
- After you complete the lane change.

Turns. In turns, check your mirrors to make sure the rear of your vehicle will not hit anything.

Merges. When merging, use your mirrors to make sure the gap in traffic is large enough for you to enter safely.

Tight Maneuvers. Any time you are driving in close quarters check your mirrors often. Make sure you have enough clearance.

How to Use Mirrors

Use mirrors correctly by checking them quickly and understanding what you see.

Checking Quickly. When you use your mirrors while driving on the road, check quickly. Look back and forth between the mirrors and the road ahead. Don't focus on the mirrors for too long. Otherwise, you will travel quite a distance without knowing what's happening ahead.

Understanding What You See. Many large vehicles have curved (convex, "fisheye," "spot," "bugeye") mirrors that show a wider area than flat mirrors. This is often helpful. But everything appears smaller in a convex mirror than it would if you were looking at it directly. Things also seem farther away than they really are. It's important to realize this and to allow for it.

2.5 COMMUNICATING

Other drivers can't know what you are going to do until you tell them.

Signal Your Intentions

Signaling what you intend to do is important for safety. Here are some general rules for signaling.

Turns. There are three good rules for using turn signals:

1. Signal early, well before you turn. It is the best way to keep others from trying to pass you.
2. Signal continuously. You need both hands on the wheel to turn safely. Don't cancel the signal until you have completed the turn.

3. Cancel your signal. Don't forget to turn off your turn signal after you've turned (if you don't have self-cancelling signals).

Lane Changes. Put your turn signal on before changing lanes. Change lanes slowly and smoothly. That way, a driver you didn't see may have a chance to honk his/her horn or avoid your vehicle.

Slowing Down. Warn drivers behind you when you see you'll need to slow down. A few light taps on the brake pedal—enough to flash the brake lights—should warn following drivers. Use the four-way emergency flashers for times when you are driving very slowly or are stopped. Warn other drivers in any of the following situations:

- **Trouble Ahead.** The size of your vehicle may make it hard for drivers behind you to see hazards ahead. If you see a hazard that will require slowing down, warn the drivers behind by flashing your brake lights.

- **Tight Turns.** Most car drivers don't know how slow you have to go to make a tight turn in a large vehicle. Give drivers behind you warning by braking early and slowing gradually.

- **Stopping on the Road.** Truck and bus drivers sometimes stop in the road to unload cargo or passengers or to stop at a railroad crossing. Warn following drivers by flashing your brake lights. Don't stop suddenly.

- **Driving Slowly.** Drivers often do not realize how fast they are catching up to a slow vehicle until they are very close. If you must drive slowly, alert following drivers by turning on your emergency flashers if it is legal. (Laws regarding the use of flashers differ from one state to another. Check the laws of the states where you will drive.)

Don't Direct Traffic. Some drivers try to help out others by signaling when it is safe to pass. You should not do this. You could cause an accident.

Communicating Your Presence

Other drivers may not notice your vehicle even when it's in plain sight. Keeping this in mind will help to prevent further accidents.

When Passing. Whenever you are about to pass a vehicle, pedestrian, or bicyclist, assume they don't see you. They could suddenly move in front of you. When it is legal, tap the horn lightly or, at night, flash your lights from low to high beam and back. Drive carefully enough to avoid a crash even if others don't see or hear you.

When It's Hard to See. At dawn or dusk or in rain or snow, you need to make yourself easier to see. If you are having trouble seeing other vehicles, other drivers will have trouble seeing you. Turn on your lights. Use the headlights, not just the identification or clearance lights. Use the low beams; high beams can bother people in the daytime as well as at night.

When Parked at the Side of the Road. When you pull off the road and stop, be sure to turn on the four-way emergency flashers. This is very important at night. Don't trust the taillights to give warning. Drivers have crashed into the rear of a parked vehicle because they thought it was moving normally.

If you must stop on a road or the shoulder of a road, you should put out your reflective triangles within ten minutes. Place your warning devices at the following locations:

- On the traffic side of the vehicle, within 10 feet of the front or rear corners—to mark the location of the vehicle. (See Figure 2-8.)

- About 100 feet behind and ahead of the vehicle, on the shoulder or in the lane you are stopped in. (See Figure 2-8.)

- Back beyond any hill, curve, or other obstruction that prevents other drivers from seeing the vehicle within 500 feet. (See Figure 2-9.)

- If you must stop on or by a one-way or divided highway, place warning devices 10 feet, 100 feet, and 200 feet toward the approaching traffic. (See Figure 2-10.)

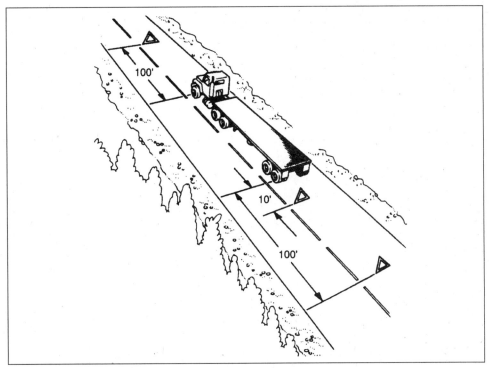

**Figure 2-8 Warning Device Placement:
Two-Lane or Undivided Highway**

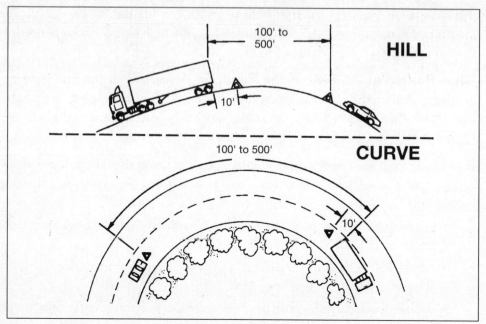

Figure 2-9 Warning Device Placement: Obstructed View

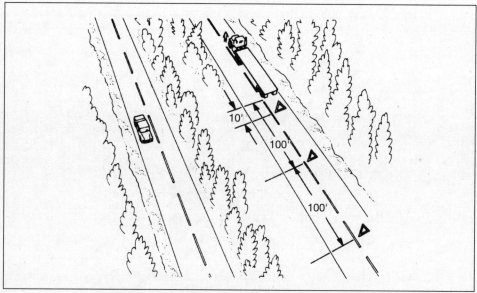

**Figure 2-10 Warning Device Placement:
One Way or Divided Highway**

When putting out the triangles, always hold them between yourself and oncoming traffic so other drivers can see you.

Use Your Horn When Needed. Your horn can let others know you're there. It can help to avoid a crash. Use your horn when needed. However, it can startle others and be dangerous when used unnecessarily.

2.6 CONTROLLING SPEED

Driving too fast is a major cause of fatal crashes. You must adjust your speed to fit driving conditions. Variables that affect conditions include traction, curves, visibility, traffic, and hills.

Speed and Stopping Distance

There are three things that add up to total stopping distance:

      Perception Distance
+ Reaction Distance
+ Braking Distance
_____
= Total Stopping Distance

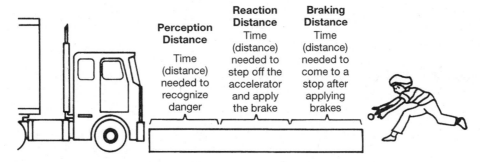

Total stopping distance after detecting danger ahead:
this distance is covered in about 6 seconds at 55 mph.

Figure 2-10.1

- **Perception distance.** This is the distance your vehicle travels from the time your eyes see a hazard until your brain recognizes it. The perception time for an alert driver is about 3/4 second. At 55 mph, you travel 60 feet in 3/4 second.

- **Reaction distance.** This is the distance traveled from the time your brain tells your foot to move from the accelerator until your foot is actually pushing the brake pedal. The average driver has a reaction time of 3/4 second. This accounts for an additional 60 feet traveled at 55 mph.

- **Braking distance.** This is the distance it takes to stop once the brakes are put on. At 55 mph on dry pavement with good brakes it can take a heavy vehicle about 170 feet to stop. This takes about 4 1/2 seconds.
- **Total stopping distance.** At 55 mph it will take about six seconds to stop and your vehicle will travel about the distance of a football field (60 + 60 + 170 = 290 feet).

The Effect of Speed on Stopping Distance. Whenever you double your speed, it takes about **four** times as much distance to stop and your vehicle will have **four** times the destructive power if it crashes. High speeds increase stopping distances greatly. By slowing down a little, you can gain a lot in reduced braking distance.

The Effect of Vehicle Weight on Stopping Distance. The heavier the vehicle, the more work the brakes must do to stop it and the more heat they absorb. But the brakes, tires, springs, and shock absorbers on heavy vehicles are designed to work best when the vehicle is fully loaded. **Empty** trucks require **greater** stopping distances, because an empty vehicle has less traction. It can bounce and lock up its wheels, giving much poorer braking. (This is not usually the case with buses.)

Matching Speed to the Road Surface

You can't steer or brake a vehicle unless you have traction. Traction is friction between the tires and the road. There are some road conditions that reduce traction and call for lower speeds.

Slippery Surfaces. It will take longer to stop and it will be harder to turn without skidding when the road is slippery. You must drive slower to be able to stop in the same distance as on a dry road. Wet roads can double stopping distance. Reduce speed by about one-third (for example, slow from 55 to about 35 mph) on a wet road. On packed snow, reduce speed by one half or more. If the surface is icy, reduce speed to a crawl and stop driving as soon as you can safely do so.

Identifying Slippery Surfaces. Sometimes it's hard to know if the road is slippery. Here are some signs of slippery roads:

- **Shaded areas.** Shady parts of the road will remain icy and slippery long after ice on sun-exposed areas has melted.
- **Bridges.** When the temperature drops, bridges will freeze before the road will. Be especially careful when the temperature is close to 32 degrees F.
- **Melting ice.** Slight melting will make ice wet. Wet ice is much more slippery than ice that is not wet.
- **Black ice.** Black ice is a thin layer of ice that is clear enough that you can see the road underneath it. It makes the road look wet. Any time the temperature is below freezing and the road looks wet, watch out for black ice.

- **Vehicle icing.** An easy way to check for ice is to open the window and feel the front of the mirror, mirror support, or antenna. If ice is starting to accumulate on these surfaces, the road surface is probably starting to ice up.
- **Just after rain begins.** Right after it starts to rain, the water mixes with oil left on the road by vehicles. This makes the road very slippery. If the rain continues, it will wash the oil away.

Hydroplaning. In some weather, water or slush collects on the road. When this happens, your vehicle can hydroplane. It's like water-skiing: the tires lose their contact with the road and have little or no traction. You may not be able to steer or brake. You can regain control by releasing the accelerator and pushing in the clutch. This will slow your vehicle and let the wheels turn freely. If the vehicle is hydroplaning, do not use the brakes to slow down. If the drive wheels start to skid, push in the clutch to let them turn freely.

It does not take a lot of water to cause hydroplaning. Hydroplaning can occur at speeds as low as 30 mph if there is a lot of water. Hydroplaning is more likely if tire pressure is low or the tread is worn. (The grooves in a tire carry away the water; if they aren't deep enough they don't work well.) Be especially careful driving through puddles. Water that appears to be shallow is often deep enough to cause hydroplaning.

Speed and Curves

Drivers must adjust their speed for curves in the road. If you take a curve too fast, two things can happen:

1. The wheels can lose their traction and continue straight ahead, causing you to skid off the road; or
2. The wheels may keep their traction, causing the vehicle to roll over. Tests have shown that trucks with a high center of gravity can roll over at the posted speed limit for a curve.

Slow to a safe speed **before** you enter a curve. Braking in a curve is dangerous because it is easier to lock the wheels and cause a skid. Slow down as needed. Don't ever exceed the posted speed limit for the curve. Be in a gear that will let you accelerate slightly in the curve. This will help you keep control.

Speed and Distance Ahead

You should always be able to stop within the distance you can see ahead. Fog, rain, or other conditions may require that you slow down to be able to stop in the distance you can see. At night, you can't see as far with low beams as you can with high beams. When you must use low beams, slow down.

Speed and Traffic Flow

When you're driving in heavy traffic, the safest speed is the speed of other vehicles. Vehicles going the same direction at the same speed are not likely to run into one another. Drive at the speed of traffic, if you can, without going at an illegal or unsafe speed. Always keep a safe following distance.

The main reason drivers exceed speed limits is to save time. But anyone trying to drive faster than the speed of traffic will not be able to save much time. The risks involved are not worth it. If you go faster than the speed of other traffic:

- You'll have to keep passing other vehicles. This increases the chance of a crash.
- It is more tiring. Fatigue increases the chance of a crash.

Going with the flow of traffic is safer and easier.

Speed on Downgrades

Your vehicle's speed will increase on downgrades because of gravity.

Your most important objective is to select and maintain a speed that is not too fast when considering these factors:

- Total weight of the vehicle and cargo.
- Length of the grade.
- Steepness of the grade.
- Road conditions.
- Weather.

If a speed limit is posted, or there is a sign indicating "Maximum Safe Speed," never exceed the speed shown. Also look for and heed warning signs indicating the length and steepness of the grade.

You must use the braking effect of the engine as the principal way of controlling your speed on downgrades. The braking effect of the engine is greatest when it is near the governed RPMs and the transmission is in the lower gears. Save your brakes so you will be able to slow or stop as required by road and traffic conditions.

Shift your transmission to a low gear before starting down the grade and use the proper braking techniques.

Going down long steep downgrades safely is discussed more in "Mountain Driving." Read that section carefully.

2.7 MANAGING SPACE

To be a safe driver, you need space all around your vehicle. When things go wrong, space gives you time to think and to take action.

To have space available when something goes wrong, you need to **manage** space. While this is true for all drivers, it is very important for those at the wheel of large vehicles. Large vehicles take up more space and require more space for stopping and turning.

Space Ahead

Of all the space around your vehicle, it is the area ahead of the vehicle—the space you're driving into—that is most important.

The Need for Space Ahead. You need space ahead in case you must suddenly stop. According to accident reports, the vehicle that trucks and buses most often run into is the one in front of them. The most frequent cause is **following too closely**. Remember, if the vehicle ahead of you is smaller than yours, it can probably stop faster than you can. You may crash if you are following too closely.

How Much Space? How much space should you keep in front of you? One good rule says you need at least one second for each 10 feet of vehicle length at speeds below 40 mph. At greater speeds, you must add one second for safety. For example, if you are driving a 40-foot vehicle, you should leave four seconds between you and the vehicle ahead. In a 60-foot rig, you'll need six seconds. Over 40 mph, you'd need five seconds for a 40-foot vehicle and seven seconds for a 60-foot vehicle.

40-Foot Truck Requires Four Seconds

When driving under 40 mph, you need
One second for each 10 feet of your vehicle length.

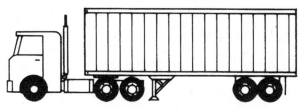

60-Foot Truck Requires Seven Seconds

When driving under 40 mph, you need the same
time plus an additional second for the higher speed.

Figure 2-10.2

To know how much space you have, wait until the vehicle ahead passes a shadow on the road, a pavement marking, or some other clear landmark. Then count off the seconds like this: "one thousand-and-one, one thousand-and-two," and so on, until you reach the same spot. Compare your count with the rule of one second for every 10 feet of length. If you are driving a 40-foot truck and only counted up to two seconds, you're too close. Drop back a little and count again until you have four seconds of following distance (or five seconds, if you're going over 40 mph). After a little practice, you will know how far back you should be. Remember to add one second for speeds above 40 mph. Also remember that when the road is slippery, you need **much more space** to stop.

Space Behind

You can't stop others from following you too closely. But there are things you can do to make it safer:

- Stay to the right.
- Deal with tailgaters safely.

Stay to the Right. Heavy vehicles are often tailgated when they can't keep up with the speed of traffic. This often happens when you're going uphill. If a heavy load is slowing you down, stay in the right lane when going uphill; you should not pass another slow vehicle unless you can get around quickly and safely.

Deal with Tailgaters Safely. In a large vehicle, it's often hard to see whether another vehicle is close behind you. You may be tailgated:

- When you are traveling slowly. Drivers trapped behind slow vehicles often follow closely.
- In bad weather. Many car drivers follow large vehicles closely during bad weather, especially when it is hard to see the road ahead.

If you find yourself being tailgated, here are some things you can do to reduce the chances of a crash:

- Avoid quick changes. If you have to slow down or turn, signal early and reduce speed very gradually.
- Increase your following distance. Opening up room in front of you will help you avoid having to make sudden speed or direction changes. It also makes it easier for the tailgater to get around you.
- Don't speed up. It's safer to be tailgated at a low speed than a high speed.
- Avoid tricks. Don't turn on your taillights or flash your brake lights. Follow the suggestions above.

Space to the Sides

Commercial vehicles are often wide and take up most of a lane. Safe drivers will manage what little space they have. You can do this by keeping your vehicle centered in your lane. Avoid driving alongside others.

Staying Centered in a Lane. You need to keep your vehicle centered in the lane to keep safe clearance on either side. If your vehicle is wide, you have little room to spare.

Traveling Next to Others. There are two dangers in traveling alongside other vehicles:

- Another driver may change lanes suddenly and turn into you.
- You may be trapped when **you** need to change lanes.

Find an open spot where you aren't near other traffic. When traffic is heavy, it may be hard to find an open spot. If you must travel near other vehicles, try to keep as much space as possible between you and them. Also, drop back or pull forward so that you are sure the other driver can see you.

Strong Winds. Strong winds make it difficult to stay in your lane. The problem is usually worse for lighter vehicles. This problem can be especially bad coming out of tunnels. When it's windy, don't drive alongside others if you can avoid it.

Space Overhead

Hitting overhead objects is a danger. Make sure you always have overhead clearance.

- Don't assume that the heights posted at bridges and overpasses are correct. Repaving or packed snow may have reduced the clearances since the heights were posted.
- The weight of a cargo van changes its height. An empty van is higher than a loaded one. Just because you got under a bridge when you were loaded does not mean that you can get under it again when you are empty.
- If you doubt you have safe space to pass under an object, go slowly. If you aren't sure you can make it, take another route. Warnings are often posted on low bridges or underpasses, but sometimes they are not.
- Some roads can cause a vehicle to tilt. There can be a problem clearing objects along the edge of the road, such as signs or trees. Where this is a problem, drive a little closer to the center of the road.
- Before you back into an area, get out and check for overhanging objects, such as trees, branches, or electric wires. It's easy to miss seeing them while you are backing. (Also check for other hazards at the same time.)

Space Below

Many drivers forget about the space under their vehicles. That space can be very small when a vehicle is heavily loaded. Railroad tracks can stick up several inches. This is often a problem on dirt roads and in unpaved yards where the surface around the tracks can wear away. Don't take a chance on getting hung up halfway across. Drainage channels across roads can cause the ends of some vehicles to drag. Cross such depressions carefully.

Space for Turns

The space around a truck or bus is important in turns. When any vehicle goes around a corner, the rear wheels follow a different path than the front wheels. This is called offtracking. Longer vehicles will offtrack more than shorter ones. Because of wide turning and offtracking, large vehicles can hit other vehicles or objects during turns.

Right Turns. Here are some rules to help prevent right-turn crashes:

- Turn slowly to give yourself and others more time to avoid problems.
- If you are driving a truck or bus that cannot make the right turn without swinging into another lane, turn wide as you complete the turn, as shown in Figure 2-11. Keep the rear of your vehicle close to the curb. This will stop other drivers from passing you on the right.
- Don't turn wide to the left as you start the turn, as shown in Figure 2-12. A following driver may think you are turning left and try to pass you on the right. You may crash into the other vehicle as you complete your turn.
- If you must cross into the oncoming lane to make a turn, watch out for vehicles coming toward you. Give them room to go by or to stop. However, don't back up for them, because you might hit someone behind you.

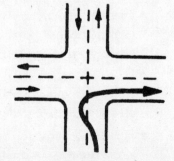

Figure 2-11 Do This.   **Figure 2-12 Don't Do This!**

Left Turns. On a left turn, make sure you have reached the center of the intersection before you start the turn. If you turn too soon, the left side of your vehicle may hit another vehicle because of offtracking.

If there are two turning lanes, always take the right-hand turn lane, as shown in Figure 2-13. Don't start in the inside lane because you may have to swing right to make the turn. Drivers on your right may be hard for you to see, and you could crash into them.

Space Needed to Cross or Enter Traffic

Be aware of the size and weight of your vehicle when you cross or enter traffic. Here are some important things to keep in mind:

- Because of slow acceleration and the space large vehicles require, you may need a much larger gap to enter traffic than you would in a car.
- Acceleration varies with the load. Allow more room if your vehicle is heavily loaded.
- Before you start across a road, make sure you can get all the way across before traffic reaches you.

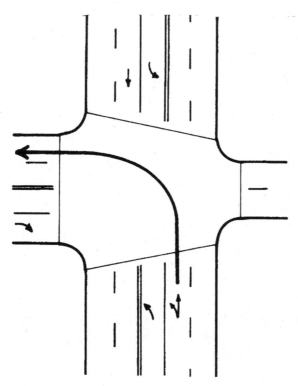

Figure 2-13 If there are two left-turn lanes, use the right-hand lane.

2.8 DRIVING AT NIGHT

It's More Dangerous

You are at greater risk when you drive at night. Drivers can't see hazards as soon as in daylight, so they have less time to respond. Drivers caught by surprise are less able to avoid a crash.

The problems of night driving involve the driver, the roadway, and the vehicle. We will discuss each of these factors.

Driver Factors

Vision. People can't see as sharply at night or in dim light. Also, the eyes need time to adjust to seeing in dim light. Most people have noticed this when walking into a dark movie theater.

Glare. Drivers can be blinded for a short time by bright light. It takes time to recover from this blindness. Older drivers are especially bothered by glare. Most people have been temporarily blinded by camera flash units or by the high beams of an oncoming vehicle. It can take several seconds to recover from glare. Even two seconds of glare blindness can be dangerous. A vehicle going 55 mph will travel more than half the distance of a football field during that time. Don't look directly at bright lights when driving. Look at the right side of the road. Watch the sidelines when someone coming toward you has very bright lights.

Fatigue and Lack of Alertness. Fatigue (being tired) and lack of alertness are bigger problems at night. The body's need for sleep is beyond a person's control. Most people are less alert at night, especially after midnight. This is particularly true if you have been driving for a long time. Drivers may not see hazards as soon or react as quickly, so the chance of a crash is greater. If you are sleepy, the only safe cure is to get off the road and get some sleep. If you don't, you risk your life and the lives of others.

Roadway Factors

Poor Lighting. In the daytime there is usually enough light to see well. This is not true at night. Some areas may have bright street lights, but many areas will have poor lighting. On most roads you will probably have to depend entirely on your headlights.

Less light means you will not be able to see hazards as well as in daytime. Road users who do not have lights are hard to see. There are many accidents at night involving pedestrians, joggers, bicyclists, and animals.

Even when there are lights, the road scene can be confusing. Traffic signals and hazards can be hard to see against a background of signs, shop windows, and other lights.

Drive slower when lighting is poor or confusing. Drive slowly enough to be sure you can stop in the distance you can see ahead.

Drunk Drivers. Drunk drivers and drivers under the influence of drugs are a hazard to themselves and to you. Be especially alert around the closing times for bars and taverns. Watch for drivers who have trouble staying in their lane or maintaining speed, stop without reason, or show other signs of being under the influence of alcohol or drugs.

Vehicle Factors

Headlights. At night your headlights will usually be the main source of light for you to see and for others to see you. You can't see nearly as much with your headlights as you can see in the daytime. With low beams you can see ahead about 250 feet and with high beams about 350 to 500 feet. You must adjust your speed to keep your stopping distance within your sight distance. This means going slowly enough to be able to stop within the range of your headlights. Otherwise, by the time you see a hazard, you will not have time to stop.

Night driving can be more dangerous if you have problems with your headlights. Dirty headlights may give only half the light they should. This cuts down your ability to see, and makes it harder for others to see you. Make sure your lights are clean and working. Headlights can be out of adjustment. If they don't point in the right direction, they won't give you a good view and they can blind other drivers. Have a qualified person make sure they are adjusted properly.

Other Lights. In order for you to be seen easily, the following must be clean and working properly:

- Reflectors.
- Marker lights.
- Clearance lights.
- Taillights.
- Identification lights.

Turn Signals and Brake Lights. At night your turn signals and brake lights are even more important for telling other drivers what you intend to do. Make sure you have clean, working turn signals and stop lights.

Windshields and Mirrors. It is more important at night than in the daytime to have clean windshields and mirrors. Bright lights at night can cause dirt on your windshield or mirrors to create a glare of its own, blocking your view. Most people have experienced driving toward the sun just as it has risen or is about to set and found that they can barely see through a windshield that seemed to look OK in the middle of the day. Clean your windshield on the inside and outside for safe driving at night.

Night Driving Procedures

Pre-Trip Procedures. Make sure you are rested and alert. If you are drowsy, **sleep before you drive!** Even a nap can save your life or the lives of others. If you wear eyeglasses, make sure they are clean and unscratched. Don't wear sunglasses at night. Do a complete pre-trip inspection of your vehicle. Check all lights and reflectors and clean those you can reach.

Avoid blinding others. Glare from your headlights can cause problems for drivers coming towards you. It can also bother drivers going in the same direction you are, when your lights shine in their rearview mirrors. Dim your lights before they cause glare for other drivers. Dim your lights within 500 feet of an oncoming vehicle and when following another vehicle within 500 feet.

Avoid glare from oncoming vehicles. Do not look directly at lights of oncoming vehicles. Look slightly to the right at a right lane or edge marking if available. If other drivers don't put their low beams on, don't try to "get back at them" by putting your own high beams on. This increases glare for oncoming drivers and increases the chance of a crash.

Use high beams when you can. Some drivers make the mistake of always using low beams. This seriously cuts down on their ability to see ahead. Use high beams when it is safe and legal to do so. Use them when you are not within 500 feet of an approaching vehicle. Also, don't let the inside of your cab get too bright. This makes it harder to see outside. Keep the interior light off and adjust your instrument lights as low as you can while still being able to read the gauges.

If you get sleepy, stop driving at the nearest safe place. People often don't realize how close they are to falling asleep even when their eyelids are falling shut. If you can safely do so, look at yourself in a mirror. If you look sleepy, or just feel sleepy, **stop driving!** You are in a very dangerous condition. The only safe cure is to sleep.

2.9 DRIVING IN WINTER

Vehicle Checks

Make sure your vehicle is ready before driving in winter weather. You should make a regular pre-trip inspection, paying extra attention to the following items:

Coolant Level and Antifreeze Amount. Make sure the cooling system is full and there is enough antifreeze in the system to protect against freezing. This can be checked with a special coolant tester.

Defrosting and Heating Equipment. Make sure the defrosters work. They are needed for safe driving. Make sure the heater is working and that you know how to operate it. If you use other heaters and expect to need them (e.g., mirror heaters, battery box heaters, fuel tank heaters), check their operation.

Wipers and Washers. Make sure the windshield wiper blades are in good condition. Make sure the wiper blades press against the window hard enough to wipe the windshield clean. If they don't, they may not sweep off snow properly. Make sure the windshield washer works and there is washing fluid in the washer reservoir. Use windshield washer antifreeze to prevent freezing of the washer liquid. If you can't see well enough while driving (for example, if your wipers fail), stop safely and fix the problem.

Tires. Make sure you have enough tread on your tires. The drive tires must provide traction to push the rig over wet pavement and through snow. The steering tires must have traction to steer the vehicle. Enough tread is especially important in winter conditions. You should have at least 4/32 inch tread depth in every major groove on front wheels and at least 2/32 inch on other wheels. The deeper the groove, the better. Use a gauge to determine if you have enough tread for safe driving.

Tire Chains. You may find yourself in conditions where you can't drive without chains, even to get to a place of safety. Carry the right number of chains and extra cross links. Make sure they will fit your drive tires. Check the chains for broken hooks, worn or broken cross links, and bent or broken side chains. Learn how to put the chains on before you need to do it in snow and ice.

Lights and Reflectors. Make sure the lights and reflectors are clean. Lights and reflectors are especially important during bad weather. Check from time to time during bad weather to make sure they are clean and working properly.

Windows and Mirrors. Remove any ice, snow, etc., from the windshield, windows, and mirrors before starting. Use a windshield scraper, snow brush, and windshield defroster as necessary.

Hand Holds, Steps, and Deck Plates. Remove all ice and snow from hand holds, steps, and deck plates which you must use to enter the cab or to move about the vehicle. This will reduce your danger of slipping.

Radiator Shutters and Winterfront. Remove ice from the radiator shutters. Make sure the winterfront is not closed too tightly. If the shutters freeze shut or the winterfront is closed too much, the engine may overheat and stop.

Exhaust System. Exhaust system leaks are especially dangerous when cab ventilation may be poor (windows rolled up, etc.). Loose connections could permit poisonous carbon monoxide to leak into your vehicle. Carbon monoxide gas will cause you to be sleepy, and in large enough amounts, can kill you. Check the exhaust system for loose parts and for sounds and signs of leaks.

Driving

Slippery Surfaces. Drive slowly and smoothly on slippery roads. If it is very slippery, you shouldn't drive at all. Stop at the first safe place.

The following are some safety guidelines:

Start gently and slowly. When first starting, get the feel of the road. Don't hurry.

Adjust turning and braking to conditions. Make turns as gently as possible. Don't brake any harder than necessary, and don't use the engine brake or speed retarder. (They can cause the driving wheels to skid on slippery surfaces.)

Adjust speed to conditions. Don't pass slower vehicles unless necessary. Go slowly and watch far enough ahead to keep a steady speed. Avoid having to slow down and speed up. Take curves at slower speeds and don't brake while in curves. Be aware that as the temperature rises to the point where ice begins to melt, the road becomes even more slippery.

Adjust space to conditions. Don't drive alongside other vehicles. Keep a longer following distance. When you see a traffic jam ahead, slow down or stop to wait for it to clear. Try hard to anticipate stops early and slow down gradually.

Wet Brakes. When driving in heavy rain or deep standing water, your brakes will get wet. Water in the brakes can cause the brakes to be weak, to apply unevenly, or to grab. This can cause lack of braking power, wheel lockups, pulling to one side or the other, and jackknifing if you are pulling a trailer.

Avoid driving through deep puddles or flowing water if possible. If you cannot, you should:

- Slow down.
- Place transmission in a low gear.
- Gently put on the brakes. This presses linings against brake drums or discs and keeps mud, silt, sand, and water from getting in.
- Increase engine RPM and cross the water while keeping light pressure on the brakes.
- When out of the water, maintain light pressure on the brakes for a short distance to heat them up and dry them out.
- Make a test stop when safe to do so. Check behind to make sure no one is following, then apply the brakes to be sure they work right. If not, dry out further as described above.

> **CAUTION:** Do not apply too much brake pressure and accelerator at the same time or you may overheat brake drums and linings.

2.10 DRIVING IN VERY HOT WEATHER

Vehicle Checks

Do a normal pre-trip inspection, but pay special attention to the following items:

Tires. Check the tire mounting and air pressure. Inspect the tires every two hours or every 100 miles when driving in very hot weather. Air pressure increases with temperature. Do not let air out or the pressure will be too low when the tires cool off. If a tire is too hot to touch, remain stopped until the tire cools off. Otherwise the tire may blow out or catch fire. Pay special attention to recapped or retreaded tires. Under high temperatures the tread may separate from the body of the tire.

Engine Oil. The engine oil helps keep the engine cool, and lubricates it as well. Make sure there is enough engine oil. If you have an oil temperature gauge, make sure the temperature is within the proper range while you are driving.

Engine Coolant. Before starting out, make sure the engine cooling system has enough water and antifreeze according to the engine manufacturer's directions. (Antifreeze helps the engine under hot conditions as well as cold conditions.) When driving, check the water temperature or coolant temperature gauge from time to time. Make sure that it remains in the normal range. If the gauge goes above the highest safe temperature, there may be something wrong that could lead to engine failure and possibly fire. Stop driving as soon as safely possible and try to find out what is wrong.

Some vehicles have sight glasses or see-through coolant overflow or recovery containers. These permit you to check the coolant level while the engine is hot. If the container is not part of the pressurized system, the cap can be safely removed and coolant added even when the engine is at operating temperature.

CAUTION: Never remove the radiator cap or any part of the pressurized system until the system has cooled. Steam and boiling water can spray under pressure and cause severe burns. If you can touch the radiator cap with your bare hand, it is probably cool enough to open.

If coolant has to be added to a system without a recovery tank or an overflow tank, follow these steps:

- Shut engine off.
- Wait until engine has cooled.
- Protect hands (use gloves or a thick cloth).

- Turn radiator cap slowly to the first stop, which releases the pressure seal.

- Step back while pressure is released from cooling system.

- When all pressure has been released, press down on the cap and turn it further to remove it.

- Visually check level of coolant and add more coolant if necessary.

- Replace cap and turn all the way to the closed position.

Engine Belts. Learn how to check V-belt tightness on your vehicle by pressing on the belts. Loose belts will not turn the water pump and/or fan properly. This will result in overheating. Also check belts for cracking, or other signs of wear.

Hoses. Make sure coolant hoses are in good condition. A broken hose while driving can lead to engine failure and even fire.

Driving

Watch for Bleeding Tar. Tar in the road pavement frequently rises to the surface in very hot weather. Spots where tar "bleeds" to the surface are very slippery.

Go Slow Enough to Prevent Overheating. High speeds create more heat for tires and the engine. In desert conditions, the heat may build up to the point where it is dangerous. The heat will increase chances of tire failure, fire, and engine failure.

2.11 DRIVING IN FOG

The best advice for driving in fog is don't. It is preferable that you pull off the road into a rest area or truck stop until visibility is better. If you must drive, be sure to consider the following:

- Obey all fog-related warning signs.

- Slow before you enter fog.

- Turn on all your lights. (Headlights should be on low beams.)

- Be prepared for emergency stops.

2.12 MOUNTAIN DRIVING

In mountain driving, gravity plays a major role. On any upgrade, gravity slows you down. The steeper the grade, the longer the grade, and/or the heavier the load—the more you will have to use lower gears to climb hills or mountains. In coming down long steep downgrades, gravity causes the speed of your vehicle to increase. You must select an appropriate safe speed, then use a low gear, and use proper braking techniques. You should plan ahead and obtain information about any long steep grades along your planned route of travel. If possible, talk to other drivers who are familiar with the grades to find out what speeds are safe.

You must go slow enough so your brakes can hold you back without getting too hot. If the brakes become too hot, they may start to "fade." This means you have to apply them harder and harder to get the same stopping power. If you continue to use the brakes hard, they can keep fading until you cannot slow down or stop at all.

Select a "Safe" Speed

Your most important consideration is to select a speed that is not too fast when considering these factors:

- Total weight of the vehicle and cargo.
- Length of the grade.
- Steepness of the grade.
- Road conditions.
- Weather.

If a speed limit is posted, or there is a sign indicating "Maximum Safe Speed," never exceed the speed shown. Also look for and heed warning signs indicating the length and steepness of the grade.

Be in the Right Gear Before Starting Down the Grade

You must use the braking effect of the engine as the principal way of controlling your speed. The braking effect of the engine is greatest when it is near the governed RPMs and the transmission is in the lower gears. Save your brakes so you will be able to slow or stop as required by road and traffic conditions.

Shift the transmission to a low gear before starting down the grade. Do not try to downshift after your speed has already built up. You will not be able to shift into a lower gear. You may not even be able to get back into any gear and all engine braking effect will be lost. Forcing an automatic transmission into a lower gear at high speed could damage the transmission and also lead to loss of all engine braking effect.

With older trucks, a rule for choosing gears is to use the same gear going down a hill that you would need to climb the hill. However, new trucks have low friction parts and streamlined shapes for fuel economy. They may also have more powerful engines. This means they can go up hills in higher gears and have less friction and air drag to hold them back going down hills. For that reason, drivers of modern trucks may have to use lower gears going down a hill than would be required to go up the hill. You should know what is right for your vehicle.

Brake Fading or Failure and Proper Braking

Brakes are designed so brake shoes or pads rub against the brake drum or disks to slow the vehicle. Braking creates heat, but brakes are designed to take a lot of heat.

However, brakes can fade or fail from excessive heat caused by using them too much and not relying on the engine braking effect.

The right way to use your brakes for long downhill grades is to drive slowly enough that a fairly light use of the brakes will keep your speed from increasing. If you drive slowly enough, the brakes will be able to get rid of the heat and they won't get too hot.

Some people believe that letting up on the brakes from time to time will allow them to cool enough so they don't become overheated. Tests have proven this is **not** true. Brake drums cool very slowly, so the amount of cooling between applications is not enough to prevent overheating. This type of braking requires heavier brake pressures than steady application does. Heavy pressure on the brakes from time to time builds up more heat than light continuous pressure does. Therefore, select the right gear, drive slowly, and maintain a lighter, steadier use of the brakes.

Escape Ramps

Escape ramps have been built on many steep mountain grades. Escape ramps are made to stop runaway vehicles safely without injuring drivers and passengers. Escape ramps use a long bed of loose soft material (pea gravel), sometimes in combination with an upgrade, to slow runaway vehicles. Know escape ramp locations on your route. Signs show drivers where ramps are located. Escape ramps save lives, equipment, and cargo. Use them if you lose your brakes.

2.13 RAILROAD CROSSINGS

Railroad crossings are always dangerous. Every such crossing must be approached with the expectation that a train is coming.

Never Race a Train to a Crossing

Never attempt to race a train to a crossing. It is extremely difficult to judge the speed of an approaching train.

Reduce Speed

Speed must be reduced in accordance with your ability to see approaching trains in any direction, and speed must be held to a point that will permit you to stop short of the tracks in case a stop is necessary.

Don't Expect to Hear a Train

Because of noise in the cab, you cannot expect to hear the train horn until the train is dangerously close to the crossing.

Don't Rely on Signals

You should not rely solely upon the presence of warning signals, gates, or flagmen to warn of the approach of trains.

Double tracks require a double check. Remember that a train on one track may hide a train on the other track. Look both ways before crossing. After one train has cleared a crossing, be sure no other trains are near before starting across the tracks.

Yard areas and grade crossings in cities and towns are just as dangerous as rural grade crossings. Approach them with as much caution.

Stop Requirements

A full stop is required at grade crossings whenever:

- The nature of the cargo makes a stop mandatory under state or federal regulations.
- Such a stop is otherwise required by law.

Crossing the Tracks

Railroad crossings with steep approaches can cause your unit to hang up on the tracks.

Never permit traffic conditions to trap you in a position where you have to stop on the tracks. Be sure you can get all the way across the tracks before you start across.

Do not shift gears while crossing railroad tracks.

2.14 SEEING HAZARDS

Importance of Seeing Hazards

What is a Hazard? A hazard is any road condition or other road user (driver, bicyclist, pedestrian) that is a possible danger. For example, a car in front of you is headed towards the freeway exit, but his brake lights come on and he begins braking hard. This could mean that the driver is uncertain about taking the off-ramp. He might suddenly return to the highway. This car is a **hazard**. If the driver of the car cuts in front of you, it is no longer just a hazard; it is an emergency.

Seeing Hazards Lets You Be Prepared. You will have more time to act if you see hazards before they become emergencies. In the example above, you might make a lane change or slow down to prevent a crash if the car suddenly cuts in front of you. Seeing this hazard gives you time to check your mirrors and signal a lane change. Being prepared reduces the danger. A driver who did not see the hazard until the slow car pulled back on the highway in front of him would have to do something very suddenly. Sudden braking or a quick lane change is much more likely to lead to a crash.

Learning to See Hazards. There are often clues that will help you see hazards. The more you drive, the better you can get at seeing hazards. This section will talk about hazards that you should be aware of.

Hazardous Roads

Slow down and be very careful if you see any of the following road hazards.

Work Zones. When people are working on the road it is a hazard. There may be narrower lanes, sharp turns, or uneven surfaces. Other drivers are often distracted and drive unsafely. Workers and construction vehicles may get in the way. Drive slowly and carefully near work zones. Use your four-way flashers or brake lights to warn drivers behind you.

Drop-Off. Sometimes the pavement drops off sharply near the edge of the road. Driving too near the edge can tilt your vehicle toward the side of the road. This can cause the top of your vehicle to hit roadside objects (signs, tree limbs). Also, it can be hard to steer as you cross the drop-off while going off the road or coming back on.

Foreign Objects. Things that have fallen on the road can be hazards. They can be a danger to your tires and wheel rims. They can damage electrical and brake lines. They can be caught between dual tires and cause severe damage. Some obstacles, which appear to be harmless, can be very dangerous. For example, cardboard boxes may be empty, but they may also contain some solid or heavy material capable of causing damage. The same is true of paper and cloth sacks. It is important to remain alert for objects of all sorts, so you can see them early enough to avoid them without making sudden, unsafe moves.

Off-ramps/On-ramps. Freeway and turnpike exits can be particularly dangerous for commercial vehicles. Off-ramps and on-ramps often have speed limit signs posted. Remember, these speeds may be safe for automobiles, **but may not be safe for larger vehicles or heavily loaded vehicles**. Exits which go downhill and turn at the same time can be especially dangerous. The downgrade makes it difficult to reduce speed. Braking and turning at the same time can be a dangerous practice. Make sure you are going slowly enough before you get on the curved part of an off-ramp or on-ramp.

Other Hazardous Situations

In order to protect yourself and others, you must know when other drivers or pedestrians may do something hazardous. Some clues to this type of hazard are as follows:

Blocked Vision. People who can't see others are a very dangerous hazard. Be alert for drivers whose vision is blocked. Vans, loaded station wagons, and cars with the rear window blocked are examples. Rental trucks should be watched carefully. Their drivers are often not used to the limited vision they have to the sides and rear of the truck. In winter, vehicles with frosted, ice-covered, or snow-covered windows are hazards.

Vehicles may be partly hidden by blind intersections or alleys. If you can only see the rear or front end of a vehicle but not the driver, then he or she can't see you. Be alert because he/she may back out or enter into your lane. Always be prepared to stop.

Delivery trucks can present a hazard. The driver's vision is often blocked by packages, or vehicle doors. Drivers of step vans, postal vehicles, and local delivery vehicles often are in a hurry and may suddenly step out of their vehicle or drive their vehicle into the traffic lane.

Parked vehicles can be hazards. People may get out of them or they may suddenly start up and drive into your way. Watch for movement inside the vehicle or movement of the vehicle itself that shows people are inside. Watch for brake lights or backup lights, exhaust, and other clues that a driver is about to move.

Be careful of a stopped bus. Passengers may cross in front of or behind the bus, and they often can't see you.

Pedestrians and bicyclists can also be hazards. Walkers, joggers, and bicyclists may be on the road with their back to the traffic, so they can't see you. Sometimes, they wear portable stereos with headsets, so they can't hear you either. This can be dangerous. On rainy days, pedestrians may not see you because of hats or umbrellas. They may be hurrying to get out of the rain and may not pay attention to the traffic.

Distractions. People who are distracted are hazards. Watch for where they are looking. If they are looking elsewhere, they can't see you. But be alert even when they are looking at you. They may believe that they have the right of way.

Children. Children tend to act quickly without checking traffic. Children playing with one another may not look for traffic and are a serious hazard.

Talkers. Drivers or pedestrians talking to one another may not be paying close attention to the traffic.

Workers. People working on or near the roadway are a hazard clue. The work creates a distraction for other drivers and the workers themselves may not see you.

Ice Cream Trucks. Someone selling ice cream is a hazard clue. Children may be nearby and may not see you.

Disabled Vehicles. Drivers changing a tire or fixing an engine often do not pay attention to the danger that roadway traffic is to them. They are often careless. Jacked-up wheels or raised hoods are hazard clues.

Accidents. Accidents are particularly hazardous. People involved in the accident may not look for traffic. Passing drivers tend to look at the accident. People often run across the road without looking. Vehicles may slow or stop suddenly.

Shoppers. Drivers and pedestrians in and around shopping areas are often not watching traffic because they are looking for stores or looking into store windows.

Confused Drivers. Confused drivers often change direction suddenly or stop without warning. Confusion is common near freeway or turnpike interchanges and major intersections. Tourists unfamiliar with the area can be very hazardous. Clues to tourists include car-top luggage and out-of-state license plates. Unexpected actions (stopping in the middle of a block, changing lanes for no apparent reason, backup lights suddenly going on) are clues to confusion. Hesitation is another clue, including driving very slowly, using brakes often, or stopping in the middle of an intersection. You may also see drivers who are looking at street signs, maps, and house numbers. These drivers may not be paying attention to you.

Slow Drivers. Motorists who fail to maintain normal speed are hazards. Seeing slow-moving vehicles early can prevent a crash. Some vehicles by their nature are slow and seeing them is a hazard clue (mopeds, farm machinery, construction machinery, tractors, etc.). Some of these will have the "slow-moving vehicle" symbol to warn you. This is a red triangle with an orange center. Watch for it.

Drivers signaling a turn may be a hazard. Drivers signaling a turn may slow more than expected or stop. If they are making a tight turn into an alley or driveway they may go very slowly. If they are blocked by pedestrians or other vehicles they may have to stop on the roadway. Vehicles turning left may have to stop for oncoming vehicles.

Drivers in a Hurry. Drivers may feel your commercial vehicle is preventing them from getting where they want to go on time. Such drivers may pass you without a safe gap in the oncoming traffic, cutting too close in front of you. Drivers entering the road may pull in front of you to avoid being stuck behind you, causing you to brake. Be aware of this and watch for drivers who are in a hurry.

Impaired Drivers. Drivers who are sleepy, have had too much to drink, are on drugs, or who are ill are hazards. Some clues to these drivers are:
- Weaving across the road or drifting from one side to another.
- Leaving the road (dropping right wheels onto the shoulder, or bumping across a curb in a turn).

- Stopping at the wrong time (stopping at a green light or waiting too long at a stop).
- Keeping the window open in cold weather.
- Speeding up or slowing down suddenly; driving too fast or too slow.

Be alert for drunk drivers and sleepy drivers late at night.

Driver Body Movement as a Clue. Drivers look in the direction they are going to turn. You may sometimes get a clue from a driver's head and body movements that a driver may be going to make a turn even though the turn signals aren't on. Drivers making over-the-shoulder checks may be about to change lanes. These clues are most easily seen in motorcyclists and bicyclists. Watch other road users and try to tell whether they might do something hazardous.

Conflicts. You are in conflict when you have to change speed and/or direction to avoid hitting someone. Conflicts occur at intersections where vehicles meet, at merges (such as turnpike on-ramps), and where there are needed lane changes (such as the end of a lane, which forces a move to another lane of traffic). Other situations include slow-moving or stalled traffic in a traffic lane, and accident scenes. Watch for other drivers who are in conflict—they are a hazard to you. When they react to this conflict, they may do something that will put them in conflict with you.

Always Have a Plan

You should always be looking for hazards. Continue to learn to see hazards on the road. However, don't forget why you are looking for the hazards: they may turn into **emergencies**. You look for the hazards in order to have time to **plan a way out of any emergency**. When you see a hazard, think about the emergencies that could develop and figure out what you would do. Always be prepared to take action based on your plans. In this way, you will be a prepared, defensive driver who will improve not only your own safety but also the safety of all road users.

2.15 EMERGENCIES

Traffic emergencies occur when two vehicles are about to collide.

Vehicle emergencies occur when tires, brakes, or other critical parts fail. Following the safety practices in this book can help prevent emergencies. But if an emergency does happen, your chances of avoiding a crash depend upon how well you take action. Actions you can take are discussed below.

Steering to Avoid a Crash

Stopping is not always the safest thing to do in an emergency. When you don't have enough room to stop, you may have to steer away from what's ahead. Remember, you can almost always turn to miss an obstacle more quickly than you can stop. (However, top-heavy vehicles and tractors with multiple trailers may flip over.)

Keep Both Hands on the Steering Wheel. In order to turn quickly, you must have a firm grip on the steering wheel with both hands. The best way to have both hands on the wheel if there is an emergency is to keep them there all the time.

How to Turn Quickly and Safely. A quick turn can be made safely, if it's done the right way. Here are some points that safe drivers use:

- **Do not** apply the brake while you are turning. It's very easy to lock your wheels while turning. If that happens, you may skid out of control.
- **Do not** turn any more than needed to clear whatever is in your way. The more sharply you turn, the greater the chances of a skid or rollover.
- Be prepared to "countersteer"—that is, to turn the wheel back in the other direction, once you've passed whatever was in your path. Unless you are prepared to countersteer, you won't be able to do it quickly enough. You should think of emergency steering and countersteering as two parts of one driving action.

Where to Steer. If an oncoming driver has drifted into your lane, a move to your right is best. If that driver realizes what has happened, the natural response will be to return to his or her own lane.

If something is blocking your path, the best direction to steer will depend on the situation.

- If you have been using your mirrors, you'll know which lane is empty and can be safely used.
- If the shoulder is clear, going right may be best. No one is likely to be driving on the shoulder but someone may be passing you on the left. You will know if you have been using your mirrors.
- If you are blocked on both sides, a move to the right may be best. At least you won't force anyone into an opposing traffic lane and a possible head-on collision.

Leaving the Road. In some emergencies, you may have to drive off the road. It may be less risky than facing a collision with another vehicle.

Most shoulders are strong enough to support the weight of a large vehicle and, therefore, offer an available escape route. Here are some guidelines, if you do leave the road.

Avoid Braking. If possible, avoid using the brakes until your speed has dropped to about 20 mph. Then brake very gently to avoid skidding on a loose surface.

Keep One Set of Wheels on Pavement if Possible. This helps to maintain control.

Stay on the Shoulder. If the shoulder is clear, stay on it until your vehicle has come to a stop. Signal and check your mirrors before pulling back onto the road.

Returning to the Road. If you are forced to return to the road before you can stop, use the following procedure:

- Hold the wheel tightly and turn sharply enough to get right back on the road safely. Don't try to edge gradually back on the road. If you do, your tires might grab unexpectedly and you could lose control.
- When both front tires are on the paved surface, **countersteer** immediately. The two turns should be made as a single "steer-countersteer" move.

How to Stop Quickly and Safely

If somebody suddenly pulls out in front of you, your natural response is to hit the brakes. This is a good response if there's enough distance to stop and you use the brakes correctly.

You should brake in a way that will keep your vehicle in a straight line and allow you to turn if it becomes necessary. You can use the "controlled braking" method or the "stab braking" method.

Controlled Braking. With this method, you apply the brakes as hard as you can without locking the wheels. Keep steering wheel movements very small while doing this. If you need to make a larger steering adjustment or if the wheels lock, release the brakes. Reapply the brakes as soon as you can.

Stab Braking.
- Apply your brakes all the way.
- Release brakes when wheels lock up.
- As soon as the wheels start rolling, apply the brakes fully again. (It can take up to one second for the wheels to start rolling after you release the brakes. If you reapply the brakes before the wheels start rolling, the vehicle won't straighten out.)

Don't Jam on the Brakes. Emergency braking does not mean pushing down on the brake pedal as hard as you can. That will only keep the wheels locked up and cause a skid. If the wheels are skidding, you cannot control the vehicle.

NOTE: If you drive a vehicle with anti-lock brakes, you should read and follow the directions found in the Owners Manual for stopping quickly.

Brake Failure

Brakes kept in good condition rarely fail. Most **hydraulic** brake failures occur for one of two reasons:

- Loss of hydraulic pressure.
- Brake fade on long hills.

(Air brakes are discussed in Chapter 5.)

Loss of Hydraulic Pressure. When the system won't build up pressure, the brake pedal will feel spongy or go to the floor. Here are some things you can do:

Downshift. Putting the vehicle into a lower gear will help to slow the vehicle.

Pump the brakes. Sometimes pumping the brake pedal will generate enough hydraulic pressure to stop the vehicle.

Use the parking brake. The parking or emergency brake is separate from the hydraulic brake system. Therefore, it can be used to slow the vehicle. However, be sure to press the release button or pull the release lever at the same time you use the emergency brake so you can adjust the brake pressure and keep the wheels from locking up.

Find an escape route. While slowing the vehicle, look for an escape route—an open field, side street, or escape ramp. Turning uphill is a good way to slow and stop the vehicle. Make sure the vehicle does not start rolling backward after you stop. Put it in low gear, apply the parking brake, and if necessary roll back into some obstacle that will stop the vehicle.

Brake Failure on Downgrades. Driving slowly enough and braking properly will almost always prevent brake failure on long downgrades. Once the brakes have failed, however, you are going to have to look outside your vehicle for something to stop it.

Your best hope is an **escape ramp**. If there is one, there will be signs telling you about it. Use it. Ramps are usually located a few miles from the top of the downgrade. Every year, hundreds of drivers avoid injury to themselves or damage to their vehicles by using escape ramps. Some escape ramps use soft gravel that resists the motion of the vehicle and brings it to a stop. Others turn uphill, using the hill to stop the vehicle and soft gravel to hold it in place.

Any driver who loses brakes going downhill should use an escape ramp if it's available. If you don't use it, your chances of having a serious crash may be greatly increased.

If no escape ramp is available, take the least hazardous escape route you can—such as an open field, or a side road that flattens out or turns uphill. Make the move as soon as you know your brakes don't work. The longer you wait, the faster the vehicle will go and the harder it will be to stop.

Tire Failure

There are four important things that safe drivers do to handle a tire failure safely:

- Be aware that a tire has failed.
- Hold the steering wheel firmly.
- Stay off the brake.
- After stopping, check all the tires.

Recognize Tire Failure. Quickly knowing you have a tire failure will let you have more time to react. Having just a few seconds to remember what it is you're supposed to do can help you. The major signs of tire failure are:

- **Sound.** The loud "bang" of a blowout is an easily recognized sign. Because it can take a few seconds for your vehicle to react, you might think it was some other vehicle. But any time you hear a tire blow, you'd be safest to assume it was yours.

- **Vibration.** If the vehicle thumps or vibrates heavily, it may be a sign that one of the tires has gone flat. With a rear tire, that may be the only sign you get.

- **Feel.** If the steering feels "heavy," it is probably a sign that one of the front tires has failed. Sometimes, failure of a rear tire will cause the vehicle to slide back and forth or "fishtail." However, dual rear tires usually prevent this.

Any of these signs is a warning of possible tire failure. You should do the following things:

- **Hold the Steering Wheel Firmly.** If a front tire fails, it can twist the steering wheel out of your hand. The only way to prevent this is to keep a firm grip on the steering wheel with both hands at all times.

- **Stay Off the Brake.** It's natural to want to brake in an emergency. However, braking when a tire has failed could cause loss of control. Unless you're about to run into something, stay off the brake until the vehicle has slowed down. Then brake very gently, pull off the road, and stop.

- **Check the Tires.** After you've come to a stop, get out and check all the tires. Do this even if the vehicle seems to be handling all right. If one of your dual tires goes, the only way you may know it is by getting out and looking at it.

2.16 SKID CONTROL AND RECOVERY

A skid happens whenever the tires lose their grip on the road. This is caused in one of four ways:

Overbraking. Braking too hard and locking up the wheels. Skids also can occur if the speed retarder is used when the road is slippery.

Oversteering. Turning the wheels more sharply than the vehicle can turn.

Overacceleration. Supplying too much power to the drive wheels, causing them to spin.

Driving Too Fast. Most serious skids result from driving too fast for road conditions. Drivers who adjust their driving to conditions don't overaccelerate and don't have to overbrake or oversteer from too much speed.

Drive-Wheel Skids

By far the most common skid is one in which the rear wheels lose traction through excessive braking or acceleration. Skids caused by acceleration usually happen on ice or snow. They can be easily stopped by taking your foot off the accelerator. (If it is very slippery, push the clutch in. Otherwise the engine can keep the wheels from rolling freely and regaining traction.)

Rear-wheel braking skids occur when the rear-drive wheels lock. Because locked wheels have less traction than rolling wheels, the rear wheels usually slide sideways in an attempt to "catch up" with the front wheels. In a bus or straight truck, the vehicle will slide sideways in a "spin-out." With vehicles towing trailers, a drive-wheel skid can let the trailer push the towing vehicle sideways, causing a sudden jackknife. (Figure 2-14).

Correcting a Drive-Wheel Braking Skid

Do the following to correct a drive-wheel braking skid:

Stop Braking. This will let the rear wheels roll again, and keep the rear wheels from sliding any further. If on ice, push in the clutch to let the wheels turn freely.

Turn Quickly. When a vehicle begins to slide sideways, **quickly** steer in the direction you want the vehicle to go—down the road. You must turn the wheel quickly.

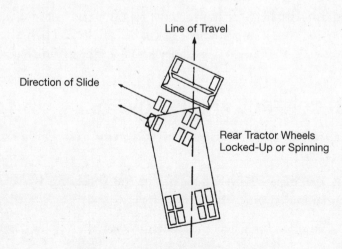

Figure 2-14 Tractor Jackknife

Countersteer. As a vehicle turns back on course, it has a tendency to keep right on turning. Unless you turn the steering wheel quickly the other way, you may find yourself skidding in the opposite direction.

Learning to stay off the brake, turning the steering wheel quickly, pushing in the clutch, and countersteering in a skid takes a lot of practice. The best place to get this practice is on a large driving range or "skid pad."

Front-Wheel Skids

Most front-wheel skids are caused by driving too fast for conditions. Other causes are: 1) lack of tread on the front tires, and 2) cargo loaded so not enough weight is on the front axle. In a front-wheel skid, the front end tends to go in a straight line regardless of how much you turn the steering wheel. On a very slippery surface, you may not be able to steer around a curve or turn.

When a front-wheel skid occurs, the only way to stop the skid is to let the vehicle slow down. Stop turning and/or braking so hard. Slow down as quickly as possible without skidding.

2.17 ACCIDENT PROCEDURES

When you're in an accident and not seriously hurt, you need to act to prevent further damage or injury. The basic steps to be taken at any accident are to:

- Protect the area.
- Notify authorities.
- Care for injured.

Protect the Area

The first thing to do at an accident scene is to keep another accident from happening at the same spot. To protect the accident area:

- If your vehicle is involved in the accident, try to get it to the side of the road. This will help prevent another accident and allow traffic to move.
- If you're stopping to help, park away from the accident. The area immediately around the accident will be needed for emergency vehicles.
- Put on your flashers.
- Set out reflective triangles to warn other traffic. Make sure they can be seen by other drivers in time for them to avoid the accident.

Notify Authorities

If you have a CB, put out a call over the emergency channel before you get out of your vehicle. If not, wait until after the accident scene has been properly protected, then phone or send someone to phone the police. Try to determine where you are so you can give the exact location.

Care for Injured

If a qualified person is at the accident site and helping the injured, stay out of the way unless asked to assist. Otherwise, do the best you can to help any injured parties. Here are some simple steps to follow in giving assistance:

- Don't move a severely injured person unless the danger of fire or passing traffic makes it necessary.
- Stop heavy bleeding by applying direct pressure to the wound.
- Keep the injured person warm.

2.18 FIRES

Truck fires can cause damage and injury. Learn the causes of fires and how to prevent them. Know what to do to extinguish fires.

Causes of Fire

The following are some causes of vehicle fires:

- **After Accidents.** Spilled fuel, improper use of flares.
- **Tires.** Underinflated tires, duals that touch.
- **Electrical System.** Short circuits due to damaged insulation or loose connections.
- **Fuel.** Driver smoking, improper fueling, or loose fuel connections.
- **Cargo.** Flammable cargo, improperly sealed or loaded cargo, or poor ventilation.

Fire Prevention

Pay attention to the following:

- **Pre-Trip Inspection.** Make a complete inspection of all tires and cargo, fuel, electrical, and exhaust systems. Be sure to check that the fire extinguisher is charged.
- **En-Route Inspection.** Check the tires, wheels, and truck body for signs of heat whenever you stop during a trip.
- **Follow Safe Procedures.** Follow correct safety procedures for fueling the vehicle, using brakes, handling flares, and other activities that can cause a fire.
- **Monitoring.** Check the instruments and gauges often for signs of overheating, and use the mirrors to look for signs of smoke from tires, or the vehicle.
- **Caution.** Use caution when handling anything flammable.

Fire Fighting

Knowing how to fight fires is important. Fires have been made worse by drivers who didn't know what to do. Here are some procedures to follow in case of fire:

Pull Off the Road. The first step is to get the vehicle off the road and stop. In doing so:

- Park in an open area, away from buildings, trees, brush, other vehicles, or anything that might catch fire.
- Don't pull into a service station!
- Use your CB to notify the police of your problem and your location.

Keep the Fire From Spreading. Before trying to put out the fire, make sure that it doesn't spread any further.

- With an **engine** fire, turn off the engine as soon as you can. Don't open the hood if you can avoid it. Shoot extinguishers through louvers, radiator, or from the underside of the vehicle.
- For a **cargo** fire in a van or box trailer, keep the doors shut, especially if your cargo contains hazardous materials. Opening the van doors will supply the fire with oxygen and can cause it to burn very fast.

Use the Right Fire Extinguisher.

- The B:C type fire extinguisher is designed to work on electrical fires and burning liquids. The A:B:C type is designed to work on burning wood, paper, and cloth as well.
- Water can be used on wood, paper, or cloth, but don't use water on an electrical fire (you could get shocked) or a gasoline fire (it will just spread the flames).
- A burning tire must be cooled. Lots of water may be required.
- If you're not sure what to use, especially on a hazardous materials fire, wait for qualified fire fighters.

Extinguish the Fire. Here are some rules to follow in putting out a fire:

- Know how the fire extinguisher works. Study the instructions printed on the extinguisher **before** you need it.
- When using the extinguisher, stay as far away from the fire as possible. Aim at the source or base of the fire, not up in the flames.
- Position yourself upwind. Let the wind carry the extinguisher to the fire rather than carrying the flames to you.

- Continue until whatever was burning has been cooled. Absence of smoke or flame does not mean the fire is completely out or cannot restart.

- Try to extinguish a fire only if you know what you are doing and it is safe to do so.

2.19 STAYING ALERT AND FIT TO DRIVE

Be Ready to Drive

Driving a vehicle for long hours is tiring. Even the best of drivers will become less alert. However, there are things that good drivers do to help stay alert and safe. Here are a few suggestions:

Get Enough Sleep. Leaving on a long trip when you're already tired is dangerous. If you have a long trip scheduled, make sure that you get a good sleep before you go. Most people require seven to eight hours of sleep every 24 hours.

Schedule Trips Safely. Your body gets used to sleeping during certain hours. If you are driving during those hours, you will be less alert. If possible, try to schedule trips for the hours you are normally awake. Many heavy motor vehicle accidents occur between midnight and 6 a.m. Tired drivers can easily fall asleep at these times, especially if they don't regularly drive at those hours. Trying to push on and finish a long trip at these times can be very dangerous.

Avoid Medication. Many medicines can make you sleepy. Those that do have a label warning against operating vehicles or machinery. The most common medicine of this type is an ordinary cold pill. If you have to drive with a cold, you are better off suffering from the cold than from the effects of the medicine.

Keep Cool. A hot, poorly ventilated cab can make you sleepy. Keep the window or vent cracked or use the air conditioner, if you have one.

Take Breaks. Short breaks can keep you alert. But the time to take them is **before** you feel really drowsy or tired. Stop often. Walk around, and inspect your vehicle. It may help to do some physical exercises.

When You Do Become Sleepy

When you are sleepy, trying to "push on" is far more dangerous than most drivers think. It is a **major cause of fatal accidents**. Here are some important rules to follow:

Stop to Sleep. When your body needs sleep, sleep is the only thing that will work. If you have to make a stop anyway, make it whenever you feel the first signs of sleepiness, even if it is earlier than you planned. By getting up a little earlier the next day, you can keep on schedule without the danger of driving while you are not alert.

Take a Nap. If you can't stop for the night, at least pull off the road and take a nap. A nap as short as a half-hour will do more to overcome fatigue than a half-hour coffee stop.

Avoid Drugs. There are no drugs that can overcome being tired. While they may keep you awake for a while, they won't make you alert. And eventually, you'll be even more tired than if you hadn't taken them at all. Sleep is the only thing that can overcome fatigue.

Alcohol and Driving

Drinking alcohol and then driving is a very serious problem. People who drink alcohol are involved in traffic accidents resulting in over 20,000 deaths every year. You should know:

- How alcohol works in the human body.
- How it affects driving.
- Laws regarding drinking and driving.
- Legal, financial, and safety risks of drinking and driving.

The Truth About Alcohol. There are many dangerous ideas about the use of alcohol. The driver who believes in these wrong ideas will be more likely to get into trouble. Here are some examples:

FALSE	THE TRUTH
Alcohol increases your ability to drive.	Alcohol is a drug that will make you less alert and reduce your ability to drive safely.
Some people can drink a lot and not be affected by it.	Everyone who drinks is affected by alcohol .
If you eat a lot first, you won't get drunk.	Food will not keep you from getting drunk.
Coffee and a little fresh air will help a drinker sober up.	Only time will help a drinker sober up—other methods just don't work.
Stick with beer—it's not as strong as wine or whiskey.	A few beers are the same as a few shots of whiskey or a few glasses of wine.

What Is a Drink? It is the alcohol in drinks that affects human performance. It doesn't make any difference whether that alcohol comes from "a couple of beers" or from two glasses of wine or two shots of hard liquor.

All of the following drinks **contain the same amount of alcohol**:
- A 12-ounce glass of 5% beer.
- A 5-ounce glass of 12% wine.
- A $1\frac{1}{2}$-ounce shot of 80 proof liquor.

How Alcohol Works. Alcohol goes directly from the stomach into the blood stream. A drinker can control the amount of alcohol that he or she takes in by having fewer drinks or none. However, the drinker cannot control how fast the body gets rid of alcohol. If you have drinks faster than the body can get rid of them, you will have more alcohol in your body and your driving will be more affected. The amount of alcohol in your body is commonly measured by the Blood Alcohol Concentration (BAC).

What Determines Blood Alcohol Concentration. BAC is determined by the amount of alcohol you drink (more alcohol means higher BAC), how fast you drink (faster drinking means higher BAC), and your weight (a small person doesn't have to drink as much to reach the same BAC).

Alcohol and the Brain. Alcohol affects more and more of the brain as BAC builds up. The first part of the brain affected controls judgement and self control. One of the bad things about this is it can keep drinkers from knowing they are getting drunk. And, of course, good judgement and self-control are absolutely necessary for safe driving.

As blood alcohol concentration continues to build up, muscle control, vision, and coordination are affected more and more. Eventually, a person will pass out.

How Alcohol Affects Driving. All drivers are affected by drinking alcohol. Alcohol affects judgement, vision, coordination, and reaction time. It causes serious driving errors, such as:
- Increased reaction time to hazards.
- Driving too fast or too slowly.
- Driving in the wrong lane.
- Running over the curb.
- Weaving.
- Straddling lanes.
- Quick, jerky starts.
- Failure to use lights or to signal.

- Running stop signs and red lights.
- Improper passing.

These effects mean increased chances of a crash and chances of losing your driver's license. Accident statistics show that the chance of a crash is much greater for drivers who have been drinking than for drivers who have not.

Other Drugs

Besides alcohol, other legal and illegal drugs are being used more often. Laws prohibit possession or use of many drugs while on duty. They prohibit being under the influence of any "controlled substance," amphetamines (including "pep pills" and "bennies"), narcotics, or any other substances which can make the driver unsafe. This could include a variety of prescription and over-the-counter drugs (cold medicines) which may make the driver drowsy or otherwise affect safe driving ability. However, possession and use of a drug given to a driver by a doctor is permitted if the doctor informs the driver that it will not affect safe driving ability.

Pay attention to warning labels of legitimate drugs and medicines and to doctor's orders regarding possible effects. Stay away from illegal drugs. Don't use any drug that hides fatigue—the only cure for fatigue is rest. Alcohol can make the effects of other drugs much worse. The safest rule is don't mix drugs with driving at all.

Use of drugs can lead to traffic accidents resulting in death, injury, and property damage. Furthermore, it can lead to arrest, fines, and jail sentences. It can also mean the end of a person's driving career.

Illness

Once in a while, you may become so ill that you cannot operate a motor vehicle safely. If this happens to you, you must not drive. However, in case of an emergency, you may drive to the nearest place where you can safely stop.

2.20 HAZARDOUS MATERIALS RULES FOR ALL COMMERCIAL DRIVERS

All drivers should know something about hazardous materials. You must be able to recognize hazardous cargo, and you must know whether or not you can haul it without having a hazardous materials endorsement to your CDL license.

NOTE: The following material covers information on hazardous materials likely to be found on the general knowledge test. This is not, however, all you need to know to pass the hazardous materials endorsement test. To review for the hazardous materials endorsement, you should study Chapter 9 in detail. (Some of the following material also appears in Chapter 9.)

What Are Hazardous Materials?

The Federal Hazardous Materials Table names materials that are hazardous. They pose a risk to health, safety, and property during transportation. You must follow the many rules about transporting them. The intent of the rules is to:

- Contain the product.
- Communicate the risk.
- Ensure safe drivers and equipment.

To Contain the Product: Many hazardous products can injure or kill on contact. To protect drivers and others from contact, the rules tell shippers how to package safely. Similar rules tell drivers how to load, transport, and unload bulk tanks. These are "containment rules."

To Communicate the Risk: The shipper uses a shipping paper and package labels to warn dockworkers and drivers of the risk. Shipping orders, bills of lading, and manifests are all examples of shipping papers. (See Figure 9-1 in Chapter 9.)

The shipping paper describes the hazardous materials being transported. Shippers put diamond-shaped hazard warning labels on most hazardous materials packages. These labels inform others of the hazard. If the diamond label won't fit on the container, shippers put the label on a tag. For example, compressed gas cylinders that will not hold a label will have tags or decals. Labels look like the examples shown in Figure 2-15.

After an accident or hazardous material leak, the driver may be unable to speak when help arrives. Firefighters and police must know the hazards involved in order to prevent more damage or injury. The driver's life, and the lives of others, may depend on quickly finding the shipping papers for hazardous cargo. For that reason, you must tab shipping papers related to hazardous materials, or keep them on top of other shipping papers. You must also keep shipping papers:

- in a pouch on the driver's door, or
- in clear view within reach while driving, or
- on the driver's seat when out of the vehicle.

Drivers must use placards to warn others of their hazardous cargo. Placards are signs placed on the outside of a vehicle to show the hazard class(es) of products on board. There are 19 different DOT placards. Each is turned upright on a point and has a diamond shape. The person who does the loading must place the placards on the front, rear, and both sides of the vehicle.

Not all vehicles carrying hazardous materials need to have placards. The rules about placards are given in Chapter 9 of this book. You can drive a vehicle that carries

Figure 2-15 Examples of Labels

hazardous materials if it does not require placards. If it requires placards, you must not drive it unless your driver license has the hazardous materials endorsement.

To ensure safe drivers and equipment: The rules require all drivers of placarded vehicles to learn how to safely load and transport hazardous products. They must have a CDL with the hazardous materials endorsement.

To get the required endorsement you must pass a written test on material found in Chapter 9 of this book. You also will need a tank endorsement if you transport hazardous products in a cargo tank on a truck larger than 26,000 pounds, gross vehicle weight rating. (Study Chapter 8).

Drivers who need the hazardous materials endorsement must learn the placard rules. If you do not know if your vehicle needs placards, ask your employer. **Never drive a vehicle needing placards unless you have the hazardous materials endorsement.** To do so is a crime. When stopped, you will be cited and you will not be allowed to drive your truck further. It will cost you time and money. A failure to placard when needed will risk your life and the lives of others if you have an accident. Emergency help will not know of your hazardous cargo.

Hazardous materials drivers must also know which products they can load together, and which they can not. These rules are also in Chapter 9. Before loading a truck with more than one type of product, you must know if it is safe to load them together. If you do not know, ask your employer.

Chapter 3 – Transporting Cargo Safely

THIS CHAPTER COVERS

❏ **Inspecting Cargo**   ❏ **Securing Cargo**
❏ **Cargo Weight & Balance**   ❏ **Cargo Needing Attention**

This chapter tells you about hauling cargo safely. You must understand basic cargo safety rules to get a CDL.

If you load cargo wrong or do not secure it, it can be a danger to others and yourself. Loose cargo that falls off a vehicle can cause traffic problems and others could be hurt or killed. Loose cargo could hurt or kill you during a quick stop or crash. Your vehicle could be damaged by an overload. Steering could be affected by how a vehicle is loaded, making it more difficult to control the vehicle.

Whether or not you load and secure the cargo yourself, you are responsible for:

- Inspecting your cargo.
- Recognizing overloads and poorly balanced weight.
- Knowing your cargo is properly secured.

These are discussed below.

If you intend to carry hazardous material that requires placards on your vehicle, you will also have to have a hazardous materials endorsement. Chapter 9 of this book has the information you need to pass the hazardous materials test.

3.1 INSPECTING CARGO

As part of your pre-trip inspection, check for overloads, poorly balanced weight, and cargo that is not secured properly.

When Should You Check Your Cargo?

You should inspect the cargo and its securing devices again within 25 miles after beginning a trip. Make any adjustments needed. Check the cargo and securing devices as often as necessary during a trip to keep the load secure. Inspect again:

- After every 3 hours or 150 miles that you drive.
- After every break you take during driving.

Federal, state, and local regulations of weight, securement, cover, and truck routes vary greatly from place to place. Know the regulations where you will be driving.

3.2 WEIGHT AND BALANCE

You are responsible for making certain that you are not being overloaded. You are also responsible for understanding how much your vehicle weighs and how much weight it can carry.

Definitions You Should Know

- **Gross Vehicle Weight (GVW).** The total weight of a single vehicle plus its load.
- **Gross Combination Weight (GCW).** The total weight of a powered unit plus trailer(s) plus the cargo.
- **Gross Vehicle Weight Rating (GVWR).** The maximum GVW specified by the manufacturer for a single vehicle plus its load.
- **Gross Combination Weight Rating (GCWR).** The maximum GCW specified by the manufacturer for a specific combination of vehicles plus its load.
- **Axle Weight.** The weight transmitted to the ground by one axle or one set of axles.
- **Tire Load.** The maximum safe weight a tire can carry at a specified pressure. This rating is stated on the side of each tire.
- **Suspension Systems.** Suspension systems have a manufacturer's weight capacity rating.
- **Coupling Device Capacity.** Coupling devices are rated for the maximum weight they can pull and/or carry.

Legal Weight Limits

You must keep weights within legal limits. States have maximums for GVWs, GCWs, and axle weights. Often, maximum axle weights are set by a bridge formula. A bridge formula permits less maximum axle weight for axles that are closer together. This is to prevent overloading bridges and roadways.

Overloading can have bad effects on steering, braking, and speed control. Overloaded trucks have to go very slowly on upgrades. Worse, they may gain too much speed on downgrades. Stopping distance increases. Brakes can fail when forced to work too hard.

During bad weather or in mountains, it may not be safe to operate at legal maximum weights. Take this into account before driving.

Don't Be Top-Heavy

The height of the vehicle's center of gravity is very important for safe handling. A high center of gravity (cargo piled up high or heavy cargo on top) means you are more likely to tip over. This is most dangerous in curves or if you have to swerve to avoid a hazard. It is very important to distribute the cargo so the center of gravity is as low as possible. Put the heaviest parts of the cargo under the lightest parts.

Balance the Weight

Poor weight balance can make vehicle handling unsafe. Too much weight on the steering axle can cause difficult steering. It can damage the steering axle and tires. Underloaded front axles (caused by shifting weight too far to the rear) can make the steering axle weight too light to steer safely. Too little weight on the driving axles can cause poor traction. The drive wheels may spin easily, and during bad weather, the truck may not be able to keep going. Weight that is loaded so there is a high center of gravity causes greater chance of rollover. On flatbed vehicles, there is also a greater chance that the load will shift to the side or fall off. Figure 3-1 shows examples of the right and wrong way to balance cargo weight.

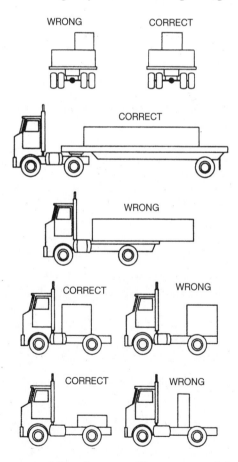

Figure 3-1 The Correct Way to Load Cargo

3.3 SECURING CARGO

Blocking and Bracing

Blocking is used in the front, back, and/or sides of a piece of cargo to keep it from sliding. Blocking is shaped to fit snugly against cargo. It is secured to the cargo deck to prevent cargo movement. **Bracing** is also used to prevent movement of cargo. Bracing goes from the upper part of the cargo to the floor and/or walls of the cargo compartment.

Cargo Tiedown

On flatbed trailers or trailers without sides, cargo must be secured to keep it from shifting and falling off. In closed vans, tiedowns can also be important to prevent cargo shifting that may affect the handling of the vehicle. Tiedowns must be of the proper type and proper strength. The combined strength of all cargo tiedowns must be strong enough to lift one-and-one-half-times the weight of the piece of cargo tied down. Proper tiedown equipment must be used, including ropes, straps, chains, and tensioning devices (winches, ratchets, clinching components). Tiedowns must be attached to the vehicle correctly (hooks, bolts, rails, rings).

Cargo should have at least one tiedown for each 10 feet of cargo. Make sure you have enough tiedowns to meet this need. No matter how small the cargo is, it should have at least two tiedowns holding it.

There are special requirements for securing various heavy pieces of metal. Find out what they are if you are to carry such loads.

Header Boards

Front-end header boards ("headache racks") protect you from your cargo in case of a collision. Make sure the front-end structure is in good condition. The front-end structure should block the forward movement of any cargo you carry.

Covering Cargo

There are two basic reasons for covering cargo:

1. To protect people from spilled cargo.
2. To protect the cargo from weather. Spill protection is a safety requirement in many states. Be familiar with the laws of the states in which you drive.

You should look at your cargo covers in the mirrors from time to time while driving. A flapping cover can tear loose, uncovering the cargo and possibly blocking your view or someone else's.

You cannot inspect sealed loads, but you should check that you don't exceed gross weight and axle weight limits.

Sealed and Containerized Loads

Containerized loads generally are used when freight is carried part way by rail or ship. Delivery by truck occurs at the beginning and/or end of the journey. Some containers have their own tiedown devices or locks that attach directly to a special frame. Others have to be loaded onto flatbed trailers. They are secured with tiedowns just like any other large cargo.

3.4 CARGO NEEDING SPECIAL ATTENTION

Dry Bulk

Dry bulk tanks require special care because they often have a high center of gravity and the load can shift. Drive slowly and carefully when going around curves and making sharp turns. (Study Chapter 8, "Tank Vehicles" to familiarize yourself with driving and inspecting a tank vehicle. Although the chapter mainly concerns itself with liquid/gas tankers, you are still required to have this endorsement to drive a dry bulk tanker.)

Hanging Meat

Hanging meat (suspended beef, pork, lamb) in a refrigerated truck can be a very unstable load with a high center of gravity. Particular caution is needed on sharp curves such as off-ramps and on-ramps. Drive slowly.

Livestock

Livestock can move around in a trailer, causing unsafe handling. With less than a full load, use false bulkheads to keep livestock bunched together. Even when bunched, special care is necessary because livestock can lean on curves. This shifts the center of gravity and makes rollover more likely.

Oversized Loads

Over length, over width, and/or over weight loads require special transit permits. Driving is usually limited to certain times. Special equipment may be necessary, such as "wide load" signs, flashing lights, flags, etc. Such loads may require a police escort or pilot vehicles bearing warning signs and/or flashing lights. These special loads require special driving care.

Tank Vehicles

Tank vehicles also require special attention, both for loading and driving. Information on tank vehicles appears in Chapter 8. You should be familiar with this information even if you are not testing for that endorsement as it may appear on the General Knowledge Test.

Chapter 4 – Transporting Passengers

THIS CHAPTER COVERS
- ❏ Definition of a Bus
- ❏ Pre-trip Inspection
- ❏ Loading
- ❏ Safe Driving with Buses

Bus and van drivers must have a commercial driver's license if they drive a vehicle designed to seat more than 15 persons, including the driver. However, you are not considered a bus driver if you only carry family members for personal reasons.

Bus drivers must have a passenger endorsement on their commercial driver's license. To get the endorsement, you must pass a written test on Chapters 2, 3, and 4 of this book. (If your bus has air brakes, you must also pass a written test on Chapter 5.) You must also pass the performance tests required for the class of vehicle you drive. This chapter has information you must know to drive a bus safely.

4.1 PRE-TRIP INSPECTION

Before driving your bus, make sure it is safe. During the pre-trip inspection, check defects reported by previous drivers. Only if defects reported earlier have been fixed should you sign the previous driver's report. This is your certification that the defects reported earlier have been fixed.

Vehicle Systems

Make sure these things are in good working order before driving:

- Service brakes including air hose couplings (if your bus has a trailer or semi-trailer).
- Parking brake.
- Steering mechanism.
- Lights and reflectors.
- Tires (front wheels must not have recapped or regrooved tires).
- Horn.
- Windshield wiper or wipers.
- Rear-vision mirror or mirrors.
- Coupling devices.
- Wheels and rims.
- Emergency equipment.

Access Doors and Panels

As you check the outside of the bus, close any open emergency exits. Also, close any open access panels (for baggage, restroom service, engine, etc.) before driving.

Bus Interior

People sometimes damage unattended buses. Always check the interior of the bus before driving to ensure rider safety. Aisles and stairwells must always be clear. The following parts of your bus must be in safe working condition:

- Each handhold and railing.
- Floor covering.
- Signaling devices, including the restroom emergency buzzer if the bus has a restroom.
- Emergency exit handles.

The seats must be safe for riders. All seats must be securely fastened to the bus. There is one exception to this rule. A charter bus carrying agricultural workers may have up to eight temporary folding seats in the aisle.

Never drive with an open emergency exit door or window. The emergency exit sign on an emergency door must be clearly visible. If there is a red emergency door light, it must work. Turn it on at night or any other time you use your outside lights.

Roof Hatches

You may lock some emergency roof hatches in a partly open position for fresh air. Do not leave them open as a regular practice. Keep in mind the bus's higher clearance while driving with them open.

Make sure your bus has the fire extinguisher and emergency reflectors required by law. The bus must also have spare electrical fuses unless equipped with circuit breakers.

Use Your Seatbelt!

The driver's seat should have a seatbelt. Always use it for safety.

4.2 LOADING AND TRIP START

Do not allow riders to leave carry-on baggage in a doorway or aisle. There should be nothing in the aisle that might trip other riders. Secure baggage and freight in ways that avoid damage and:

- Allow the driver to move freely and easily.

- Allow riders to exit by any window or door in an emergency.
- Protect riders from injury if carry-ons fall or shift.

Hazardous Materials

Watch for cargo or baggage containing hazardous materials. Most hazardous materials cannot be carried on a bus.

The Federal Hazardous Materials Table shows which materials are hazardous. They pose a risk to health safety and property during transportation. The rules require shippers to mark containers of hazardous material with the material's name, ID number, and hazard label. There are nine different four-inch diamond shaped hazard labels like the examples shown in Figure 4-1. Watch for the diamond shaped labels. Do not transport any hazardous material unless you are sure the rules allow it.

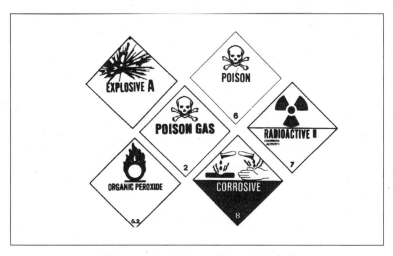

Figure 4-1 Examples of Labels.

Forbidden Hazardous Materials

Buses may carry small-arms ammunition labeled ORM-D, emergency hospital supplies, and drugs. You can carry small amounts of some other hazardous materials if the shipper cannot send them any other way. Buses must never carry:

- Class 2 poison, **liquid** Class 6 poison, tear gas, irritating material.
- More than 100 pounds of **solid** Class 6 poisons.
- Explosives in the space occupied by people, except small-arms ammunition.
- Labeled radioactive materials in the space occupied by people.
- More than 500 pounds total of allowed hazardous materials, and no more than 100 pounds of any one class.

Riders sometimes board a bus with an unlabeled hazardous material. They may not know it is unsafe. Do not allow riders to carry on common hazards such as car batteries or gasoline.

Standee Line

No rider may stand forward of the rear of the driver's seat. Buses designed to allow standing must have a two inch line on the floor or some other means of showing riders where they cannot stand. This is called the standee line. All standing riders must stay behind it.

At Your Destination

When arriving at the destination or intermediate stops announce:

- The location.
- Reason for stopping.
- Next departure time.
- Bus number.

Remind riders to take carry-ons with them if they get off the bus. If the aisle is on a lower level than the seats, remind riders of the step-down. It is best to tell them before coming to a complete stop.

Charter bus drivers should not allow riders on the bus until departure time. This will help prevent theft or vandalism of the bus.

4.3 ON THE ROAD

Passenger Supervision

While Driving. Many charter and intercity carriers have passenger comfort and safety rules. Mention rules about smoking, drinking, or the use of radio and tape players at the start of the trip. Explaining the rules at the start will help to avoid trouble later on.

While driving, scan the interior of your bus as well as the road ahead, to the sides, and to the rear. You may have to remind riders about rules or about keeping arms and heads inside the bus.

At Stops. Riders can stumble when getting on or off and when the bus starts or stops. Caution riders to watch their step when leaving the bus. Wait for them to sit down or brace themselves before starting. Start and stop as smoothly as possible to avoid rider injury.

Occasionally, you may have a drunk or disruptive rider. You must ensure this rider's safety as well as that of others. Don't discharge such riders where it would be unsafe for them. It may be safer at the next scheduled stop, or a well-lighted area where there are other people. Many carriers have guidelines for handling disruptive riders.

Common Accidents

The Most Common Bus Crashes. Bus crashes often happen at intersections. Use caution even if a signal or stop sign controls other traffic. School and mass transit buses sometimes scrape off mirrors or hit passing vehicles when pulling out from a bus stop. Remember the clearance your bus needs, and watch for poles and tree limbs at stops. Know the size of the gap your bus needs to accelerate and merge with traffic. Wait for the gap to open before leaving the stop. Never assume other drivers will brake to give you room when you signal or start to pull out.

Speed on Curves

Crashes on curves kill people and destroy buses. They result from excessive speed, often when rain or snow has made the road slippery. Every banked curve has a safe "design speed." In good weather, the posted speed is safe for cars, but it may be too high for many buses. With good traction, the bus may roll over; with poor traction, it might slide off the curve. **Reduce speed for curves!** If your bus leans toward the outside on a banked curve, you are driving too fast.

Railroad Crossings

Stop at R.R. Crossings. Stop your bus between 15 and 50 feet before railroad crossings. Listen and look in both directions for trains. You should open your forward door if it improves your ability to see or hear an approaching train. Before crossing after a train has passed, make sure there isn't another train coming in the other direction on other tracks. If your bus has a manual transmission, never change gears while crossing the tracks.

You do not have to stop but you must slow down and carefully check for other vehicles:

- At street car crossings.
- At railroad tracks used only for industrial switching within a business district.
- Where a police officer or flagman is directing traffic.
- If a traffic signal shows green.
- At crossings marked "exempt crossing."

Drawbridges

Stop at Drawbridges. Stop at drawbridges that do not have a signal light or traffic control attendant. Stop at least 50 feet before the draw of the bridge. Look to make sure the draw is completely closed before crossing. You do not need to stop, but you must slow down and make sure it's safe when:

- There is a traffic light showing green.
- The bridge has an attendant or traffic officer who controls traffic whenever the bridge opens.

4.4 AFTER-TRIP VEHICLE INSPECTION

Inspect your bus at the end of each shift. If you work for an interstate carrier, you must complete a written inspection report for each bus driven. The report must specify each bus and list any defect that would affect safety or result in a breakdown. If there are no defects, the report should say so.

Riders sometimes damage safety-related parts such as hand-holds, seats, emergency exits, and windows. If you report this damage at the end of a shift, mechanics can make repairs before the bus goes out again. Mass transit drivers should also make sure passenger signaling devices and brake-door interlocks work properly.

4.5 PROHIBITED PRACTICES

Avoid fueling your bus with riders on board unless absolutely necessary. Never refuel in a closed building with riders on board.

Don't talk with riders or engage in any other distracting activity while driving.

Do not tow or push a disabled bus with riders aboard either vehicle, unless getting off would be unsafe. Only tow or push the bus to the nearest safe spot to discharge passengers. Follow your employer's guidelines on towing or pushing disabled buses.

4.6 USE OF BRAKE-DOOR INTERLOCKS

Urban mass transit coaches may have a brake and accelerator interlock system. The interlock applies the brakes and holds the throttle in idle position when the rear door is open. The interlock releases when you close the rear door. Do not use this safety feature in place of the parking brake.

Chapter 5 – Air Brakes

THIS CHAPTER COVERS
- ❑ Air Brake System Parts
- ❑ Dual Air Brake Systems
- ❑ Inspecting Air Brakes
- ❑ Using Air Brakes

This section tells you about air brakes. You need this information for the safe operation of air brakes used on trucks and buses. If you want to pull a trailer with air brakes, you also need to read Chapter 6: Combination Vehicles.

Air brakes use **compressed air** to make the brakes work. You can apply all the braking force you need to each of the wheels of a heavy vehicle, even units pulling two or three trailers. Air brakes are a safe way of stopping large vehicles if the brakes are well maintained and used properly. However, you must know more about air brakes than you need to know with the simpler brake systems used on light vehicles. Therefore, it is important for you to study this chapter.

Air brake systems are three braking systems combined: the service brake system, the parking brake system, and the emergency brake system.

- The **service brake** system applies and releases the brakes when you use the brake pedal during normal driving.
- The **parking brake** system applies and releases the parking brakes when you use the parking brake control.
- The **emergency brake** system uses parts of the service and parking brake systems to stop the vehicle in the event of a brake system failure.

The parts of these systems are discussed in greater detail below.

5.1 THE PARTS OF AN AIR BRAKE SYSTEM

There are many parts to an air brake system. You should know about the parts discussed here.

Air Compressor

The air compressor pumps air into the air storage tanks (reservoirs). The air compressor is connected to the engine through gears or a V-belt. The compressor may be air cooled or may be cooled by the engine cooling system. It may have its own oil supply or be lubricated by engine oil. If the compressor has its own oil supply, check the oil level before driving.

Air Compressor Governor

The governor controls when the air compressor will pump air into the air storage tanks. When air tank pressure rises to the cut-out level (around 125 pounds per square inch, or "psi"), the governor stops the compressor from pumping air. When the tank pressure falls to the cut-in pressure (around 100 psi), the governor allows the compressor to start pumping again.

Air Storage Tanks

Air storage tanks are used to hold compressed air. The number and size of air tanks vary among vehicles. The tanks will hold enough air to allow the brakes to be used several times even if the compressor stops working.

Air Tank Drains

Compressed air usually has some water and some compressor oil in it which is bad for the air brake system. For example, the water can freeze in cold weather and cause brake failure. The water and oil tend to collect in the bottom of the air tank. Therefore, each air tank is equipped with a drain valve in the bottom. There are two types:

- Manual—the water and oil are expelled by turning the drain valve a quarter turn (shown in Figure 5-1) or by pulling a cable. You must drain the tanks yourself at the end of each day of driving. **Be sure that you drain the air tanks completely.**

- Automatic—the water and oil are automatically expelled. They may be equipped for manual draining as well. (The automatic types are available with electric heating devices. These help prevent freeze-up of the automatic drain in cold weather.)

Alcohol Evaporator

Some air brake systems have an alcohol evaporator to put alcohol into the air system. This helps to reduce the risk of ice in air brake valves and other parts during cold weather. Ice inside the system can make the brakes stop working.

Check the alcohol container and fill up as necessary every day during cold weather. **Daily air tank drainage is still needed to get rid of water and oil** (unless the system has automatic drain valves).

Safety Valve

A safety relief valve is installed in the first tank to which the air compressor pumps. The safety valve protects the tank and the rest of the system from too much pressure. The valve is usually set to open at 150 psi. If the safety valve releases air, something is wrong. Have the fault fixed by a mechanic.

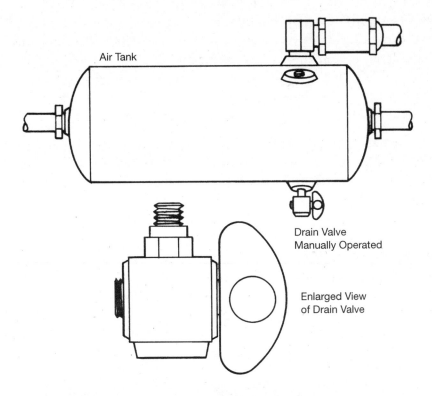

Air Tank

Drain Valve
Manually Operated

Enlarged View
of Drain Valve

Figure 5-1 Manual Drain Valve

The Brake Pedal

You put on the brakes by pushing down the brake pedal. (It is also called the foot valve or treadle valve.) Pushing the pedal down harder applies more air pressure. Letting up on the brake pedal reduces the air pressure and releases the brakes. Releasing the brakes lets some compressed air go out of the system, so the air pressure in the tanks is reduced. It must be made up by the air compressor. Pressing and releasing the pedal unnecessarily can let air out faster than the compressor can replace it. If the pressure gets too low, the brakes won't work.

When you push the brake pedal down, two forces push back against your foot. One force comes from a spring. The second force comes from the air pressure going to the brakes. This resistance lets you feel how much air pressure is being applied to the brakes.

Foundation Brakes

Foundation brakes are used at each wheel. The most common type is the S-cam drum brake shown in Figure 5-2.

Brake Drums, Shoes, and Linings. Brake drums are located on each end of the vehicle's axles. The wheels are bolted to the drums. The braking mechanism is inside the drum. To stop, the brake shoes and linings are pushed against the inside of the drum. This causes friction, which slows the vehicle (and creates heat). The heat a drum can take without damage depends on how hard and how long the brakes are used. Too much heat can make the brakes stop working.

S-Cam Brakes. When you push the brake pedal, air is let into each brake chamber (see Figure 5-2). Air pressure pushes the rod out, moving the slack adjuster, thus twisting the brake cam shaft. This turns the S-cam (so called because it is shaped like the letter S). The S-cam forces the brake shoes away from one another and presses them against the inside of the brake drum. When you release the brake pedal, the S-cam rotates back and a spring pulls the brake shoes away from the drum, letting the wheels roll freely again.

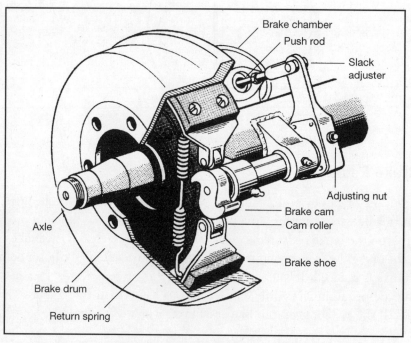

Figure 5-2 S-Cam Air Brake

Wedge Brakes. In this type brake, the chamber push rod pushes a wedge directly between the ends of two brake shoes. This shoves them apart and against the inside of the brake drum. Wedge brakes may have a single brake chamber, or two brake chambers pushing wedges in at both ends of the brake shoes. Wedge type brakes may be self-adjusting or may require manual adjustment.

Disc Brakes. In air-operated disc brakes, air pressure acts on a brake chamber and slack adjuster, like S-cam brakes. But instead of the S-cam, a power screw is used.

The pressure of the brake chamber on the slack adjuster turns the power screw. The power screw clamps the disc or rotor between the brake lining pads of a caliper, similar to a large C-clamp.

Wedge brakes and disc brakes are less common than S-cam brakes.

Supply Pressure Gauges

All air-braked vehicles have a pressure gauge connected to the air tank. If the vehicle has a dual air brake system, there will be a gauge for each half of the system (or a single gauge with two needles). Dual systems will be discussed later. These gauges tell you how much pressure is in the air tanks.

Application Pressure Gauge

This gauge shows how much air pressure you are applying to the brakes. (This gauge is not on all vehicles.) When going down steep grades, increasing application pressure to hold the same speed means the brakes are fading. You should slow down and use a lower gear. The need for increased pressure can also be caused by brakes out of adjustment, air leaks, or mechanical problems.

Low Air Pressure Warning

A low air pressure warning signal is required on vehicles with air brakes. A warning signal you can see must come on before the air pressure in the tanks falls below 60 psi (or one-half the compressor governor cutout pressure on older vehicles). The warning is usually a red light. A buzzer may also come on.

Another type of warning is the "wig wag." This device drops a mechanical arm into your view when the pressure in the system drops below 60 psi. An automatic wig wag will rise out of your view when the pressure in the system goes above 60 psi. The manual reset type must be placed in the "out of view" position manually. It will not stay in place until the pressure in the system is above 60 psi.

On large buses, it is common for the low pressure warning devices to signal at 80 to 85 psi.

Stop Light Switch

Drivers behind you must be warned when you put your brakes on. The air brake system does this with an electric switch that works by air pressure. The switch turns on the brake lights when you put on the air brakes.

Front Brake Limiting Valve

Some older vehicles (made before 1975) have a front-brake limiting valve and a control in the cab. The control is usually marked "normal" and "slippery." When you put the control in the "slippery" position, the limiting valve cuts the "normal" air pressure to the front brakes by half. Limiting valves were used to reduce the chance of the front wheels skidding on slippery surfaces. However, they actually reduce the stopping power of the vehicle. Front-wheel braking is good under all conditions. Tests have shown that front wheel skids from braking are not likely, even on ice. **Make sure the control is in the normal position to have normal stopping power.**

Many vehicles have automatic front wheel limiting valves. They reduce the air to the front brakes except when the brakes are put on very hard (60 psi or more application pressure). These valves cannot be controlled by the driver.

Spring Brakes

All trucks, truck tractors, and buses must be equipped with emergency brakes and parking brakes. They must be held on by mechanical force (because air pressure can eventually leak away). Spring brakes are usually used to meet these needs. When driving, powerful springs are held back by air pressure. If the air pressure is removed, the springs put on the brakes. A parking brake control in the cab allows the driver to let the air out of the spring brakes. This lets the springs put the brakes on. A leak in the air brake system which causes all the air to be lost, will also cause the springs to put on the brakes.

Tractor and straight truck spring brakes will come fully on when air pressure drops to a range of 20 to 45 psi (typically 20 to 30 psi). Do not wait for the brakes to come on automatically. When the low air pressure warning light and buzzer first come on, bring the vehicle to a safe stop right away while you can still control the brakes.

The braking power of spring brakes depends on the brakes being in adjustment. If the brakes are not adjusted correctly, neither the regular brakes nor the emergency/parking brakes will work properly.

Parking Brake Controls

In newer vehicles with air brakes, you put on the parking brakes using a **diamond shaped, yellow, push-pull control knob.** You pull the knob out to put the parking brakes (spring brakes) on and push it in to release them. On older vehicles, the parking brakes may be controlled by a lever. Use the parking brakes whenever you park.

> **CAUTION:** Never push the brake pedal down when the spring brakes are on. If you do, the brakes could be damaged by the combined forces of the springs and the air pressure. Many brake systems are designed so this will not happen. But not all systems are set up that way, and those that are may not always work. It is much better to develop the habit of not pushing the brake pedal down when the spring brakes are on.

Modulating control valves. In some vehicles, a control handle on the dashboard may be used to apply the spring brakes gradually. This is called a modulating valve. It is spring loaded so you have a feel for the braking action. The more you move the control lever, the harder the spring brakes come on. They work this way so you can control the spring brakes if the service brakes fail. When parking a vehicle with a modulating control valve, move the lever as far as it will go and hold it in place with the locking device.

Dual parking control valves. When main air pressure is lost, the spring brakes come on. Some vehicles, such as buses, have a separate air tank which can be used to release the spring brakes. This separate release is so you can move the vehicle in an emergency. One of the valves is a push-pull type and is used to put on the spring brakes for parking. The other valve is spring loaded in the "out" position. When you push the control in, air from the separate air tank releases the spring brakes so you can move. When you release the button, the spring brakes come on again. There is only enough air in the separate tank to do this a few times. Therefore, plan carefully when moving. Otherwise, you may be stopped in a dangerous location when the separate air supply runs out.

5.2 DUAL AIR BRAKE SYSTEMS

Most newer heavy-duty vehicles use dual air brake systems for safety. A dual air brake system has two separate air brake systems which use a single set of brake controls. Each system has its own air tanks, hoses, lines, etc. One system typically operates the regular brakes on the rear axle or axles. The other system operates the regular brakes on the front axle (and possibly one rear axle). Both systems supply air to the trailer (if there is one). The first system is called the "primary" system. The other is called the "secondary" system.

Before driving a vehicle with a dual air system, allow time for the air compressor to build up a minimum of 100 psi pressure in both the primary and secondary systems. Watch the primary and secondary air pressure gauges (or needles, if the system has two needles in one gauge). Pay attention to the low-air-pressure warning light and buzzer. The warning light and buzzer should shut off when air pressure in both systems rises to a value set by the manufacturer. This value must be greater than 60 psi.

The warning light and buzzer should come on before the air pressure drops below 60 psi in either system. If this happens while driving, you should stop right away and safely park the vehicle. If one air system is very low on pressure, either the front or the rear brakes will not be operating fully. This means it will take you longer to stop. Bring the vehicle to a safe stop and have the air brake system fixed.

5.3 INSPECTING AIR BRAKE SYSTEMS

You should use the basic seven-step inspection procedure described in Chapter 2 to inspect your vehicle. There are more things to inspect on a vehicle with air brakes than one without them. We discuss these things below in the order in which they fit into the seven-step method.

During Step 2 – Engine Compartment Checks

Check Air Compressor Drive Belt (if compressor is belt driven). If the air compressor is belt-driven, check the condition and tightness of the belt. The belt should be in good condition.

During Step 5 – Walkaround Inspection

Check Manual Slack Adjusters on S-Cam Brakes. Park on level ground and chock the wheels to prevent the vehicle from moving. Turn off the parking brakes so you can move the slack adjusters. Use gloves and pull hard on each slack adjuster that you can reach. If a slack adjuster moves more than about one inch where the push rod attaches to it, it probably needs adjustment. Adjust it or have it adjusted. Vehicles with too much brake slack can be very hard to stop. Out-of-adjustment brakes are the most common problem found in roadside inspections. Be safe; check the slack adjusters.

Check Brake Drums (or Discs), Linings, and Hoses. Brake drums (or discs) must not have cracks longer than one half the width of the friction area. Linings (friction material) must not be loose or soaked with oil or grease. They must not be dangerously thin. Mechanical parts must be in place, not broken or missing. Check the air hoses connected to the brake chambers to make sure they aren't cut or worn due to rubbing.

Step 7 – Final Air Brake Check

Do the following checks instead of the hydraulic brake check shown in Chapter 2, "Step 7: Check Brake System."

Test Low Pressure Warning Signal. Shut the engine off when you have enough air pressure that the low pressure warning signal is not on. Turn the electrical power on and step on and off the brake pedal to reduce air tank pressure. The low-air-pressure warning signal must come on before the pressure drops to less than 60 psi in the air tank (or tank with the lowest air pressure in dual air systems).

If the warning signal doesn't work, you could lose air pressure and you would not know it. This could cause sudden emergency braking in a single-circuit air system.

In dual systems, the stopping distance will be increased. Only limited braking can be done before the spring brakes come on.

Check That the Spring Brakes Come on Automatically. Chock the wheels, release the parking brakes when you have enough air pressure to do it, and shut the engine off. Step on and off the brake pedal to reduce the air tank pressure. The parking brake knob should pop out when the air pressure falls to the manufacturer's specification (usually in a range between 20 to 40 psi). This causes the spring brakes to come on.

Check Rate of Air Pressure Buildup. With the engine at operating RPM, the pressure should build from 85 to 100 psi within 45 seconds in dual air systems. (If the vehicle has larger than minimum air tanks, the buildup time can be longer and still be safe. Check the manufacturer's specifications.) In single air systems (pre-1975), typical requirements are pressure buildup from 50 to 90 psi within three minutes with the engine at an idle speed of 600 to 900 RPM.

If air pressure does not build up fast enough, your pressure may drop too low during driving, requiring an emergency stop. Don't drive until you get the problem fixed.

Test Air Leakage Rate. With a fully-charged air system (typically 125 psi), turn off the engine, turn the key to the "on" position, release the service brake, and time the air pressure drop. The loss rate should be less than 2 psi in one minute for single vehicles, less than 3 psi in one minute for combination vehicles. Then, apply 90 psi or more with the brake pedal. After the initial pressure drop, if the air pressure falls more than 3 psi in one minute for single vehicles (more than 4 psi for combination vehicles), the air loss rate is too much. Check for air leaks and fix before driving the vehicle. Otherwise, you could lose your brakes while driving.

Check Air Compressor Governor Cut-in and Cut-out Pressures. Pumping by the air compressor should start at about 100 psi and stop at about 125 psi. (Check manufacturer's specifications.) Run the engine at a fast idle. The air governor should cut-out the air compressor at about the manufacturer's specified pressure. The air pressure shown by your gauge(s) will stop rising. With the engine idling, step on and off the brake to reduce the air tank pressure. The compressor should cut-in at about the manufacturer's specified cut-in pressure. The pressure should begin to rise.

If the air governor does not work as described above, it may need to be fixed. A governor that does not work right may not keep enough air pressure for safe driving.

Test Parking Brake. Stop the vehicle, put the parking brake on, and gently pull against it in a low gear to test that the parking brake will hold.

Test Service Brakes. Wait for normal air pressure, release the parking brake, move the vehicle forward slowly (about 5 mph), and apply the brakes firmly, using the brake pedal. Note if the vehicle "pulls" to one side or if there is an unusual feel or delayed stopping action.

This test may show you problems which you otherwise wouldn't know about until you needed the brakes on the road.

5.4 USING AIR BRAKES

Normal Stops

Push the brake pedal down. Control the pressure so the vehicle comes to a smooth, safe stop. If you have a manual transmission, don't push the clutch in until the engine RPM is down close to idle. When stopped, select a starting gear.

Emergency Stops

You should brake so you can steer and so your vehicle stays in a straight line. Use one of the following two methods.

Controlled Braking. With this method, you apply the brakes as hard as you can **without** locking the wheels. Keep steering wheel movements very small while doing this. If you need to make a larger steering adjustment or if the wheels lock, release the brakes. Reapply the brakes as soon as you can.

Stab Braking. a) Press on the brake pedal as hard as you can. b) Release the brakes when the wheels lock up. c) As soon as the wheels start rolling, put on the brakes fully again. It can take up to one second for the wheels to start rolling after you release the brakes. Make sure you stay off the brakes long enough to get the wheels rolling again. Otherwise, the vehicle may not stay in a straight line.

NOTE: If you drive a vehicle with anti-lock brakes, you should read and follow the directions found in the owner's manual for stopping quickly.

Stopping Distance

We talked about stopping distance in Chapter 2 under "Speed and Stopping Distance." With air brakes there is an added delay: the time required for the brakes to work after the brake pedal is pushed. With hydraulic brakes (used on cars and light/medium trucks), the brakes work instantly. However, with air brakes, it takes a little time (one half second or more) for the air to flow through the lines to the brakes. Thus, the total stopping distance for vehicles with air brake systems is made up of four different factors.

Perception Distance
+ Reaction Distance
+ Brake Lag Distance
+ Effective Braking Distance
─────────────────────────
= Total Stopping Distance

The air brake lag distance at 55 mph on dry pavement adds about 32 feet. So at 55 mph for an average driver under **good** traction and brake conditions, the total stopping distance is over 300 feet. This is longer than a football field.

Braking on Downgrades

Brakes are designed so brake shoes or pads rub against the break drum or disks to slow the vehicle. This friction creates heat. Brakes can take a lot of heat. However, brakes will stop working if there is too much heat. Excessive heat is caused by trying to slow down from too high a speed too many times or too quickly. Brakes will fade when they get too hot. So, you will have to push harder on the pedal to get the same stopping force. Brakes can fade so much that they will not slow you down.

The right way to go down long grades is to use a low gear and drive slowly enough that a fairly light, steady use of the brakes will keep you from speeding up. If you drive slowly enough, the brakes will be able to get rid of the heat, so they will work as they should.

Some people believe that using the brakes hard going downhill but letting up on them from time to time will allow them to cool. Tests have shown this is **not** true. Brakes cool very slowly, so the cooling between hard brakings is not enough to prevent overheating. Also, the vehicle picks up speed when the brakes are let up, which means more hard braking will be needed to slow it back down. Braking in this way, on-and-off, builds up more heat than the light, steady method does. Therefore, drive slowly enough, use the right gear, and maintain light, steady pressure on the brakes.

It is always important for the brakes to be adjusted properly. However, it is **especially important when going down steep grades.** In addition to proper slack adjustment, the air brake system should be balanced to give about the same braking at each of the wheels. Otherwise, some brakes will do more work than others. They will heat up and lose some of their stopping power. Brake balance can be tested and fixed by good air brake mechanics.

Brake Fading or Failure

Remember that excessive use of the service brakes results in overheating and can lead to brake fade or failure. Brake fade results from excessive heat causing chemical changes in the brake lining, which reduces friction and also causes expansion of the brake drums. As the overheated drums expand, the brake shoes and linings have to move farther to contact the drums, and the force of this contact is also reduced. Continued overuse may increase brake fade until the vehicle cannot be slowed down or stopped at all.

Brake fade is also affected by adjustment. To safely control a vehicle, every brake must do its share of the work. Brakes out of adjustment will stop doing their share before those that are in adjustment. The other brakes can then overheat and fade and there will not be sufficient braking available to control the vehicle(s). Brakes can get out of adjustment quickly, especially when they are hot. Therefore, brake adjustment must be checked frequently.

Proper Braking Technique

Remember: The use of brakes on a long and/or steep downgrade should be used as a supplement to the braking effect of the engine. Once the vehicle is in the proper low gear, the following is the proper braking technique:

- Apply the brakes just hard enough to feel a definite slowdown.
- When your speed has been reduced to approximately 5 m.p.h. below your "safe" speed, release the brakes. [This brake application should last for about 3 seconds.]
- When your speed has increased to your "safe" speed, repeat steps 1 and 2.

For example, if your "safe" speed is 40 m.p.h., you would not apply the brakes until your speed reaches 40 m.p.h. You now apply the brakes hard enough to gradually reduce your speed to 35 m.p.h. and then release the brakes. Repeat this as often as necessary until you have reached the end of the downgrade.

Low Air Pressure Warning

If the low air pressure warning comes on, **stop and safely park your vehicle as soon as possible.** There might be an air leak in the system. Controlled braking is possible only while enough air remains in the air tanks. The spring brakes will come on when the air pressure drops into the range of 20 to 45 psi. A heavily loaded vehicle will take a longer distance to stop, because the spring brakes do not work on all axles. Lightly loaded vehicles or vehicles on slippery roads may skid out of control when the spring brakes come on. It is much safer to stop while there is enough air in the tanks to use the foot brake.

Parking Brakes

Any time you park, use the parking brakes, except as noted below. Pull the parking brake control knob out to apply the parking brakes, push it in to release them. The control will be a yellow, diamond-shaped knob labeled "parking brakes" on newer vehicles. On older vehicles, it may be a round blue knob or some other shape (including a lever that swings from side to side or up and down).

Exceptions:

Don't use the parking brakes if the brakes are very hot (from just having come down a steep grade), or if the brakes are very wet in freezing temperatures. If they are used while they are very hot, they can be damaged by the heat. If they are used in freezing temperatures when the brakes are very wet, they can freeze so the vehicle can not move. Use wheel chocks to hold the vehicle. Let hot brakes cool before using the parking brakes. If the brakes are wet, use the brakes lightly while driving in a low gear to heat and dry them.

If your vehicle does not have automatic air tank drains, drain your air tanks at the end of each working day to remove moisture and oil. Otherwise, the brakes could fail.

> **Never leave your vehicle unattended without applying the parking brakes or chocking the wheels. Your vehicle might roll away and cause injury and damage.**

Chapter 6 – Combination Vehicles

THIS CHAPTER COVERS
- ❏ Driving Combinations
- ❏ Coupling and Uncoupling
- ❏ Inspecting Combinations

This chapter provides information needed to pass the tests for combination vehicles (tractor-trailer, doubles, triples, straight truck and trailer). The information is only to give you the minimum knowledge needed for driving common combination vehicles. You should also study Chapter 7 if you need to pass the tests for doubles and triples.

6.1 DRIVING COMBINATION VEHICLES SAFELY

Combination vehicles are usually heavier, longer, and require more driving skill than single commercial vehicles. This means that drivers of combination vehicles need more knowledge and skill than drivers of single vehicles. In this chapter, we talk about some important safety factors that apply specifically to combination vehicles.

Rollover Risks

More than half of truck driver deaths in crashes are from truck rollovers. When more cargo is piled up in a truck, the "center of gravity" moves higher up from the road. The truck becomes easier to turn over. Fully loaded rigs are 10 times more likely to roll over in a crash than empty rigs.

Do the following two things to help prevent rollover: **keep the cargo as close to the ground as possible, and drive slowly around turns.** Keeping cargo low is even more important in combination vehicles than in straight trucks. Also, keep the load centered on your rig. If the load is to one side so it makes a trailer lean, a rollover is more likely. Make sure your cargo is centered and spread out as much as possible. (See Chapter 3.)

Rollovers happen when you turn too quickly. Drive slowly around corners as well as on on-ramps and off-ramps. Avoid quick lane changes, especially when fully loaded.

Steer Gently

Trucks with trailers have a dangerous crack-the-whip effect. When you make a quick lane change, the crack-the-whip effect can turn the trailer over. There are many accidents where only the trailer has overturned.

"Rearward amplification" causes the crack-the-whip effect. Figure 6-1 shows eight types of combination vehicles and the rearward amplification each has in a quick lane change. Rigs with the least crack-the-whip effect are shown at the top and those with the most at the bottom. Rearward amplification of 2.0 in the chart means that the rear trailer is twice as likely to turn over as the tractor. You can see that triples have a rearward amplification of 3.5. This means you can roll the last trailer of triples 3.5 times as easily as a five-axle tractor-semi.

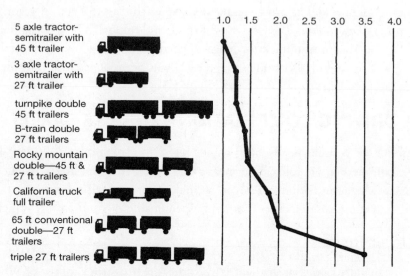

(from R.D. Ervin, R.L. Nisonger, C.C. MacAdam, and P.S. Fancher, "Influence of size and weight variables on the stability and control properties of heavy trucks," U. of Michigan Trans. Research Institute, 1983.)

Figure 6-1 Influence of Combination Type on Rearward Amplification

Steer gently and smoothly when you are pulling trailers. If you make a sudden movement with your steering wheel, you could tip over a trailer. Follow far enough behind other vehicles (at least one second for each 10 feet of your vehicle length, plus another second if going over 40 mph). Look far enough down the road to avoid being surprised and having to make a sudden lane change. At night, drive slowly enough to see obstacles with your headlights before it is too late to change lanes or stop gently. Slow down to a safe speed before going into a turn.

Brake Early

Control your speed whether fully loaded or empty. Large combination vehicles that are empty take longer to stop than those that are fully loaded. When lightly loaded, the very stiff suspension springs and strong brakes give poor traction and make it very easy to lock up the wheels. Your trailer can swing out and strike other vehicles. Your tractor can jackknife very quickly (Figure 6-2). You also must be very careful about driving "bobtail" tractors (tractors without semi-trailers). Tests have shown that bobtails can be very hard to stop smoothly. It takes them longer to stop than a trac-tor-semitrailer loaded to maximum gross weight.

In any combination rig, allow a lot of following distance and look far ahead, so you can brake early. Don't be caught by surprise and have to make a "panic" stop.

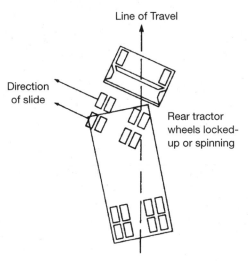

Figure 6-2 Tractor Jackknife

Prevent Trailer Skids

When the wheels of a trailer lock up, the trailer will tend to swing around. This is more likely to happen when the trailer is empty or lightly loaded. This type of jack-knife is often called a "trailer jackknife." This is shown in Figure 6-3. The procedure for stopping a trailer skid is as follows:

Recognize the skid. The earliest and best way to recognize that the trailer has started to skid is by seeing it in your mirrors. Any time you apply the brakes hard, check the mirrors to make sure the trailer is staying where it should be. Once the trailer swings out of your lane, it's very difficult to prevent a jackknife.

Stop using the brake. Release the brakes to get traction back. Do **not** use the trailer hand brake (if you have one) to "straighten out the rig." This is the wrong thing to do since it is the brakes on the trailer wheels that caused the skid in the first place. Once the trailer wheels grip the road again, the trailer will start to follow the tractor and straighten out.

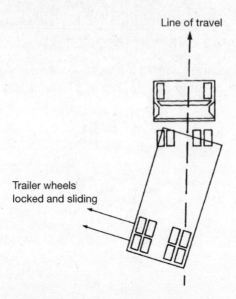

Line of travel

Trailer wheels
locked and sliding

Figure 6-3 Trailer Jackknife

Turn Wide

When a vehicle goes around a corner, the rear wheels follow a different path than the front wheels. This is called **offtracking** or "cheating." Figure 6-4 shows how offtracking causes the path followed by a tractor-semi to be wider than the rig itself. Longer vehicles will offtrack more. The rear wheels of the powered unit (truck or tractor) will offtrack somewhat, and the rear wheels of the trailer will offtrack even more. If there is more than one trailer, the rear wheels of the last trailer will offtrack the most. Steer the front end wide enough around a corner so the rear end does not run over the curb, pedestrians, other vehicles, etc. However, keep the rear of your vehicle close to the curb. This will stop other drivers from passing you on the right. If you cannot complete your turn without entering another traffic lane, turn wide as you **complete the turn** (Figure 6-5). This is better than swinging wide to the left before starting the turn because it will keep other drivers from passing you on the right. If drivers pass on the right, you might crash into them when you turn (Figure 6-6).

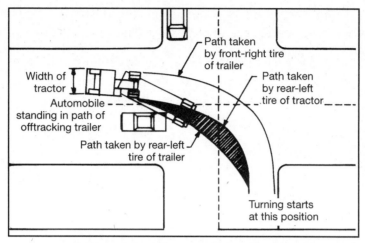

Offtracking Space Requirements

Due to the wide path required for turning a tractor-trailer at intersections, special care must be taken to avoid damage to your vehicle and others.

Figure 6-4 Offtracking in a 90 degree turn

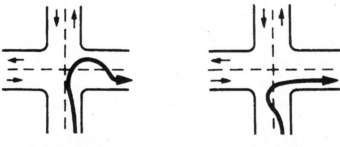

Figure 6-5
Do this so cars don't try
to pass you on the right.

Figure 6-6
Don't do this!

6.2 COMBINATION VEHICLE AIR BRAKES

You should study Chapter 5, "Single Vehicle Air Brakes" to gain an understanding of air brake systems. The following section describes the additional parts that control the trailer brakes on a combination vehicle.

Trailer Hand Valve

The trailer hand valve (also called the trolley valve or Johnson bar) works the trailer brakes. The trailer hand valve should be used only to test the trailer brakes. Do **not** use it while driving because of the danger of making the trailer skid. The foot brake sends air to all of the brakes on the vehicle (including the trailer(s)). There is much less danger of causing a skid or jackknife when using just the foot brake.

Never use the hand valve for parking, because all the air might leak out, unlocking the brakes (in trailers that don't have spring brakes). Always use the **parking brakes** when parking. If the trailer does not have spring brakes, use wheel chocks to keep the trailer from moving.

Tractor Protection Valve

The tractor protection valve keeps air in the tractor or truck should the trailer break away or develop a bad leak. The tractor protection valve is controlled by the "trailer air supply" control valve in the cab. The control valve allows you to open and shut the tractor protection valve. The tractor protection valve will close automatically if air pressure is low (in the range of 20 to 45 psi). When the tractor protection valve closes, it stops any air from going out of the tractor. It also lets the air out of the trailer emergency line. This causes the trailer emergency brakes to come on. (Emergency brakes are covered later.)

Trailer Air Supply Control

The trailer air supply control on newer vehicles is a red eight-sided knob that you use to control the tractor protection valve. You push it in to supply the trailer with air, and pull it out to shut the air off and put on the trailer emergency brakes. The valve will pop out (thus closing the tractor protection valve) when the air pressure drops into the range 20 to 45 psi. Tractor protection valve controls or "emergency" valves on older vehicles may not operate automatically. There may be a lever rather than a knob. The "normal" position is used for pulling a trailer. The "emergency" position is used to shut the air off and put on the trailer emergency brakes.

Trailer Air Lines

Every combination vehicle has two air lines, the **service** line and the **emergency** line. They run between each vehicle (tractor to trailer, trailer to dolly, dolly to second trailer, etc.).

Service Air Line. The **service** line (also called the control line or signal line) carries air, which is controlled by the foot brake or the trailer hand brake. Depending on how hard you press the foot brake or hand valve, the pressure in the service line will similarly change. The service line is connected to **relay valve(s)** on the trailer(s) to apply more or less pressure to the trailer brakes. The relay valve connects the trailer air tanks to the trailer air brakes. As pressure builds up in the service line, the relay valve opens and sends air pressure from the trailer air tank to the trailer brake chambers, thus putting on the trailer brakes.

Emergency Air Line. The emergency line (also called the supply line) has two purposes. First, it supplies air to the trailer air tanks. Second, the emergency line controls the emergency brakes on combination vehicles. **Loss of air pressure** in the emergency line causes the trailer emergency brakes to come on. The pressure loss could be caused by a trailer breaking loose, thus tearing apart the emergency air hose. Or it could be caused by a hose, metal tubing, or other part that breaks, letting the air out. When the emergency line loses pressure, it also causes the tractor protection valve to close (the air supply knob will pop out).

Emergency lines are often coded with the color **red** (red hose, red couplers, or other parts) to keep from getting them mixed up with the **blue** service line.

Hose Couplers (Glad Hands)

Glad hands are coupling devices used to connect the service and emergency air lines from the truck or tractor to the trailer. The couplers have a rubber seal which prevents air from escaping. Clean the couplers and rubber seals before a connection is made. When connecting the glad hands, press the two seals together with the couplers at a 90 degree angle to each other. A turn of the glad hand attached to the hose will join and lock the couplers.

Some vehicles have "dead end," or dummy, couplers to which the hoses may be attached when they are not in use. This will prevent water and dirt from getting into the coupler and the air lines. Use the dummy couplers when the air lines are not connected to a trailer. If there are no dummy couplers, the glad hands can sometimes be locked together (depending on the couplings). It is very important to keep the air supply clean.

When coupling, make sure to couple the proper glad hands together. To help avoid mistakes, colors are sometimes used. Blue is used for the service lines and red for the emergency (supply) lines. Sometimes, metal tags are attached to the lines with the words "service" and "emergency" stamped on them.

If you do cross the air lines, supply air will be sent to the service line instead of going to charge the trailer air tanks. Air will not be available to release the trailer spring brakes (parking brakes). If the spring brakes don't release when you push the trailer air supply control, check the air line connections.

Older trailers do not have spring brakes. If the air supply in the trailer air tank has leaked away, there will be no emergency brakes, and the trailer wheels will turn freely. If you crossed the air lines, you could drive away but you wouldn't have trailer brakes. **This would be very dangerous.** Always test the trailer brakes before driving, with the hand valve or by pulling the air supply (tractor protection valve) control. Pull gently against them in a low gear to make sure the brakes work.

Trailer Air Tanks

Each trailer and converter dolly has one or more air tanks. They are filled by the **emergency (supply) line** from the tractor. They provide the air pressure used to operate trailer brakes. Air pressure is sent from the air tanks to the brakes by relay valves. The pressure in the **service line** tells how much pressure the relay valves should send to the trailer brakes. The pressure in the service line is controlled by the brake pedal (and the trailer hand brake).

It is important that you don't let water and oil build up in the air tanks. If you do, the brakes may not work right. Each tank has a drain valve on it, and you should drain each tank every day. If your tanks have automatic drains, they will keep most moisture out. But you should still open the drains to make sure.

Shut-Off Valves

Shut-off valves (also called cut-out cocks) are used in the service and supply air lines at the back of trailers that tow other trailers. These valves permit closing off of the air lines when another trailer is not being towed. You must check that all shut-off valves are in the **open** position except the ones at the back of the last trailer which must be **closed**.

Trailer Service, Parking, and Emergency Brakes

Newer trailers have spring brakes just like trucks and truck tractors. However, converter dollies and trailers built before 1975 are not required to have spring brakes. Those that do not have spring brakes have emergency brakes, which work from the air stored in the trailer air tank. The emergency brakes come on whenever air pressure in the emergency line is lost. **These trailers have no parking brake.** The emergency brakes come on whenever the air supply knob is pulled out or the trailer is disconnected. But the brakes will hold only as long as there is air pressure in the trailer air tank. Eventually, the air will leak away, and then there will be no brakes. Therefore, **it is very important for safety that you use wheel chocks when you park trailers without spring brakes.**

A major leak in the **emergency** line will cause the tractor protection valve to close and the trailer emergency brakes to come on.

You may not notice a major leak in the **service** line until you try to put the brakes on. Then, the air loss from the leak will lower the air tank pressure quickly. If it goes low enough, the trailer emergency brakes will come on.

6.3 COUPLING AND UNCOUPLING

Knowing how to couple and uncouple correctly is basic to safe operation of combination vehicles. Wrong coupling and uncoupling can be very dangerous. General coupling and uncoupling steps are listed below. There are differences between different rigs, so learn the details of coupling and uncoupling the truck(s) you will operate.

Coupling Tractor-Semitrailers

Step 1. Inspect Fifth Wheel

- Check for damaged/missing parts.
- Check to see that mounting to tractor is secure, no cracks in frame, etc.
- Be sure that the fifth wheel plate is greased as required. Failure to keep the fifth wheel plate lubricated could cause steering problems because of friction between the tractor and trailer.
- Check if fifth wheel is in proper position for coupling:
    - Wheel tilted down towards rear of tractor.
    - Jaws open.
    - Safety unlocking handle in the automatic lock position.
- If you have a sliding fifth wheel, make sure it is locked.
- Make sure the trailer kingpin is not bent or broken.

Step 2. Inspect Area and Chock Wheels

- Make sure area around the vehicle is clear.
- Be sure trailer wheels are chocked or spring brakes are on.
- Check that cargo (if any) is secured against movement due to tractor being coupled to the trailer.

Step 3. Position Tractor

- Put the tractor directly in front of the trailer. (Never back under the trailer at an angle, because you might push the trailer sideways and break the landing gear.)
- Check position, using outside mirrors, by looking down both sides of the trailer.

Step 4. Back Slowly

- Back until fifth wheel just touches the trailer.
- Don't hit the trailer.

Step 5. Secure Tractor

- Put on the parking brake.
- Put transmission in neutral.

Step 6. Check Trailer Height

- The trailer should be low enough that it is raised slightly by the tractor when the tractor is backed under it. Raise or lower the trailer as needed. (If trailer is too low, tractor may strike and damage nose of trailer; if trailer is too high, **it may not couple correctly.**)
- Check that the kingpin and fifth wheel are aligned.

Step 7. Connect Air Lines to Trailer

- Check glad hand seals and connect tractor emergency air line to trailer emergency glad hand.
- Check glad hand seals and connect tractor service air line to trailer service glad hand.
- Make sure air lines are safely supported where they won't be crushed or caught while tractor is backing under the trailer.

Step 8. Supply Air to Trailer

- From cab, push in "air supply" knob or move tractor protection valve control from the "emergency" to the "normal" position to supply air to the trailer brake system.
- Wait until the air pressure is normal.
- Check brake system for crossed air lines:
    - Shut engine off so you can hear the brakes.
    - Apply and release trailer brakes, listen for sound of trailer brakes being applied and released. You should hear the brakes move when applied and air escape when the brakes are released.
    - Check air brake system pressure gauge for signs of major air loss.
- When you are sure trailer brakes are working, start engine.
- Make sure air pressure is up to normal.

Step 9. Lock Trailer Brakes

- Pull out the "air supply" knob, or move the tractor protection valve control from "normal" to "emergency."

Step 10. Back Under Trailer

- Use lowest reverse gear.
- Back tractor slowly under trailer to avoid hitting the kingpin too hard.
- Stop when the kingpin is locked into the fifth wheel.

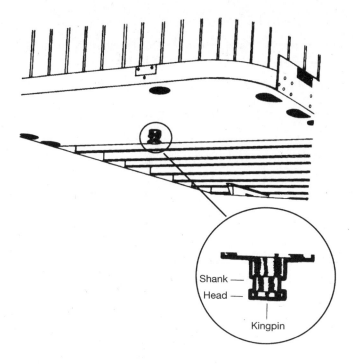

Figure 6-7 Trailer Kingpin

Step 11. Check Connection for Security

- Raise trailer landing gear **slightly** off ground.
- Pull tractor **gently** forward while the trailer brakes are still locked to check that the trailer is locked onto the tractor.

Step 12. Secure Vehicle

- Put transmission in neutral.
- Put parking brakes on.
- Shut off the engine and **take the key with you so someone else won't move the truck while you are under it.**

Step 13. Inspect Coupling

- Use a flashlight if necessary.
- Make sure there is **no space between upper and lower fifth wheel**. If there is space, something is wrong (kingpin may be on **top** of closed fifth wheel jaws; trailer would come loose very easily).
- Go under trailer and look into the back of the fifth wheel. Make sure the fifth wheel jaws have closed around the shank of the kingpin (see Figure 6-7).

- Check that the locking lever is in the "lock" position.
- Check that the safety catch is in position over locking lever. (On some fifth wheels the catch must be put in place by hand.)
- If the coupling isn't right, **don't drive the coupled unit**; get it fixed.

Step 14. Connect the Electrical Cord and Check Air Lines

- Plug the electrical cord into the trailer and fasten the safety catch.
- Check both air lines and electrical line for signs of damage.
- Make sure air and electrical lines will not hit any moving parts of vehicle.

Step 15. Raise Front Trailer Supports (Landing Gear)

- Use low gear range (if so equipped) to begin raising the landing gear. Once free of weight, switch to the high gear range.
- Raise the landing gear all the way up. (Never drive with landing gear only part way up as it may catch on railroad tracks or other things.)
- After raising landing gear, secure the crank handle safely.
- When full weight of trailer is resting on tractor:
  - Check for enough clearance between rear of tractor frame and landing gear. (When tractor turns sharply it must not hit landing gear.)
  - Check that there is enough clearance between the top of the tractor tires and the nose of the trailer.

Step 16. Remove Trailer Wheel Chocks

- Remove and store wheel chocks in a safe place.

Uncoupling Tractor-Semitrailers

The following steps will help you to uncouple safely:

Step 1. Position Rig

- Make sure surface of parking area can support weight of trailer.
- Have tractor lined up with the trailer. (Pulling out at an angle can damage landing gear.)

Step 2. Ease Pressure on Locking Jaws

- Shut off trailer air supply to lock trailer brakes.
- Ease pressure on fifth wheel locking jaws by backing up gently (this will help you release the fifth wheel locking lever).
- Put parking brakes on while tractor is pushing against the kingpin. This will hold rig with pressure off the locking jaws.

Step 3. Chock Trailer Wheels

- Chock the trailer wheels if the trailer doesn't have spring brakes or if you're not sure. (The air could leak out of the trailer air tank, releasing its emergency brakes. The trailer could then move if it didn't have chocks.)

Step 4. Lower The Landing Gear

- If trailer is empty—lower the landing gear until it makes firm contact with ground.
- If trailer is loaded—after the landing gear makes firm contact with the ground—turn crank in low gear a few extra turns; this will lift some weight off the tractor. (Do not lift trailer off the fifth wheel.) This will:
  - – Make it easier to unlatch fifth wheel.
  - – Make it easier to couple next time.

Step 5. Disconnect Air Lines and Electrical Cable

- Disconnect air lines from trailer. Connect air line glad hands to dummy couplers at back of cab, or couple them together.
- Hang electrical cable with plug down to prevent moisture from entering it.
- Make sure lines are supported so they won't be damaged while driving the tractor.

Step 6. Unlock Fifth Wheel

- Raise release handle lock.
- Pull the release handle to "open" position.
- Keep legs and feet clear of the rear tractor wheels to avoid serious injury in case the vehicle moves.

Step 7. Pull Tractor Partially Clear of Trailer

- Pull tractor forward until fifth wheel comes out from under the trailer.
- Stop with tractor frame under trailer (prevents trailer from falling to ground if landing gear should collapse or sink).

Step 8. Secure Tractor

- Apply parking brake.
- Place transmission in neutral.

Step 9. Inspect Trailer Supports

- Make sure ground is supporting trailer.
- Make sure landing gear is not damaged.

Step 10. Pull Tractor Clear of Trailer

- Release parking brakes.
- Check the area and drive tractor clear.

6.4 INSPECTING A COMBINATION VEHICLE

Use the seven-step inspection procedure described in Chapter 2 to inspect your combination vehicle. There are more things to inspect on a combination vehicle than on a single vehicle. Many of these additional things are just more of what are on a single vehicle. (For example, tires, wheels, lights, reflectors, etc.) However, there are also some new things to check. These are discussed below.

Additional Things to Check During a Walkaround Inspection

Do these checks in addition to those already listed in Chapter 2, "Step 5: Do Walkaround Inspection."

Coupling System Areas

- Check fifth wheel (lower):
  - Securely mounted to frame.
  - No missing, damaged parts.
  - Enough grease.
  - No visible space between upper and lower fifth wheel.
  - Locking jaws around the shank, **not** the head of kingpin.
  - Release arm properly seated and safety latch/lock engaged.
- Fifth wheel (upper):
  - Glide plate securely mounted to trailer frame.
  - Kingpin not damaged.
- Air and electric lines to trailer:
  - Electrical cord firmly plugged in and secured.
  - Air lines properly connected to glad hands, no air leaks, properly secured with enough slack for turns.
  - All lines free from damage.
- Sliding fifth wheel:
  - Slide not damaged or parts missing.
  - Properly greased:
  - All locking pins present and locked in place.
  - If air powered—no air leaks.

– Check that fifth wheel is not so far forward that tractor frame will hit landing gear or the cab hit the trailer, during turns.

Landing Gear

- Fully raised, no missing parts, not bent or otherwise damaged.
- Crank handle in place and secured.
- If power operated, no air or hydraulic leaks.

Combination Vehicle Brake Check

Do these checks **in addition** to Chapter 5, "Inspecting Air Brake Systems."

The following section explains how to check air brakes on combination vehicles. Check the brakes on a double or triple trailer as you would any combination vehicle.

Check that Air Flows to All Trailers. Use the tractor parking brake and/or chock the wheels to hold the vehicle. Wait for air pressure to reach normal, then push in the red "trailer air supply" knob. This will supply air to the emergency (supply) lines. Use the trailer handbrake to provide air to the service line. Go to the rear of the rig. Open the emergency line shut-off valve at the rear of the last trailer. You should hear air escaping, showing the entire system is charged. Close the emergency line valve. Open the service line valve to check that service pressure goes through all the trailers (this test assumes that the trailer handbrake or the service brake pedal is on), then close the valve. If you do NOT hear air escaping from both lines, check that the shut-off valves on the trailer(s) and dolly(ies) are in the OPEN position.

> **CAUTION: You MUST have air all the way to the back for ALL the brakes to work.**

Test Tractor Protection Valve. Charge the trailer air brake system. (That is, build up normal air pressure and push the "air supply" knob in). Shut the engine off. Step on and off the brake pedal several times to reduce the air pressure in the tanks. The trailer air supply control (also called the tractor protection valve control) should pop out (or go from "normal" to "emergency" position) when the air pressure falls into the pressure range specified by the manufacturer (usually within the range of 20 to 45 psi).

If the tractor protection valve doesn't work properly, an air hose or trailer brake leak could drain all the air from the tractor. This would cause the emergency brakes to come on, with possible loss of control.

Test Trailer Emergency Brakes. Charge the trailer air brake system and check that the trailer rolls freely. Then stop and pull out the trailer air supply control (also called tractor protection valve control or trailer emergency valve) or place it in the "emergency" position. Pull gently on the trailer with the tractor to check that the trailer emergency brakes are on.

Test Trailer Service Brakes. Check for normal air pressure, release the parking brakes, move the vehicle forward slowly, and apply trailer brakes with the hand control (trolley valve), if so equipped. You should feel the brakes come on. This tells you the trailer brakes are connected and working. (The trailer brakes should be **tested** with the hand valve but controlled in normal operation with the **foot pedal**, which applies air to the service brakes at all wheels.)

Chapter 7 – Doubles and Triples

THIS CHAPTER COVERS
❏ **Pulling Double/Triple Trailers**
❏ **Coupling and Uncoupling**
❏ **Inspecting Doubles and Triples**
❏ **Checking Air Brakes**

7.1 PULLING DOUBLE/TRIPLE TRAILERS

Take special care when pulling two and three trailers. There are more things that can go wrong, and doubles/triples are less stable than other commercial vehicles. Some areas of concern are discussed below.

Prevent Trailers from Rolling Over

To prevent trailers from rolling over, you must steer gently and go slowly around corners, on-ramps, off-ramps, and curves. A safe speed on a curve for a straight truck or a single trailer combination vehicle may be too fast for a set of doubles or triples.

Beware of the Crack-the-Whip Effect

Doubles and triples are more likely to turn over than other combination vehicles because of the "crack-the-whip" effect. You must steer gently when pulling trailers. The last trailer in a combination is most likely to turn over. If you don't understand the crack-the-whip effect, study Chapter 6, "Driving Combination Vehicles Safely," and review Figure 6-1.

Inspect Completely

There are more critical parts to check when you have two or three trailers. Check them all. Follow the procedures described later in this chapter.

Look Far Ahead

Doubles and triples must be driven very smoothly to avoid rollover or jackknife. Therefore, **look far ahead** so you can slow down or change lanes gradually when necessary.

Manage Space

Doubles and triples take up more space than other commercial vehicles. They are not only longer, but also need more space because they can't be turned or stopped suddenly. Allow more following distance. Make sure you have large enough gaps before entering or crossing traffic. Be certain you are clear at the sides before changing lanes.

Be More Careful in Adverse Conditions

In bad weather, slippery conditions, and mountain driving, you must be especially careful if you drive double and triple bottoms. You will have greater length and more dead axles to pull with your drive axles than other drivers. There is more chance for skids and loss of traction.

7.2 COUPLING AND UNCOUPLING

Knowing how to couple and uncouple correctly is basic to safe operation and doubles and triples. Wrong coupling and uncoupling can be very dangerous. Coupling and uncoupling steps for doubles and triples are listed below:

Coupling Twin or Double Trailers

NOTE: You will not be tested on coupling twin trailers unless you want to get a double/triple trailer endorsement on your license.

Secure Second (Rear) Trailer

- If the second trailer doesn't have spring brakes, drive the tractor close to the trailer, connect the emergency line, charge the trailer air tank, and disconnect the emergency line. This will set the trailer emergency brakes (if the slack adjusters are correctly adjusted). Chock the wheels if you have any doubt about the brakes.

Couple Tractor and First Semitrailer as Described Earlier.

> **CAUTION:** For safe handling on the road, the more heavily loaded semi-trailer must always be in first position behind the tractor. The lighter trailer should be in the rear.

Position Converter Dolly in Front of Second (Rear) Trailer

- Release dolly brakes by opening the air tank petcock. (Or, if the dolly has spring brakes, use the dolly parking brake control.)
- If distance is not too great, wheel dolly into position by hand so it is in line with the kingpin.
- Or, use tractor and first semi-trailer to pick up the converter dolly:
  - Position combination as close as possible to converter dolly.
  - Move dolly to rear of first semi-trailer and couple it to the trailer.

– Lock pintle hook.

– Secure dolly support in raised position.

– Pull dolly into position as close as possible to nose of the second semi-trailer.

– Lower dolly support.

– Unhook dolly from first trailer.

– Wheel dolly into position in front of second trailer in line with the kingpin.

Connect Converter Dolly to Front Trailer

- Back first semitrailer into position in front of dolly tongue.
- Hook dolly to front trailer:
  – Lock pintle hook.
  – Secure converter gear support in raised position.

Connect Converter Dolly to Rear Trailer

- Make sure trailer brakes are locked and/or wheels chocked.
- Make sure trailer height is correct. (It must be slightly lower than the center of the fifth wheel, so trailer is raised slightly when dolly is pushed under.)
- Back converter dolly under rear trailer.
- Raise landing gear slightly off ground to prevent damage if trailer moves.
- Test coupling by pulling against pin of number two semi-trailer.
- Make visual check of coupling. (No space between upper and lower fifth wheel; locking jaws closed on kingpin.)
- Connect safety chains, air hoses, and light cords.
- Close converter dolly air tank petcock, and shut-off valves at rear of second trailer (service and emergency shut-offs).
- Open shut-off valves at rear of first trailer (and on dolly if so equipped).
- Raise landing gear completely.
- Charge trailers (push "air supply" knob in) and check for air at rear of second trailer by opening the emergency line shut-off. If air pressure isn't there, something is wrong and the brakes won't work.

Uncoupling Twin or Double Trailers

NOTE: You will not be tested on uncoupling twins unless you want to get a double/triple trailer endorsement on your license.

Uncouple Rear Trailer

- Park rig in a straight line on firm, level ground.
- Apply parking brakes so rig won't move.
- Chock wheels of second trailer if it doesn't have spring brakes.
- Lower landing gear of second semi-trailer enough to remove some weight from dolly.
- Close air shut-offs at rear of first semi-trailer (and on dolly if so equipped).
- Disconnect all dolly air and electric lines and secure them.
- Release dolly brakes.
- Release converter dolly fifth wheel latch.
- Slowly pull tractor, first semi-trailer and dolly forward to pull dolly out from under rear semi-trailer.

Uncouple Converter Dolly

- Lower dolly landing gear.
- Disconnect safety chains.
- Apply converter gear spring brakes or chock wheels.
- Release pintle hook on first semi-trailer.
- Slowly pull clear of dolly.

CAUTION: Never unlock the pintle hook with the dolly still under the rear trailer. The dolly tow bar may fly up, possibly causing injury, and making it very difficult to re-couple.

Coupling and Uncoupling Triple Trailers

NOTE: You will not be tested on this unless you want to get a double/triple trailer endorsement on your license.

Couple Second and Third Trailers

- Couple second and third trailers using the method for coupling doubles.
- Uncouple tractor and pull away from second and third trailers.

Couple Tractor/First Semi-trailer to Second/Third Trailers

- Couple tractor to first trailer. Use the method already described for coupling tractor/semi-trailers.
- Move converter dolly into position and couple first trailer to second trailer using the method for coupling doubles. Triples rig is now complete.

Uncouple Triple-Trailer Rig

- Uncouple third trailer by pulling the dolly out and then unhitching the dolly using the method for uncoupling doubles.
- Uncouple remainder of rig as you would any double-bottom rig using the method already described.

Coupling and Uncoupling Other Combinations

The methods described so far apply to the more common tractor-trailer combinations. However, there are other ways of coupling and uncoupling the many types of truck-trailer and tractor-trailer combinations that are in use. Learn the right way to couple the vehicle(s) you will drive according to the manufacturer and/or owner.

7.3 INSPECTING DOUBLES AND TRIPLES

Use the seven-step inspection procedure described in Chapter 2 to begin your inspection. Then continue your inspection as detailed in Chapter 6, "Inspecting a Combination Vehicle." In the case of doubles and triples, there are additional areas to check. They are discussed below.

Additional Things to Check During a Walkaround Inspection

Double and Triple Trailers

- Shut-off valves (at rear of trailers in service and emergency lines):
    - Rear of front trailers: OPEN.
    - Rear of last trailer: CLOSED.
    - Converter dolly air tank drain valve: CLOSED.
- Be sure air lines are supported and glad hands are properly connected.
- If spare tire is carried on converter gear (dolly), make sure it's secured.
- Be sure pintle-eye of dolly is in place in pintle hook of trailer(s).
- Make sure pintle hook is latched.
- Safety chains should be secured to trailer(s).
- Be sure light cords are firmly in sockets on trailers.

Air Brakes Check

Check the brakes on a double or triple trailer as you would any other combination vehicle. Do the checks in Chapter 5, "Inspecting Air Brake Systems," and Chapter 6, "Combination Vehicle Brake Check." Make certain that you check all trailers.

Chapter 8 – Tank Vehicles

THIS CHAPTER COVERS
❏ **Inspecting Tank Vehicles**   ❏ **Driving Tank Vehicles**

This chapter has information needed to pass the CDL knowledge test for driving a tank vehicle. (You should also study Chapters 2, 5, and 6). A "tank vehicle" is used to carry any liquid or liquid gas in a tank of 1000 gallons or more. (This endorsement is also needed for dry bulk tankers.)

Before loading, unloading, or driving a tanker, inspect the vehicle. This ensures that the vehicle is safe to carry the liquid or gas and is safe to drive.

8.1 INSPECTING TANK VEHICLES

Tank vehicles have special items that you need to check. Tank vehicles come in many types and sizes. You need to check the vehicle's operator's manual to make sure you know how to inspect your tank vehicle.

Leaks

On all tank vehicles, the most important item to check for is leaks. Check under and around the vehicle for signs of any leaking. Don't carry liquids or gases in a leaking tank. In general, check the following:

- Check the tank's body or shell for dents or leaks.
- Check the intake, discharge, and cut-off valves. Make sure the valves are in the correct position before loading, unloading, or moving the vehicle.
- Check pipes, connections, and hoses for leaks, especially around joints.
- Check manhole covers and vents. Make sure the covers have gaskets and they close correctly. Keep the vents clear so they work correctly.
- Check special purpose equipment. If your vehicle has any of the following equipment, make sure it works:
    - Vapor recovery kits.
    - Grounding and bonding cables.
    - Emergency shut-off systems.
    - Built-in fire extinguisher.

    Make sure you know how to operate your special equipment.
- Check the emergency equipment required for your vehicle. Find out what equipment you're required to carry and make sure you have it (and that it works).

8.2 DRIVING TANK VEHICLES

Hauling liquids in tanks requires special skills.

High Center of Gravity

High center of gravity means that much of the load's weight is carried high up off the road. This makes the vehicle top-heavy and easy to roll over. Liquid tankers are especially prone to rollover. Tests have shown that **tankers can turn over at the speed limits posted for curves. Take highway curves and on-ramp/off-ramp curves well below the posted speeds.**

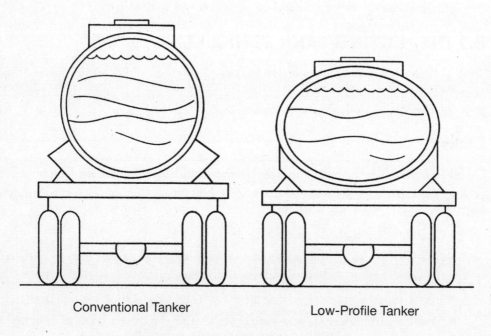

Conventional Tanker

Low-Profile Tanker

Both tankers hold the same number of gallons,
but the low-profile tanker has the advantage of a lower center of gravity

Figure 8-1 Tankers With Different Centers of Gravity

Danger of Surge

Liquid surge results from movement of the liquid in partially filled tanks. This movement can have bad effects on handling. For example, when coming to a stop, the liquid will surge back and forth. When the wave hits the end of the tank, it tends to push the truck in the direction the wave is moving. If the truck is on a slippery surface such as ice, the wave can shove a stopped truck out into an intersection. The driver of a liquid tanker must be very familiar with the handling of the vehicle.

Bulkheads

Some liquid tankers are divided into several smaller tanks by bulkheads. When loading and unloading the smaller tanks, the driver must pay attention to weight distribution. **Don't put too much weight on the front or rear of the vehicle.**

Baffled Tanks

Baffled liquid tanks have bulkheads in them with holes that let the liquid flow through. The baffles help to control the forward and backward liquid surge. Side-to-side surge can still occur. This can cause a roll over. **Drive slowly and carefully when taking curves or making sharp turns with a partially loaded tanker.**

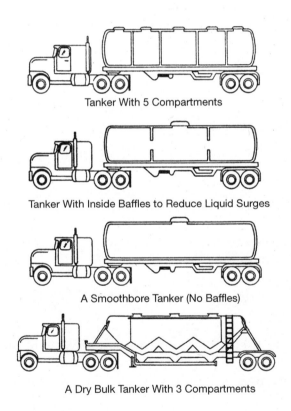

Tanker With 5 Compartments

Tanker With Inside Baffles to Reduce Liquid Surges

A Smoothbore Tanker (No Baffles)

A Dry Bulk Tanker With 3 Compartments

Figure 8-2

Unbaffled Tanks

Unbaffled liquid tankers (sometimes called "smooth bore" tanks) have nothing inside to slow down the flow of the liquid. Therefore, forward-and-back surge is very strong. Unbaffled tanks are usually those that transport food products (milk, for example). (Sanitation regulations forbid the use of baffles because of the difficulty in cleaning the inside of the tank.) Be extremely cautious in driving smooth bore tanks, especially when starting and stopping.

Outage

Never load a cargo tank totally full. Liquids expand as they warm and you must leave room for the expanding liquid. This is called "outage." Since different liquids expand by different amounts, they require different amounts of outage. You must know the outage requirement when hauling liquids in bulk.

How Much to Load?

A full tank of dense liquid (such as some acids) may exceed legal weight limits. For that reason, you may often only partially fill tanks with heavy liquids. The amount of liquid to load into a tank depends on:

- The amount the liquid will expand in transit.
- The weight of the liquid.
- Legal weight limits.

8.3 SAFE DRIVING RULES

To drive tank vehicles safely, you must remember to follow all the safe driving rules. A few of these rules are:

Drive Smoothly

Drive smoothly. Because of the high center of gravity and the surge of the liquid, you must start, slow down, and stop very smoothly. Also, make smooth turns and lane changes.

Braking

If you must make a quick stop to avoid a crash, use controlled or stab braking. If you do not remember how to stop using these methods, review Section 2.15. Also, remember that if you steer quickly while braking, your vehicle may roll over.

Curves

Slow down before curves, then accelerate slightly through the curve. The posted speed for a curve may be too fast for a tank vehicle.

Stopping Distance

Keep in mind how much space you need to stop your vehicle. Remember that wet roads double the normal stopping distance. Empty tank vehicles may take longer to stop than full ones.

Skids

Don't oversteer, overaccelerate, or overbrake. If you do, your vehicle may skid. On tank trailers, if your drive wheels or trailer wheels begin to skid, your vehicle may jackknife. When any vehicle starts to skid, you must take action to restore traction to the wheels.

Chapter 9 – Hazardous Materials

THIS CHAPTER COVERS

- ❏ The Intent of the Regulations
- ❏ Driver Responsibilities
- ❏ Communication Rules
- ❏ Loading and Unloading
- ❏ Bulk Tank Marking, Loading, and Unloading
- ❏ Driving and Parking Rules
- ❏ Emergencies

Hazardous materials are products that pose a risk to health, safety, and property during transportation. The term often is shortened to HAZMAT, which you may see on road signs, or to HM in government regulations. Hazardous materials include explosives, various types of gas, solids, flammable and combustible liquid, and other materials. Because of the risks involved and the potential consequences these risks impose, the handling of hazardous materials is very heavily regulated by all levels of government.

The Hazardous Materials Regulations (HMR) are found in parts 171–180 of title 49 of the Code of Federal Regulations. The common reference for these regulations is 49 CFR 171–180.

The Hazardous Materials Table in these regulations contains a list of these items. However, this list is not all-inclusive. Whether or not a material is considered hazardous is based on its characteristics and the shipper's decision on whether or not the material meets a definition of a hazardous material in the regulations.

The regulations require vehicles transporting certain types or quantities of hazardous materials to display diamond-shaped, square on-point warning signs called placards.

This chapter is designed to assist you in understanding your role and responsibilities in hauling hazardous materials. Due to the constantly changing nature of government regulations, it is impossible to guarantee absolute accuracy of the information in this chapter. It is essential for you to have an up-to-date copy of the complete regulations. Included in these regulations is a complete glossary of terms.

You must have a commercial driver license (CDL) with a hazardous materials endorsement before driving vehicles carrying hazardous material that require placards. You must pass a written test on the regulations and requirements to get this endorsement.

This chapter will help you prepare for the written test. However, this is only a beginning. Most drivers need to know much more on the job. You can learn more by reading and understanding the federal and state rules applicable to hazardous materials as well as attending hazardous materials training courses. These courses are usually offered by your employer, colleges and universities, and various associations. You can get copies of the Federal Regulations (49 CFR) from your local Government Printing Office bookstore and various industry publishers. Union or company offices often have copies of the rules for driver use. Find out where you can get your own copy to use on the job.

The regulations require training and testing for all drivers involved in transporting hazardous materials. Your employer or a designated representative is required to provide this training and testing. Hazardous materials employers are required to keep a record of that training on each employee as long as that employee is working with hazardous materials, and for 90 days thereafter. The regulations require that hazardous materials employees be trained and tested at least once every two years.

The regulations also require that drivers have special training before driving a vehicle transporting certain flammable gas materials or highway route-controlled quantities of radioactive materials. In addition, drivers transporting cargo tanks and portable tanks must receive specialized training. Each driver's employer or a designated representative must provide such training.

Some locations require permits to transport certain explosives or bulk hazardous wastes. States and counties also may require drivers to follow special hazardous material routes. The federal government may require permits or exemptions for special hazardous materials cargo such as rocket fuel. Find out about permits, exemptions, and special routes for places you drive.

NOTE: Regulations also exist for the transportation of hazardous materials in busses or other passenger vehicles. This information is in Chapter 4 "Loading and Trip Start."

9.1 THE INTENT OF THE REGULATIONS

Contain the Material

Many hazardous materials can injure or kill people. To protect drivers and others, and the environment, the rules tell shippers how to package hazardous materials safely. Similar rules tell drivers how to load, transport, and unload bulk tanks. These are "containment rules."

Communicate the Risk

To communicate the risk, shippers must warn drivers and others about the material's hazards. The regulations require shippers to put hazard warning labels on packages, provide proper shipping papers, emergency response information, and placards. These steps communicate the hazard to the shipper, the carrier, and the driver. Drivers must also warn others if there is an accident or leak.

Assure Safe Drivers and Equipment

To get a hazardous materials endorsement on a CDL, you must pass a written test about transporting hazardous materials. To pass the test, you must know how to:

- Identify hazardous materials.
- Safely load shipments.
- Properly placard your vehicle in accordance with the rules.
- Safely transport shipments.

Learn the rules and follow them. Following the rules reduces the risk of injury from hazardous materials. Taking shortcuts by breaking rules is unsafe. Rule breakers can be fined and put in jail.

Inspect your vehicle before and during each trip. Law enforcement officers may stop and inspect your vehicle. When stopped, they may check your shipping papers, vehicle placards, the hazardous materials endorsement on your driver license, and your knowledge of hazardous materials.

9.2 HAZARDOUS MATERIALS TRANSPORTATION: WHO DOES WHAT?

The Shipper

- Sends products from one place to another by truck, railroad, ship, or airplane.
- Uses the hazardous materials regulations to decide the product's:
  - Proper shipping name.
  - Hazard class.
  - Identification number.
  - Correct packaging.
  - Correct label and markings.
  - Correct placard.
- Must package, mark, and label the materials; prepare shipping papers; provide emergency response information; and supply placards.
- Must certify on the shipping paper that the shipment has been prepared according to the rules (unless you are pulling cargo tanks supplied by you or your employer).

The Carrier

- Takes the shipment from the shipper to its destination.
- Checks that the shipper correctly named, labeled, and marked the shipment.
- Refuses improper shipments.
- Reports accidents and incidents involving hazardous materials to the proper government agency.

The Driver

- Makes sure the shipper has identified, marked, and labeled the product.
- Refuses leaking shipments.
- Placards his vehicle when loading, if needed.
- Safely transports the shipment without delay.
- Follows all special rules about transporting hazardous material.
- Keeps hazardous material shipping papers in the proper place.

9.3 COMMUNICATION RULES

Definitions

Some words and phrases have special meanings when used with hazardous materials. The meanings may differ from common use. The words and phrases in this chapter may be on your test. The meanings of other important words are in the glossary at the end of this chapter.

A material's **hazard class** reflects the risks associated with it. There are nine different hazard classes. Figure 9-1 tells the exact meaning of each hazard class.

The **shipping paper** describes a shipment of hazardous material. Each item description on the shipping paper shows the material's hazard class. Shipping orders, bills of lading, and manifests are all shipping papers. Figure 9-2 shows an example of a shipping paper.

After an accident or hazardous material leak, you may be unable to speak. Firefighters and police can prevent more damage or injury if they know the hazards involved. Your life, and the lives of others, may depend on their quickly finding the shipping papers for hazardous cargo. For that reason the rules:

- Require shippers to describe shipments correctly on shipping papers and to include emergency response numbers.
- Require carriers and drivers to put tabs on shipping papers related to hazardous materials, or keep them on top of other shipping papers, and to keep emergency response information with the shipping papers.

Class	Division	Name of Class or Division	Example
1	1.1	Mass Explosives	Dynamite
	1.2	Projection Hazards	Flares
	1.3	Mass Fire Hazards	Display Fireworks
	1.4	Minor Hazards	Ammunition
	1.5	Very Insensitive	Blasting Agents
	1.6	Extremely Insensitive	Explosive Devices
2	2.1	Flammable Gases	Propane
	2.2	Non-Flammable Gases	Helium
	2.3	Poisonous/Toxic Gases	Fluorine, Compressed
3	—	Flammable Liquids	Gasoline
4	4.1	Flammable Solids	Ammonium Picrate, Wetted
	4.2	Spontaneously Combustible	White Phosphorus
	4.3	Spontaneously Combustible When Wet	Sodium
5	5.1	Oxidizers	Ammonium Nitrate
	5.2	Organic Peroxides	Methyl Ethyl Ketone Peroxide
6	6.1	Poison (Toxic Material)	Potassium Cyanide
	6.2	Infectious Substances	Anthrax Virus
7	—	Radioactive	Uranium
8	—	Corrosives	Battery fluid
9	—	Miscellaneous Hazardous Materials	Polychlorinated Biphenyls (PCBs)
None	—	ORM-D (Other Regulated Material—Domestic)	Food Flavorings, Medicines
None	—	Combustible Liquids	Fuel Oil

Figure 9-1 Hazardous Materials Hazard Class/Division Table

- Require drivers to keep shipping papers for hazardous cargo:
    - In a pouch on the driver's door.
    - In clear view within reach while driving.
    - On the driver's seat when out of the vehicle.

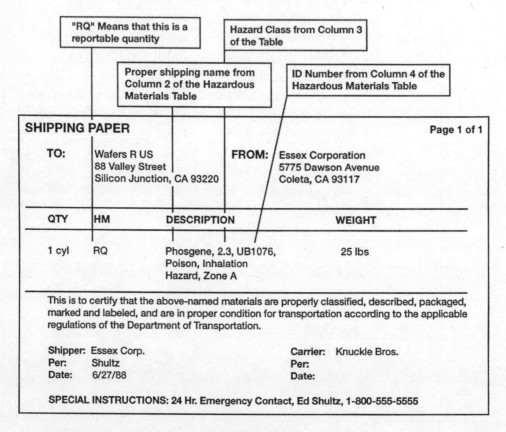

Figure 9-2 Example of Shipping Paper

Package Labels

Shippers put diamond shaped labels on hazardous material packages. These labels warn others of the hazard. If the diamond label won't fit on the package, shippers put the label on a tag. For example, compressed gas cylinders that will not hold a label will have tags or decals. Labels look like the example in Figure 9-3. (Others are shown in Chapter 4, Figure 4.1.)

Figure 9-3 Example of Labeled Package

Placards are used to warn others about hazardous cargo. Placards are signs put on the outside of a vehicle to show the hazard class of the cargo. A placarded vehicle must have at least four identical placards. They are put on the front, rear, and both sides (see Figure 9-4). Placards must be readable from all four directions. They are 10 3/4 inches square, turned upright on a point, in a diamond shape. Cargo tanks show the ID number of their contents on placards, orange panels, or white square on-point displays that are the same size as placards.

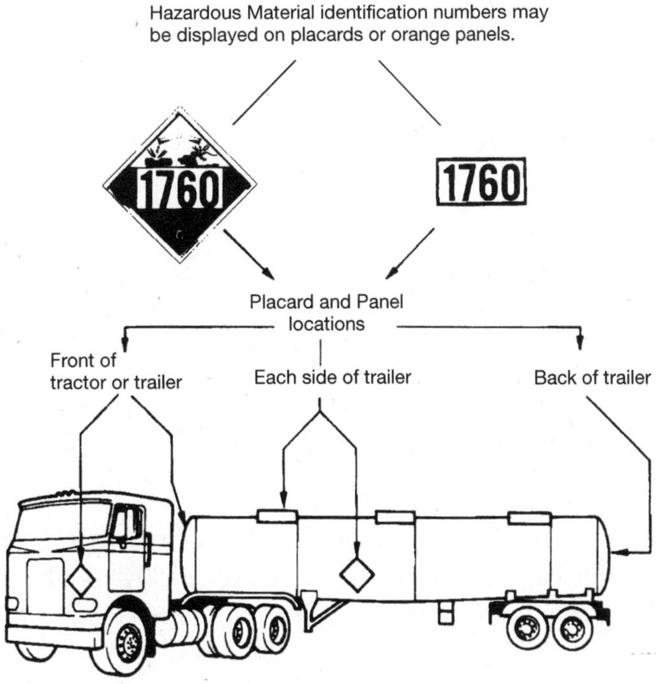

Hazardous Material identification numbers may be displayed on placards or orange panels.

1760

1760

Placard and Panel locations

Front of tractor or trailer

Each side of trailer

Back of trailer

Figure 9-4 Placard and Panel Locations

Lists of Regulated Products

There are three main lists used by shippers, carriers, and drivers when trying to identify hazardous materials. Before transporting a material, look for its name on three lists. Some materials are on all lists, others on only one. Always check the following lists:

- Section 172.101, the Hazardous Materials Table.
- Appendix A to Section 172.101, the List of Hazardous Substances and Reportable Quantities.
- Appendix B to Section 172.101, the List of Marine Pollutants.

The Hazardous Materials Table. Figure 9-5 shows part of the Hazardous Materials Table. Column 1 tells which shipping mode(s) the entry affects and other information concerning the shipping description. The next five columns show each material's shipping name, hazard class or division, ID number, packaging group, and required labels.

Five different symbols may appear in Column 1 of the table.

(+) Shows the proper shipping name, hazard class, and packing group to use, even if the material doesn't meet the hazard class definition.

(A) Means the hazardous material described in Column 2 is subject to the HMR only when offered or intended for transport by air unless it is a hazardous substance or hazardous waste.

(W) Means the hazardous material described in Column 2 is subject to the HMR only when offered or intended for transportation by water unless it is a hazardous substance, hazardous waste, or marine pollutant.

(D) Means the proper shipping name is appropriate for describing materials for domestic transportation, but may not be proper for international transportation.

(I) Identifies a proper shipping name that is used to describe materials in international transportation. A different shipping name may be used when only domestic transportation is involved.

Column 2 lists the proper shipping names and descriptions of regulated materials. Entries are in alphabetical order so you can more quickly find the right entry. The table shows proper shipping names in regular type. The shipping paper must show proper shipping names. Names shown in *italics* are not proper shipping names.

Column 3 shows a material's hazard class or division, or the entry "Forbidden." Never transport a "Forbidden" material. You placard shipments based on the quantity and hazard class. You can decide which placards to use if you know these three things:

- Material's hazard class.

§ 172.101 Hazardous Materials Table

(1)	(2)	(3)	(4)	(5)	(6)	(7)	(8) Packaging authorizations (§ 173.***)		
							Exceptions (8A)	Non-bulk packaging (8B)	Bulk packaging (8C)
Symbols	Hazardous materials descriptions and proper shipping names	Hazard class or Division	Identification Numbers	Packing Group	Label(s) required (if not excepted)	Special provisions			
—	Poisonous, solids, self heating, n.o.s. ...	6.1	UN3124	1	POISON, SPONTANEOUSLY COMBUSTIBLE	A5	None	211	241

Figure 9-5 Part of the Hazardous Materials Table

- Amount being shipped.
- Amount of all hazardous materials of all classes on your vehicle.

Column 4 lists the identification number for each proper shipping name. Identification numbers are preceded by the letters "UN" or "NA." The letters "NA" are associated with proper shipping names that are only used within the United States and to and from Canada. The identification number must appear on the shipping paper as part of the shipping description and also appear on the package. It also must appear on cargo tanks and other bulk packaging. Police and firefighters use this number to quickly identify the hazardous materials.

Column 5 shows the packing group assigned to a material.

Column 6 shows the hazard warning label(s) shippers must put on packages of hazardous materials. Some products require use of more than one label due to a dual hazard being present. No label is needed where the table shows the word NONE.

Column 7 lists the additional (special) provisions that apply to this material. When there is an entry in this column, you must refer to the federal regulations for specific information.

Column 8 is a three-part column showing the section numbers covering the packaging requirements for each hazardous material.

NOTE: Columns 9 and 10 (not shown) do not apply to transportation by highway.

Appendix A to §172.101 – The list of Hazardous Substances and Reportable Quantities. The DOT and the EPA want to know about spills of **hazardous substances**. They are named in the List of Hazardous Substances and Reportable Quantities (see Figure 9-6). Column 3 of the list shows each product's reportable quantity (RQ). When these materials are being transported in a reportable quantity or greater in one package, the shipper displays the letters RQ on the shipping paper and package. The letters RQ may appear before or after the basic description. You or your employer must report any spill of these materials that occurs in a **reportable quantity**.

If the words INHALATION HAZARD appear on the shipping paper or package, the rules require display of the POISON or POISON GAS placards, as appropriate. These placards must be used in addition to other placards which may be required by the product's hazard class. Always display the hazard class placard and the POISON placard, even for small amounts.

Spills of 10 pounds or
more must be reported.

List of Hazardous Substances and Reportable Quantities – Continued		
Hazardous Substance	**Synonyms**	**Reportable Quantity (RQ) Pounds (Kilograms)**
Phenyl mercaptan @	Benzinethiol Thiophenol	100 (45.4)
Phenylmercuric acetate	Mercury, (acetato-0) phenyl	100 (45.4)
N-Phenylthiourea	Thiourea, phenyl	100 (45.4)
Phorate	Phosphorodithioic acid, O,O-diethyl S- (ethylthio), methylester	10 (4.54)
Phosgene	Carbonyl chloride	10 (4.54)
Phosphine	Hydrogen Phosphide	100 (45.4)
Phosphoric acid		5000 (2270)
Phosphoric acid, diethyl 4-nitrophenyl ester	Diethyl-p nitrophenyl phosphate	100 (45.4)
Phosphoric acid, lead salt	Lead phosphate	1 (0.454)

Figure 9-6 List of Hazardous Substances

The Shipping Paper

The shipping paper shown in Figure 9-2 describes a shipment. The shipping paper for a hazardous material must include:

- The number of pages of shipping papers. The first page must tell the total number of pages, for example, "Page 1 of 1."
- A proper description of the hazardous product.
- A "shipper's certification," signed by the shipper, saying he/ she prepared the shipment according to the regulations.

The Item Description

If the shipping paper describes both hazardous and non-hazardous products, the hazardous materials will be either:

- Described first.
- Highlighted in a contrasting color.

- Identified by an "X" placed before the shipping name in a column captioned "HM." The letters "RQ" may be used instead of "X" if the shipment is a reportable quantity.

The basic description of hazardous materials includes the proper shipping name, hazard class or division, the identification number, and the packing group, if any, in that order. The packing group is displayed in Roman numerals and may be preceded by "PG."

Shipping name, hazard class, and ID number must not be abbreviated unless specifically authorized in the hazardous materials regulations. The description must also show:

- The total quantity and unit of measure.
- The letters RQ, if a reportable quantity.
- If the letters RQ appear, the name of the hazardous substance.
- For "n.o.s." and generic descriptions, the technical name of the hazardous material.

Shipping papers also must list an emergency response telephone number. The emergency response telephone number is the responsibility of the shipper. It can be used by emergency responders to obtain information about any hazardous materials involved in a spill or fire.

Shippers also must provide emergency response information to the motor carrier for each hazardous material being shipped. The emergency response information must be able to be used away from the motor vehicle and must provide information on how to safely handle incidents involving the material. It must include information on the shipping name of the hazardous materials, risks to health, fire, explosion, and initial methods of handling spills, fires, and leaks of the materials.

Such information can be on the shipping paper or some other document that includes the basic description and technical name of the hazardous material. Or, it may be in a guidance book such as the Emergency Response Guidebook (ERG). Motor carriers may assist shippers by keeping an ERG on each vehicle carrying hazardous materials. The driver must provide the emergency response information to any federal, state, or local authority responding to a hazardous materials incident or investigating one.

Total quantity must appear before or after the basic description. The packaging type and the unit of measurement may be abbreviated. For example:

10 ctns. Paint, 3, UN1263, PG II, 500 lbs.

The shipper of hazardous wastes must put the word WASTE before the proper shipping name of the material on the shipping paper (hazardous waste manifest). For example:

Waste Acetone, 3, UN1090, PG 11.

A non-hazardous material may **not** be described by using a hazard class or an ID number.

Shipper's Certification

When the shipper packages a hazardous material, the shipper certifies that the package has been prepared according to the regulations. The signed shipper's certification appears on the original shipping paper. The only exceptions are when a shipper is a private carrier transporting his or her own product, and when the package is provided by the carrier (for example, a cargo tank). The glossary at the end of this chapter shows acceptable shipper certifications. Unless a package is clearly unsafe or does not comply with the HMR, you may accept the shipper's certification concerning proper packaging. Some carriers have additional rules about transporting hazardous products. Follow your employer's rules when accepting shipments.

Package Markings and Labels

Shippers print required markings directly on the package, an attached label, or tag. The most important package marking is the name of the hazardous material. It is the same name as the one on the shipping paper. When required, the shipper will put the following on the package:

- The name and address of shipper or consignee.
- The hazardous material's shipping name and identification number.
- The labels required.

If the rules require it, the shipper also will put RQ or INHALATION-HAZARD on the package. Cartons with liquid containers inside may also have "This Side Up" markings. The labels used always reflect the hazard class of the product. If a package needs more than one label, the labels will be close together, near the proper shipping name.

Recognizing Hazardous Materials

Learn to recognize shipments of hazardous materials. To find out if the shipment includes a hazardous material, look at the shipping paper. Does it have:

- An entry with a proper shipping name, hazard class, and ID number?
- A highlighted entry, or one with an X or RQ in the HM column?

Other clues that suggest hazardous materials are:

- The business of the shipper. Paint dealers, chemical and scientific suppliers, pest control or agricultural suppliers, and explosives, munitions, or fireworks dealers may be shipping hazardous materials.
- Tanks with diamond labels or placards on the premises.
- The type of package being shipped. Cylinders and drums are often used for hazardous materials shipments.
- A hazard class label, proper shipping name, or ID number on the package.
- Handling precautions.

Hazardous Waste Manifest

When transporting hazardous waste, you must sign and carry a Uniform Hazardous Waste Manifest. The name and EPA registration number of the shipper, carriers, and destination must appear on the manifest. The shipper will prepare, date and sign the manifest. Treat the manifest as a shipping paper when transporting the waste. You may only deliver the waste shipment to another registered carrier or treatment facility. Each carrier transporting the shipment must sign the manifest. After you deliver the shipment, keep your copy of the manifest. Each copy must have all needed signatures and dates, including those of the person to whom you delivered the waste.

Placarding

Attach the right placards as you load the vehicle and before you drive it. You may move an improperly placarded vehicle only in an emergency to protect life or property.

Placards must appear on both sides and ends of the vehicle. Each placard must be:

- Easily seen from the direction it faces.
- Placed so the words or numbers are level and read from left to right.
- At least three inches away from any other markings.
- Kept clear of attachments or devices such as ladders, doors, and tarpaulins.
- Kept clean and undamaged so that the color, format, and message are easily seen.

To decide which placards to use, you need to know:

- The hazard class of the materials.
- The amount of hazardous materials shipped.
- The total weight of all classes of hazardous materials in your vehicle.

PLACARD TABLE 1—ANY AMOUNT

IF YOUR VEHICLE CONTAINS ANY AMOUNT OF...	PLACARD AS...
1.1	EXPLOSIVE 1.1
1.2	EXPLOSIVE 1.2
1.3	EXPLOSIVE 1.3
2.3	POISON GAS
4.3	DANGEROUS WHEN WET
6.1 (PG I, inhalation hazard only)	POISON
7 (Radioactive Yellow III label only)	RADIOACTIVE

Figure 9–7 Placard Table 1—Any Amount

Always make sure that the shipper shows the correct basic description on the shipping paper and verifies that the proper labels are shown on the packages. If you are not familiar with the material, ask the shipper to contact your office.

There are two placard tables. Always use placards to transport **any** amount of material listed in Table 1.

The hazard classes in Table 2 need placards only if the amount transported is 1,000 lbs. or more, including the package. Add the amounts from all shipping papers for all the Table 2 products you have on board. You may use DANGEROUS placards instead of separate placards for each Table 2 hazard class when:

- You have two or more Table 2 hazard classes, requiring different placards that total 1,000 lbs. or more.

- You have **not** loaded 5,000 lbs. or more of any Table 2 hazard class material at any one place. (You must use the specific placard for this material.)

- If the words INHALATION HAZARD are on the shipping paper or package, the rules require POISON placards. You must use POISON placards in addition to any others needed by the product's hazard class. Always show the hazard class placard and the POISON placard, even for small amounts.

You need not use EXPLOSIVES 1.5, OXIDIZER, and DANGEROUS placards if a vehicle contains Division 1.1 or 1.2 explosives and is placarded with EXPLOSIVES 1.1 or 1.2 placards. You need not use a Division 2.2 NON-FLAMMABLE GAS placard on a vehicle displaying a Division 2.1 FLAMMABLE GAS or for oxygen a Division 2.2 OXYGEN placard.

PLACARD TABLE 2

Category of Material (Hazard class or division number and additional description, as appropriate)	Placard Name
1.4	EXPLOSIVES 1.4
1.5	EXPLOSIVES 1.5
1.6	EXPLOSIVES 1.6
2.1	FLAMMABLE GAS
2.2	NON-FLAMMABLE GAS
3	FLAMMABLE
Combustible liquid	COMBUSTIBLE*
4.1	FLAMMABLE SOLID
4.2	SPONTANEOUSLY COMBUSTIBLE
5.1	OXIDIZER
5.2	ORGANIC PEROXIDE
6.1 (PG I or II, other than PG I inhalation hazard)	POISON
6.1 (PG III)	KEEP AWAY FROM FOOD
6.2	(NONE)
8	CORROSIVE
9	CLASS 9**
ORM-D	(NONE)

* FLAMMABLE placard may be used in place of a COMBUSTIBLE placard on a cargo tank or portable tank.

** Class 9 Placard is not required for domestic transportation.

Figure 9–8 Placard Table 2—1000 lbs. or more

Placards used to identify the primary hazard class of a material must have the hazard class or division number displayed in the lower corner of the placard. No hazard class or division number is allowed on placards used to identify a secondary hazard class of a material.

Placards may be displayed for hazardous materials even if not required so long as the placard identifies the hazard of the material being transported.

9.4 LOADING AND UNLOADING

General Loading Requirements

- Do all you can to protect containers of hazardous materials. Don't use any tools which might damage containers or other packaging during loading. Don't use hooks.

- Before loading or unloading, set the parking brake. Make sure the vehicle will not move.

- Many products are more hazardous in the heat. Load hazardous materials away from heat sources.

- Watch for signs of leaking or damaged containers: LEAKS SPELL TROUBLE! Do not transport leaking packages. Depending on the material, you, your truck, and others could be in danger.

Containers of Class 1 (explosives), Class 3 (flammable liquids), Class 4 (flammable solids), Class 5 (oxidizers), Class 8 (corrosives), Class 2 (gases), and Division 6.1 (poisons) must be braced to prevent movement of the packages during transportation.

No Smoking. When loading hazardous materials, keep fire away. Don't let people smoke nearby. Never smoke around:

Class 1	Division 2.1	Class 4
(EXPLOSIVES)	(FLAMMABLE GAS)	(FLAMMABLE SOLIDS)

Class 5	Class 3
(OXIDIZERS)	(FLAMMABLE LIQUIDS)

Secure Against Movement. Make sure containers don't move around in transit. Brace them so they will not fall, slide, or bounce around. Be very careful when loading containers that have valves or other fittings.

Do not open any package between the points of origin and destination. Never transfer hazardous products from one package to another. You may empty a cargo tank, but do not empty any other package while it is on the vehicle.

Cargo Heater Rules. There are special cargo heater rules for loading:

Class 1	Class 3	Division 2.1
(EXPLOSIVES)	(FLAMMABLE LIQUID)	(FLAMMABLE GAS)

The rules usually forbid use of cargo heaters, including automatic cargo heater/air conditioner units. Unless you have read all the related rules, don't load the above products in a cargo space that has a heater.

Use Closed Cargo Space. You cannot have overhang or tailgate loads of:

Class 1	Class 4	Class 5
(EXPLOSIVES)	(FLAMMABLE SOLIDS)	(OXIDIZERS)

You must load these hazards into a closed cargo space unless all packages are:

- Fire and water resistant.
- Covered with a fire and water resistant tarp.

Precautions for Specific Hazards

Explosives. Before loading or unloading any explosive, turn your engine off. Then check the cargo space.

- You must disable cargo heaters. Disconnect heater power sources and drain heater fuel tanks.
- There must be no sharp points that might damage cargo. Look for bolts, screws, nails, broken side panels, and broken floor boards.
- Use a floor lining with Division 1.1, 1.2, or 1.3 (Class A or B explosives). The floors must be tight and the liner must be either non-metallic material or non-ferrous metal.

Use extra care to protect explosives. Never use hooks or other metal tools. Never drop, throw, or roll the shipment. Protect explosive packages from other cargo that might cause damage.

Do not transfer a Division 1.1, 1.2, or 1.3 (Class A or B explosive) from one vehicle to another on a public roadway except in an emergency. If safety requires an emergency transfer, set out red warning reflectors, flags, or electric lanterns. You must warn other highway users.

Never transport damaged packages of explosives. Do not take a package that shows any dampness or an oily stain.

Do not transport Division 1.1 or 1.2 (Class A explosives) in triples or in vehicle combinations if:

- There is a marked or placarded cargo tank in the combination.
- The other vehicle in the combination contains:
    - Division 1.1 A (initiating explosives).
    - Packages of Class 7 (radioactive) materials labeled "Yellow III."
    - Division 2.3 (poisonous gas) or Division 6.1 (poisonous) materials.
    - Hazardous materials in a portable tank, on a DOT Spec 106A or 110A tank.

Class 8 (Corrosive Materials). If loading by hand, load breakable containers of corrosive liquid one by one. Keep them right side up. Do not drop or roll the containers. Load them onto an even floor surface. Only stack carboys if the lower tiers can bear the weight of the upper tiers safely.

Do not load nitric acid above any other product, or stack more than two high.

Load charged storage batteries so their liquid won't spill. Keep them right side up. Make sure other cargo won't fall against or short circuit them.

Never load corrosive liquids next to or above:
- Division 1.4 (Explosives C).
- Class 4 (Flammable Solids).
- Class 5 (Oxidizers).
- Division 2.3, Zone B (Poisonous Gases).

Never load corrosive liquids with:
- Division 1.1 or 1.2 (Explosives A).
- Division 1.2 or 1.3 (Explosives B).
- Division 1.5 (Blasting Agents).
- Division 2.3, Zone A (Poisonous Gases).
- Division 4.2 (Spontaneously Combustible Materials).
- Division 6.1, PGI, Zone A (Poison Liquids).

Class 2 (Compressed Gases, Including Cryogenic Liquids). If your vehicle doesn't have racks to hold cylinders, the cargo space floor must be flat. The cylinders must be:
- Held upright or braced laying down flat.
- In racks attached to the vehicle.
- In boxes that will keep them from turning over.

Division 2.3 (Poisonous Gas) or Division 6.1 (Poisonous Materials). Never transport these materials in containers with interconnections. Never load a package labeled POISON, POISON GAS, or IRRITANT in the driver's cab or sleeper or with food for human or animal consumption.

Class 7 (Radioactive Materials). Some packages of Class 7 radioactive materials bear a number called the "transport index." The shipper labels these packages Radioactive II or Radioactive III, and prints the package's transport index on the label. Radiation surrounds each package, passing through all nearby packages. To deal with this problem, the number of packages you can load together is controlled. Their closeness to people, animals, and unexposed film is also controlled. The

DO NOT LOAD...	IN THE SAME VEHICLE WITH...
Division 6.1 or 2.3 (POISON or poison gas labeled material)	animal or human food unless the poison package is overpacked in an approved way. Foodstuffs are anything you swallow. However, mouthwash, toothpaste, and skin creams are not foodstuff.
Division 2.3 (poisonous) gas Zone A or Division 6.1 (poison) liquids, PGI, Zone A	Division 5.1 (oxidizers), Class 3 (flammable liquids), Class 8 (corrosive liquids), Division 5.2 (organic peroxides), Division 1.1, 1.2, 1.3 (Class A or B) explosives, Division 1.5 (blasting agents), Division 2.1 (flammable gases), Class 4 (flammable solids).
Charged storage batteries	Division 1.1 (Class A Explosives).
Class 1 (Detonating primers)	any other explosives unless in authorized containers or packagings.
Division 6.1 (Cyanides or cyanide mixtures)	acids, corrosive materials, or other acidic materials which could release hydrocyanic acid from cyanides. For example: Cyanides, Inorganic, n.o.s. Silver Cyanide Sodium Cyanide
Nitric acid (Class 8)	other materials unless the nitric acid is not loaded above any other material and not more than two tiers high.

Figure 9-9 Prohibited Loading Combinations

transport index tells the degree of control needed during transportation. The total transport index of all packages in a single vehicle must not exceed 50.

The appendix at the end of this chapter has rules for each transport index. It shows how long you can load radioactive materials and how close you can load them to people, animals, or film. For example, you can't leave a package with a transport index of 1.1 within 2 feet of people or cargo space walls.

Mixed loads. The rules require some products to be loaded separately. Do not load them together in the same cargo space. Figure 9-9 lists some examples. **The regulations (the Segregation and Separation Chart) name other materials you must keep apart.**

9.5 BULK TANK MARKING, LOADING, AND UNLOADING

Bulk packaging is any packaging, including a transport vehicle or freight container, that can hold more than 118.9 gallons of a liquid or 881.9 pounds of a solid, or that has a water capacity greater than 1,000 pounds for a gas. **Cargo tanks** are bulk containers permanently attached to a vehicle. Cargo tanks remain on the vehicle when you load and unload them. **Portable tanks** are bulk containers that are not permanently attached to a vehicle. They are loaded or unloaded with the product while off the vehicle. Portable tanks are then put on a vehicle for transportation. There are many types of cargo tanks in use. The most common are MC306 for liquids and MC331 for gases.

Tank Markings

You must display the ID number of the contents of portable tanks and cargo tanks. Product ID numbers are in column 3a of the Hazardous Materials Table. The rules require black four-inch numbers on orange panels, DOT placards, or a white, diamond-shaped background if no placards are required. Specification cargo tanks must show retest date markings.

Portable tanks must also show the lessee or owner's name and the shipping name and ID number of the contents on two opposing sides. The letters must be at least two inches tall. The ID number must appear on each side and each end of tanks that hold 1,000 gallons or more. The ID numbers must still show when the portable tank is on the vehicle. If they don't, you must display the ID number on both sides and ends of the vehicle.

Tank Loading

The person in charge of loading and unloading a cargo tank must be sure someone is always watching. The person watching the loading or unloading must:
- Be alert.
- Have a clear view of the cargo tank.
- Be within 25 feet of the tank.
- Be aware of the hazards.

- Know the procedures to follow in an emergency.
- Be authorized to move the cargo tank and able to do so.

Close all manholes and valves before moving a tank of hazardous materials. It does not matter how small the amount in the tank or how short the distance. Manholes and valves must not leak.

Flammable Liquids

Turn off your engine before loading or unloading any flammable liquid. Only run the engine if needed to operate a pump. Ground a cargo tank correctly before filling it through an open filling hole. Ground the tank before opening the filling hole, and maintain the ground until after closing the filling hole.

Compressed Gas

Keep liquid discharge valves on a compressed gas tank closed except when loading and unloading. Unless your engine runs a pump for product transfer, turn it off when loading or unloading. If you use the engine, turn it off after product transfer, before unhooking the hose. Unhook all loading/unloading connections before coupling, uncoupling, or moving a chlorine cargo tank. Always chock trailers and semi-trailers to prevent motion when uncoupled from the power unit.

9.6 HAZARDOUS MATERIALS: DRIVING AND PARKING RULES

Parking with Division 1.1, 1.2, or 1.3 (Class A or B) Explosives

Never park with Division 1.1, 1.2, or 1.3 (Class A or B) explosives when you are within five feet of the travelled part of the road. Unless your work requires it, do not park within 300 feet of:

- A bridge, tunnel, or building.
- A place where people gather.
- An open fire.

If you must park to do your job, do so only briefly.

Don't park on private property unless the owner is aware of the danger. Someone must always watch the parked vehicle. You may let someone else watch it for you only if your vehicle is:

- On the shipper's property.
- On the carrier's property.
- On the consignee's property.

You can leave your vehicle unattended in a safe haven. A safe haven is a government-approved place for parking unattended vehicles loaded with explosives.

Parking When Placarded But Not Transporting Division 1.1, 1.2, or 1.3 (Class A or B) Explosives

You may park a placarded vehicle (not carrying explosives) within five feet of the travelled part of the road only if your work requires it. Do so only briefly. Someone must always watch the vehicle when parked on a public roadway or shoulder. Do not uncouple a trailer and leave it with hazardous material on a public street. Do not park within 300 feet of an open fire.

Watching Parked Vehicles

The person watching a placarded vehicle must:

- Be in the vehicle, awake, and not in the sleeper berth, or within 100 feet of the vehicle and have it within clear view.
- Be aware of the hazards.
- Know what to do in emergencies.
- Be able to move the vehicle if needed.

No Flares!

You might break down and have to use stopped-vehicle signals. Use reflective triangles or red electric lights. Never use burning signals, such as flares or fuses, around a:

- Tank used for Class 3 (flammable liquid) or Division 2.1 (flammable gas) whether loaded or empty.
- Vehicle loaded with Division 1.1, 1.2, or 1.3 (Class A or B) explosives.

Route Restrictions

Some states and counties require permits to transport hazardous material or waste. They may limit the routes you can use. Local rules about routes and permits change often. It is your job as driver to find out if you need permits or must use special routes. Make sure you have all required papers before starting.

If you work for a carrier, ask your dispatcher about route limits or permits. If you are an independent and are planning a new route, check with state agencies where you plan to travel. Some localities prohibit transportation of hazardous materials through tunnels, over bridges or other roadways. Check before you start.

Whenever placarded, avoid heavily populated areas, crowds, tunnels, narrow streets, and alleys. Take other routes, even if inconvenient, unless there is no other way. Never drive a placarded vehicle near open fires unless you can safely pass without stopping.

If transporting Division 1.1, 1.2, or 1.3 (Class A or B) explosives, you must have a written route plan and follow that plan. Carriers prepare the route plan in advance, and give the driver a copy. You may plan the route yourself if you pick up the explosives at a location other than your employer's terminal. Write out the plan in advance. Keep a copy of it with you while transporting the explosives. Deliver shipments of explosives only to authorized persons or leave them in locked rooms designed for explosives storage.

A carrier must choose the safest route to transport placarded radioactive material. After choosing the route, the carrier must tell the driver about the radioactive materials and show the route to be taken.

No Smoking

Do not smoke within 25 feet of a placarded tank used for Class 3 (flammable liquids) or Division 2.1 (gases). Also, do not smoke or carry a lighted cigarette, cigar, or pipe within 25 feet of any vehicle which contains:

Class 1	Class 3
(EXPLOSIVES)	(FLAMMABLE LIQUIDS)
Class 4	Class 5
(FLAMMABLE SOLIDS)	(OXIDIZERS)

Refuel with Engine Off

Turn off your engine before fueling a placarded vehicle. Someone must always be at the nozzle, controlling fuel flow.

10 B:C Fire Extinguisher

The power unit of placarded vehicles must have a fire extinguisher with a UL rating of 10 B:C or more.

Check Tires Every 2 hours/100 miles

Make sure your tires are properly inflated. Check placarded vehicles with dual tires at the start of each trip and when you park. You must stop and check the tires every 2 hours or 100 miles, whichever is less. The only acceptable way to check tire pressure is to use a tire pressure gauge.

Do not drive with a tire that is leaking or flat except to the nearest safe place to fix it. Remove any overheated tire. Place it a safe distance from your vehicle. Don't drive until you correct the cause of the overheating. Remember to follow the rules about parking and watching placarded vehicles. They apply even when checking, repairing, or replacing tires.

Where to Keep Shipping Papers

Do not take a hazardous material shipment without a properly prepared shipping paper. A shipping paper for hazardous material must always be easily recognized. Other people must be able to find it quickly after an accident.

- Clearly distinguish hazardous material shipping papers from others by tabbing them or keeping them on top of the stack of papers.
- When you are behind the wheel, keep shipping papers within your reach (with your seat belt on), or in a pouch on the driver's door. They must be easily seen by someone entering the cab.
- When not behind the wheel, leave shipping papers in the driver's door pouch or on the driver's seat.
- Emergency response information must be kept in the same location as the shipping paper.

Papers for Division 1.1, 1.2, or 1.3 (Class A or B) Explosives

A carrier must give each driver transporting Division 1.1, 1.2, or 1.3 (Class A or B) explosives a copy of FMCSR part 397. The carrier must also give written instructions on what to do if delayed or in an accident. The written instructions must include:

- The names and telephone numbers of people to contact (including carrier agents or shippers).
- The nature of the explosives transported.
- The precautions to take in emergencies such as fires, accidents, or leaks.

You must be familiar with, and have in your possession while driving, the:

- Shipping papers.
- Written emergency instructions.
- Written route plan.
- A copy of FMCSR part 397.

Equipment for Chlorine

A driver transporting chlorine in cargo tanks must have an approved gas mask in the vehicle. The driver must also have an emergency kit for controlling leaks in dome-cover plate fittings on the cargo tank.

Stop Before Railroad Crossings

Stop before crossing a railroad if your vehicle:

- Is placarded.
- Carries any amount of chlorine.
- Has cargo tanks, whether loaded or empty, used for hazardous materials.

You must stop 15 to 50 feet before the nearest rail. Proceed only when you are sure no train is coming. Don't shift gears while crossing the tracks.

9.7 HAZARDOUS MATERIALS: EMERGENCIES

No Smoking

Warn Others

Keep People Away

Avoid Contact or Inhaling

Emergency Response Guidebook

The U.S. Department of Transportation has a guidebook for firefighters, police, and industry personnel. The guidebook tells them what to do first to protect themselves and the public from hazardous materials. The guide is indexed by shipping name and hazardous material ID number. Emergency personnel look for these things on the shipping paper. That is why it is vital that the shipping name, ID number, label, and placards are correct.

Accidents/Incidents

As a professional driver, your job at the scene of an accident is to:

- Keep people away from the area.
- Limit the spread of material, but only if you can safely do so.
- Communicate the danger to emergency response personnel.
- Provide emergency responders with the shipping papers and emergency response information.

Follow this checklist:

1. Check to see that your driving partner is OK.
2. Keep shipping papers with you.
3. Keep people far away and upwind.

4. Warn others of the danger.

5. Send for help.

6. Follow your employer's instructions.

Fires

You might have to control minor truck fires on the road. **However, unless you have the training and equipment to do so safely, don't fight hazardous material fires.** Dealing with hazardous material fires requires special training and protective gear.

When you discover a fire, send someone for help. You may use the fire extinguisher to keep minor truck fires from spreading to cargo before firefighters arrive. Feel trailer doors to see if they are hot before opening them. If hot, you may have a cargo fire and should not open the doors. Opening doors lets air in and may make the fire flare up. Without air, many fires only smolder until firefighters arrive, and less damage is done. If your cargo is already on fire, it is not safe to fight the fire. Keep the shipping papers with you to give to emergency personnel as soon as they arrive. **Warn other people of the danger and keep them away.**

Leaks

If you discover a cargo leak, identify the material by using shipping papers, labels, or package location. **Do not touch any leaking material.** Many people, under the stress of handling an accident or leak, forget and injure themselves this way. Do not try to identify material or find the source of a leak by smell. Many toxic gases destroy one's sense of smell. They can injure or kill you even if they don't smell. Do not eat, drink, or smoke around a leak or spill.

If hazardous material is spilling from your vehicle, do not move it any more than safety requires. You may move off the road and away from places where people gather, if doing so serves safety. Only move your vehicle if you can do so without danger to yourself or others.

Never continue driving with hazardous material leaking from your vehicle to find a phone booth, truck stop, help, or for any similar reason. Remember that the carrier pays for the cleanup of contaminated parking lots, roadways, and drainage ditches. The costs are enormous, so don't leave a lengthy trail of contamination. If hazardous material is spilling from your vehicle:

- Park it.
- Secure the area.
- Stay there.
- Send someone else for help.

When sending someone for help, give that person:

- A description of the emergency.
- Your exact location and direction of travel.
- Your name, the carrier's name, and the name of the community or city where your terminal is located.
- The shipping name, hazard class, and ID number of the material, if you know them.

This is a lot for someone to remember. It is a good idea to **write it all down** for the person you send for help. The emergency response team must know these things to find you and to handle the emergency. They may have to travel miles to get to you. This information will help them to bring the right equipment the first time, without having to go back for it.

Never move your vehicle if doing so will cause contamination or damage to the vehicle. Keep downwind and away from roadside rests, truckstops, cafes, and businesses. Never try to repack leaking containers. Unless you have the training and equipment to repair leaks safely, don't try it. Call your dispatcher or supervisor for instructions, and, if needed, emergency personnel.

Response to Specific Hazards

Class 1 (Explosives). If your vehicle breaks down or is in an accident while carrying explosives, warn others of the danger. Keep bystanders away. Do not allow smoking or an open fire near the vehicle.

Remove all explosives before pulling apart vehicles involved in a collision. Place the explosives at least 200 feet from the vehicles and occupied buildings. If there is a fire, warn everyone of the danger of explosion. Stay a safe distance away.

Class 2 (Compressed Gases). If compressed gas is leaking from your vehicle, warn others of the danger. Permit only those involved in removing the hazard or wreckage to get close. You must notify the shipper of the compressed gas of any accident.

Unless you are fueling machinery used in road construction or maintenance, do not transfer a flammable compressed gas from one tank to another on any public roadway.

Class 3 (Flammable Liquids). If you are transporting a flammable liquid and have an accident or your vehicle breaks down, prevent bystanders from gathering. Warn people of the danger. Keep them from smoking.

Never transport a leaking cargo tank farther than needed to reach a safe place. If safe to do so, get off the roadway. Don't transfer flammable liquid from one vehicle to another on a public roadway except in an emergency.

Class 4 and Class 5 (Flammable Solids and Oxidizing Materials). If a flammable solid or oxidizing material spills, warn others of the fire hazard. Do not open smoldering packages of flammable solids. Remove them from the vehicle if you can safely do so. Gather and remove any broken packages if safe to do so. Also, remove unbroken packages if it will decrease the fire hazard.

Class 6 (Poisonous Materials and Infectious Substances). You must protect yourself, other people, and property from harm. Remember that many products classed as poison are also flammable. If you think a leaking poison liquid or gas might be flammable, take the added precautions needed for flammable liquids or gases. Do not allow smoking, open flame, or welding. Warn others of the hazards of fire, of inhaling vapors, or coming in contact with the poison.

A vehicle involved in a leak of Division 2.3 (Poison Gases) or Division 6.1 (Poisons) must be checked for stray poison before being used again.

Class 7 (Radioactive Materials). If a leak or broken package involves radioactive material, tell your dispatcher or supervisor as soon as possible. If there is a spill, or if an internal container might be damaged, do not touch or inhale the material. Do not use the vehicle until it is cleaned and checked with a survey meter.

Class 8 (Corrosive Materials). If corrosives spill or leak in transit, be careful to avoid further damage or injury when handling the containers. Parts of the vehicle exposed to a corrosive liquid must be thoroughly washed with water. Wash out the interior as soon after unloading as possible, before reloading the vehicle.

If further transportation of a leaking tank would be unsafe, get off the road. If safe to do so, try to contain any liquid leaking from the vehicle. Keep spectators away from the liquid and its fumes. Do everything possible to prevent injury to other highway users.

Required Notifications

The National Response Center helps coordinate emergency response to chemical hazards. They are a resource to the local police and fire fighters. The person in charge of a vehicle involved in an accident may have to phone the National Response Center. This call will be in addition to any made to police or fire fighters. You or your employer must phone when **any** of the following occur as **a direct result of a hazardous materials incident**.

- A person is killed.

- A person receives injuries requiring hospitalization.
- Estimated carrier or other property damage exceeds $50,000.
- The general public is evacuated for one or more hours.
- One or more major transportation arteries or facilities are closed or shut down for one hour or more.
- Fire, breakage, spillage, or suspected radioactive contamination occurs.
- Fire, breakage, spillage, or suspected contamination occurs involving shipment of etiologic agents (bacteria or toxins).
- A situation exists of such a nature (e.g., continuing danger to life exists at the scene of an incident) that, in the judgment of the carrier, should be reported.

National Response Center
(800) 424-8801

The person making the immediate telephone report should be ready to give:
- Name and address of the carrier they work for.
- Phone number where they can be reached.
- Date, time, and location of incident.
- The extent of injuries, if any.
- Classification, name, and quantity of hazardous materials involved, if such information is available.
- Type of incident and nature of hazardous material involvement and whether a continuing danger to life exists at the scene.
- If a reportable quantity of hazardous substance was involved, the caller should give:
    - The name of the shipper.
    - The quantity of the hazardous substance discharged.

Be prepared to give your employer the required information. Carriers must make detailed written reports within 15 days.

The Chemical Transportation Emergency Center (CHEMTREC) in Washington also has a 24-hour toll-free line. CHEMTREC was created to provide emergency personnel with technical information about the physical properties of hazardous products. The National Response Center and CHEMTREC are in close communication. If you call either one, it will tell the other about the problem when appropriate.

CHEMTREC
(800) 424-9300

APPENDIX I: RADIOACTIVE SEPARATION TABLE

(**NOTE:** You will not be tested on the numbers in this table.)

Do not leave radioactive Yellow II or Yellow III labeled packages near people, animals, or film longer than shown in this table.

MINIMUM DISTANCE IN FEET:

Total Transport Index	To Nearest Undeveloped Film					To People or Cargo Compartment Partitions
	0 - 2 Hours	2-4 Hours	4-8 Hours	8-12 Hours	Over 12 Hours	
None	0	0	0	0	0	0
0.1 to 1.0	1	2	3	4	5	1
1.1 to 5.0	3	4	6	8	11	2
5.1 to 10.0	4	6	9	11	15	3
10.1 to 20.0	5	8	12	16	22	4
20.1 to 30.0	7	10	15	20	29	5
30.1 to 40.0	8	11	17	22	33	6
40.1 to 50.0	9	12	19	24	36	

APPENDIX II: HAZARDOUS MATERIALS GLOSSARY

This glossary presents definitions of certain terms used in this chapter. A complete glossary of terms can be found in the federal Hazardous Materials Rules (49 CFR 171.8). You should have an up-to-date copy of these rules for your reference.

(**NOTE:** You will not be tested on the glossary.)

Blasting Agent—a material designed for blasting, but so insensitive that there is very little probability of ignition during transport. Ammonium nitrate-fuel oil mixture.

Bulk packaging—a packaging, including a transport vehicle or freight container, with a capacity greater than:

- 119 gallons for a liquid.
- 882 pounds for a solid.
- Water capacity greater than 1,000 lbs. for a gas.

Carboy—a bottle or rectangular container that holds from 5 to 15 gallons of liquid. Carboys are made of glass, plastic, or metal and are often cushioned in a wooden box.

Cargo tank—any bulk liquid or compressed gas packaging, whether or not permanently attached to any motor vehicle, which by reason of its size, construction, or attachment to a motor vehicle, is loaded or unloaded without being removed from the motor vehicle. Any packaging fabricated under specifications for cylinders is not a cargo tank.

Carrier—a person engaged in the transportation of passengers or property by land or water (as a common, contract, or private carrier), or by civil aircraft.

Combustible liquid—any liquid, such as kerosene or fuel oil, having a flash point at or above 100°F and below 200°F as determined by tests listed in 173.115(d). Exceptions are listed in 173.11 5(b).

Compressed Gas—any material kept in a container with a pressure exceeding 40 psi at 70°F, or 104 psi at 130°F.

Consignee—the business or person to whom a shipment is delivered.

Corrosive Material—liquid or solid that causes visible destruction or irreversible alterations in human skin tissue at the site of contact. Liquids that severely corrode steel are included. Examples include: Bromine, soda lime, hydrochloric acid, sodium hydroxide solution, and battery acid.

Cryogenic liquid—a refrigerated liquefied gas having a boiling point colder than -130°F.

Cylinder—a pressure vessel designed for pressures higher than 40 psi.

Division—a subdivision of a hazard class.

EPA—the U. S. Environmental Protection Agency.

Etiologic agents—a living micro-organism, or its toxin, which causes or may cause human disease. Examples include: salmonella and polio virus.

Explosives—chemical compounds, mixtures, or devices, the primary or common purpose of which is to function by explosion, unless such compound, mixture, or device is otherwise classified. Explosives are divided into three subclasses as follows:

Explosives A—detonate with a shock wave greater than the speed of sound and are of maximum hazard. Dynamite and nitroglycerin are examples.

Explosives B—generally function by rapid combustion rather than detonation and are a flammable hazard. For example: torpedoes and propellant explosives.

Explosives C—manufactured articles, such as small arms ammunition, that contain restricted quantities of Class A and/or Class B explosives, and certain types of fireworks. Class C explosives are of minimum hazard. These include: toy caps, trick matches, signal flares, and some fireworks.

Flammable liquid—Any liquid having a flash point below 100°F as determined by tests listed in 173.115(d). Examples include ethyl alcohol, gasoline, acetone, benzene, and dimethyl sulfide. Exceptions are listed in 173.115(a).

Flammable solid—Any solid material, other than an explosive, liable to cause fires through friction or retained heat from manufacturing or processing, or which can be ignited readily creating a serious transportation hazard because it burns vigorously and persistently. For example: nitrocellulose (film), phosphorus, and charcoal.

FMCSR—The Federal Motor Carrier Safety Regulations.

Freight container—a reusable container, with a volume of 64 cubic feet or more, designed and constructed to permit being lifted with its contents intact and intended primarily for containment of packages (in unit form) during transportation.

Gross weight—the weight of the packaging plus the weight of its contents.

Hazard class—the category of hazard assigned to a hazardous material. A material may meet the defining criteria for more than one hazard class, but is assigned to only one hazard class.

Hazardous material—any material that poses an unreasonable risk to health, safety, and property during transportation. These materials are named by DOT in the Hazardous Materials Table.

Hazardous substance—a material, including its mixtures and solutions, that:

- Is listed in Appendix A to Sec. 172.101;
- Is in a quantity, in one package, which equals or exceeds the reportable quantity (RQ) listed in Appendix A to Sec. 172.101; and
- When in a mixture or solution–
    - For radionuclides, conforms to paragraph 6 of Appendix A to Sec. 172.101.
    - For other than radionuclides, is in a concentration by weight which equals or exceeds the concentration corresponding to the RQ of the material, as shown in the following table:

RQ Pounds (Kilograms)	Concentration by Weight	
	Percent	PPM
5,000 (2270)	10	100,000
1,000 (454)	2	20,000
100 (45.4)	.02	2,000
10 (4.54)	0.02	200
1 (0.454)	0.002	20

This definition does not apply to petroleum products that are lubricants or fuels (see 40 CFR 300.6).

Hazardous waste—for the purposes of this chapter, means any material that is subject to the Hazardous Waste Manifest Requirements of the U.S. Environmental Protection Agency specified in 40 CFR Part 262.

Irritating material—a liquid or solid substance that, on contact with fire or when exposed to air, gives off dangerous or intensely irritating fumes. Examples are tear gas, monochloroacetone, and diphenylchloroarsine. Poison A materials excluded.

Limited quantity—the maximum amount with specific placarding, labeling, and packaging exceptions, except for Poison B materials.

Marking—applying the descriptive name, instructions, cautions, weight, or specification marks required to be placed on outside containers of hazardous materials.

Mixture—a material containing more than one chemical compound or element.

Name of contents—the proper shipping name as specified in the Hazardous Materials Table or the Optional Table.

Non-bulk packaging—means a packaging which has:
- A maximum capacity of 450 L (119 gallons) as a receptacle for a liquid;
- A maximum net mass less than 400 kg (882 pounds) and a maximum capacity of 450 L (119 gallons) or less as a receptacle for a solid; or
- A water capacity greater than 454 kg (1,000 pounds) or less as a receptacle for a gas as defined in Sec. 173.115.

N.O.S.—not otherwise specified.

ORM—(Other Regulated Materials.) Any regulated material that does not meet the definition of the other hazard classes. ORM are divided into five subcategories as follows:

ORM-A—a material which has an anesthetic, irritating, noxious, toxic, or similar property, and can cause extreme annoyance or discomfort to passengers and crew in the event of leakage during transportation.

ORM-B—a material capable of causing significant damage to a transport vehicle or vessel if leaked. This class includes materials that may be corrosive to aluminum.

ORM-C—a material which has other inherent characteristics not described as an ORM-A or ORM-B, but which make it unsuitable for shipment unless properly identified and prepared for transportation. Each ORM-C material is specifically named in the Hazardous Materials Table.

ORM-D—a material, such as a consumer commodity that, although otherwise subject to regulation, presents a limited hazard during transportation due to its form, quantity, and packaging.

ORM-E—a material that is not included in any other hazard class, but is subject to regulation. Materials in this class include hazardous wastes and hazardous substances named in the List of Hazardous Substances and Reportable Quantities but not in the Hazardous Materials Table.

Outage (or Ullage)—the amount by which a packaging falls short of being full of liquid, usually expressed in percent by volume. The amount of outage required for liquids in cargo tanks depends on how much the material will expand with temperature change during transit. Different materials expand at different rates. Enough outage must be allowed so that the tank will still not be full at 130°F.

Overpack—an enclosure used by a single shipper to provide protection or easy use in handling of a package or to combine two or more packages. "Overpack" does not include a freight container.

Oxidizer—a substance such as chlorate, permanganate, inorganic peroxide, or a nitrate that yields oxygen readily to stimulate the combustion of organic matter.

Poison A—extremely dangerous poison gases or liquids belong to this class. Very small amounts of these gases or vapors of these liquids, mixed with air, are dangerous to life. For example: hydrocyanic acid, bromoacetone, and nitric oxide.

Poison B—substances, liquids, or solids (including pastes and semi-solids), other than Poison A or irritating materials, that are known to be toxic to humans. These materials cause serious sickness or death within 48 hours following skin contact, inhalation, or ingestion by mouth. In the absence of adequate data on human toxicity, materials are presumed to be toxic to humans if they are toxic to laboratory animals exposed under specified conditions. Examples include: phenol, cyanide, mercury based pesticides, and disinfectants.

Portable tank—a bulk package (except a cylinder having a 1,000 lbs. or less water capacity) with a capacity greater than 110 U.S. gallons, designed primarily to be loaded in, on, or temporarily attached to a transport vehicle. A portable tank is equipped with skids, mounting, or accessories to facilitate handling of the tank by mechanical means.

Proper shipping name—the name of the hazardous material shown in roman print (not italics) in the Hazardous Materials Table.

P.s.i. (psi)—pounds per square inch.

P.s.i.a. (psia)—pounds per square inch absolute.

Radioactive material—a material that spontaneously emits ionizing radiation having a specific activity greater than 0.002 microcuries per gram. Further classifications are made within this category according to levels of radioactivity. Examples include: thorium nitrate and uranium hexafluoride.

Reportable quantity (RQ)—the quantity (per single package) that equals or exceeds the quantity specified in column 3 of the List of Hazardous Substances and Reportable Quantities. Reportable quantities are treated as hazardous materials and have reporting requirements.

RSPA—Research and Special Programs Administration, U.S. Department of Transportation, Washington, DC 20590.

Shipper's certification—a statement on a shipping paper, signed by the shipper, saying he/she prepared the shipment properly according to law.

> "This is to certify that the above named materials are properly classified, described, packaged, marked, and labeled, and are in proper condition for transportation according to the applicable regulations of the Department of Transportation."

> or

> "I hereby declare that the contents of this consignment are fully and accurately described above by proper shipping name and are classified, packed, marked, and labeled, and are in all respects in proper condition for transport by * according to applicable international and national governmental regulations."

* Words may be inserted here to indicate mode of transportation (rail, aircraft, motor vehicle, vessel).

Shipping paper—a shipping order, bill of lading, manifest, or other shipping document serving a similar purpose and containing the information required by the regulations.

Technical name—a recognized chemical name currently used in scientific and technical handbooks.

Transport vehicle—a cargo-carrying vehicle such as an automobile, van, tractor, truck, semitrailer, tank car or rail car used for the transportation of cargo by any mode. Each cargo-carrying body (trailer, rail car, etc.) is a separate transport vehicle.

UN Standard packaging—means a specification packaging conforming to the requirements in Subpart L and M of Part 178.

UN—United Nations.

Water-reactive material (solid)—any solid material (including sludges and pastes) that, when mixed with water, is likely to ignite or give off flammable or toxic gases in dangerous quantities. Water-reactive material must have DANGEROUS WHEN WET and FLAMMABLE SOLID labels.

HAZARDOUS MATERIALS INFORMATION

At the time this book was printed, changes in rules which apply to hazardous materials were being made by the federal government. The most recent information should be obtained from:

U.S. Department of Transportation
Research and Special Programs Administration
OHMT/DHM—51
Washington, DC 20590

PART III: CDL SKILLS TEST REVIEW

Chapter 10 – The Skills Tests

When you pass the required Knowledge Tests, you can take the CDL Skills Test. As mentioned before, there are three parts of the CDL Skills Test: the pre-trip inspection test, the basic control skills test, and the road test. These are described in detail below. If you wish to obtain a license for a particular vehicle, you must take these tests in that type of vehicle.

10.1 PRE-TRIP INSPECTION TEST

This test is an informal procedure. You will be asked to perform a pre-trip inspection on the truck you will be using to take the driving tests. To prepare for this test, you should keep in mind these objectives:

- Know and observe vehicle inspection safety rules.
- Recognize the vehicle component(s) involved in each tractor- trailer inspection step.
- Know the purpose of each tractor-trailer inspection step.
- Know the inspection criteria for each tractor-trailer inspection step.

This test will cover safety rules, engine compartment checks, engine start checks, and walkaround inspection.

GUIDE TO VEHICLE INSPECTION

Safety Rules

Follow these safety rules:

1. Make sure you keep the examiner in sight.
2. Make sure the vehicle can't move before getting in front, behind, or under! USE CHOCKS!
3. Enter/exit vehicle using correct procedure.

The following are items the examiner will want you to check.

Engine Compartment Inspection

Oil level check: You should pull out the dipstick and see where the oil level is relative to the full or refill mark. The level must be above the refill mark.

Coolant level check: You should look at the sight glass or reservoir, or remove the radiator cap and look to see the level. Adequate level will show in sight glass or be visible in the radiator when the cap is removed.

NOTE: If the engine is hot, do not remove the radiator cap! If there is no sight glass, indicate that you would remove the cap. If there is a sight glass, do not remove the radiator cap—you will be marked incorrect if you do.

Power steering fluid check: With the engine stopped, you must pull out the dipstick and see where the fluid level is relative to the refill mark. The level must be above the refill mark.

Water pump, alternator, and air compressor drive belt checks: With the engine off, you should point to, touch, or press the belt to test that it is tight enough. You must inspect that the belt is not frayed, has no visible cracks, loose fibers, or other signs of wear. If the belt appears worn or loose, you should push the belt with your hand and look for excessive deflection.

NOTE: Make sure you are inspecting the correct belt. The air compressor may not be belt driven—if this is the case, mention this. You may be marked incorrect if you do not.

Fluid leaks: Make sure to check for signs of fluid puddles, or dripping fluids on the ground under the engine, or the underside of the engine.

Engine Start

Proper clutch/gear shift operation: You should depress the clutch before turning on the starter, to prevent vehicle from moving and to reduce the load on the starter motor. (On an automatic transmission, the selector should be in the "park" position if available, or in the "neutral" position if not.)

Engine oil pressure check: After the engine starts, check that oil pressure is building to normal. The oil gauge should either show increasing or normal oil pressure. Make sure the warning light is not on.

Ammeter/voltmeter check: You should check the gauge which shows that the alternator or generator is charging. Make sure the warning light is not on.

Air brake checks: You should perform the following checks:

1. Let air pressure build to governed or cut-out pressure.

2. With engine off, wheels chocked, and parking brake released, fully apply footbrake to see if air pressure drops more than three pounds in one minute (single vehicle) or more than four pounds in one minute (for combination vehicles).

3. Start fanning off the air pressure by rapidly applying and releasing the footbrake: low-air-pressure warning alarm should activate before air pressure drops below 60 psi.

4. Continue to fan off the air pressure: at approximately 40 pounds pressure on a combination vehicle, the tractor protection valve should close (pop out); on straight vehicles, the spring brake push/pull valve should pop out. On truck tractors, the parking brake push/pull valve should pop out before the pressure has dropped below 20 psi.

Steering wheel play check: You should work the steering wheel back and forth to determine whether less than 5 to 10 degrees (less than 2" at the rim of a 20" wheel) of free play exists. (With power steering, you must perform this with the engine running, while observing the left front wheel to see that it does not move.)

Parking brake check: You must check that the parking brake will hold the vehicle, by gently trying to pull forward with the parking brake on.

Mirror checks: You must check all mirrors for proper adjustment, cracked or loose glass or fittings, and cleanliness.

Windshield checks: You should check the windshield for cracks, dirt, and illegal stickers or other obstructions to your view.

Wiper checks: You should check to make sure that the wipers operate and appear securely mounted. Washer (if present) should be checked, as well as the performance of the wiper blades.

Lighting indicator checks: Check the dashboard indicator lights for turn signals, flashers, and headlight high beam.

Horn checks: Check that the electric and/or air horns work.

Heater/defroster check: Make sure that heater/defroster will blow air on windshield as required by safety regulations.

Safety/emergency equipment checks: You should check for the presence of three red reflective triangles (or flares), for a properly charged and rated fire extinguisher (one rated 5B:C or more, or two rated 4B:C), and for electrical fuses (if used in the vehicle).

Walkaround Inspection

Suspension inspection (repeat at each wheel as appropriate, depending on construction and accessibility): Look for broken spring leaves, leaves that have shifted and are close to or contacting tires, rim, brake drum, frame, or body; missing or broken leaves in the spring. For coil springs, look for broken or distorted springs. For air suspension, you should listen for audible air leaks.

You should check that the **torsion bar assembly, torque arm, or control arm** (as applicable) is not cracked, broken or missing.

Check all **brackets, bolts, and bushings** used for attaching spring to axle and vehicle frame. You should check for cracked or broken **spring hangers**; broken, missing or loose bolts; missing or damaged bushings; broken, loose, or missing axle mounting parts.

Make sure that the **shock absorber mounting** is secure; no fluid should be leaking.

Wheel inspection (repeated at each wheel as appropriate):
- **Rims.** You should check for damaged or bent rims; rims should not have welding repairs and should not have rust areas indicating that the rims or lug nuts are loose.
- **Tires.** Check tread depth, tire inflation, and that tires are evenly worn. Look for cuts or other damage. Make sure that valve caps and stems are not broken or damaged and that treads are not separating from the tire.

NOTE: Minimum tread depth is 4/32 inch on front tires and 2/32 inch on other tires. A proper check of inflation requires the use of a tire pressure gauge. A tire mallet or iron can be used on dual tires to check that one tire is not flat. **You will be marked incorrect if you simply kick a tire, especially a front tire!**

Tire Inflation

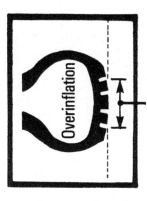

Overinflation

Tread Contact With Road

Overinflation

Tires Run Hard, Causes Irregular Wear.

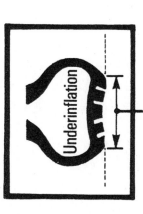

Underinflation

Tread Contact With Road

Underinflation

Causes Irregular Wear, Abnormal Tire Deflection, Excessive Heat Build-Up.

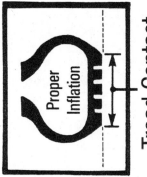

Proper Inflation

Tread Contact With Road

Proper Inflation

Full Contact With Road.

Figure 10-1

- **Axle seals.** On driving wheels, the drive axle flange gaskets should be checked for leaks (any sign of lubricant coming from the hub area).

- **Hub oil seals.** Wheels that are not powered (for example, most front wheels) may have hub oil seals which are transparent to permit checking oil level, or have removable plastic caps that permit checking oil level. Level should be checked, and all types of hubs should be checked for signs of lubricant leaks.

- **Lug nuts.** Check that all lug nuts are present; that nuts are not loose (try to turn nuts; look for rust trails around nuts); that no cracks radiate from lug bolt holes; that there is no distortion of the holes.

- **Spacers of dual wheels.** The driver should check that dual wheels are evenly separated, and that the tires are not touching one another.

Brake checks (at each wheel):

- **Slack adjuster.** Make sure to check for broken, loose, or missing parts. Make sure the angle between the push rod and adjuster arm is slightly more than 90 degrees when the brakes are applied or pulled by hand. When the slack adjuster is pulled by hand, the brake rod should not move outward more than approximately one inch.

- **Brake chamber and hoses.** The brake chamber should not be cracked or dented, and it should be securely mounted. The hoses carrying air to the brake chamber should not be frayed, cracked, or abraded from rubbing on other vehicle parts.

- **Brake drums.** Check for cracked drums, brake shoes or pads with oil, grease, or brake fluid on them. Make sure brake shoes are not worn dangerously thin, or are missing.

Fuel tank: Check for leaks from fuel tanks and for secure mounting of the fuel tank.

Front-of-vehicle inspection: Check **headlights** (high and low beams), **turn signals, clearance lights, and identification lights** for illumination, cleanliness, unbroken lenses, and secure fastening.

Check that the **steering box** is secure (no loose or missing nuts or bolts, no broken parts), with no power steering leaks, and that the power steering hoses are in safe condition.

Check **steering linkage** (no loose or missing nuts or bolts; connecting links, arms, rods not worn or cracked; joints or sockets not worn or loose).

Walkaround Sequence

1. Left Side of Cab Area
2. Front of Cab Area
3. Right Side of Tractor Area
4. Right Saddle Tank Area
5. Coupling System Area
6. Right Rear Tractor Wheels Area
7. Rear of Tractor Area
8. Trailer Frontal Area
9. Right Side of Trailer Area
10. Right Rear Trailer Wheels Area
11. Rear of Trailer Area
12. Left Rear Trailer Wheels Area
13. Left Side of Trailer Area
14. Left Saddle Tank Area

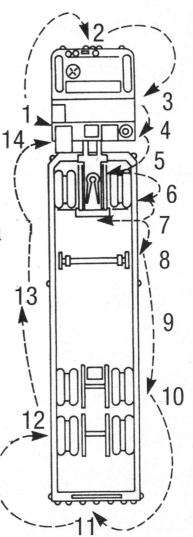

Figure 10-2

Under-vehicle checks: Make sure that the drive shaft is not bent or cracked and that universal joints and fasteners appear to be secure.

Check the **exhaust system** (if it's underneath), making sure that all visible parts are securely mounted and that there are no cracks, holes, or severe dents.

Check the **frame of the vehicle** (no cracks or bends in longitudinal frame members; no loose, cracked, bent, broken, or missing cross members; no signs of breaks or holes in floor of cargo area).

Bus items: Make sure that **passenger emergency exits** (doors, roof hatches, designated windows) work correctly and are secured properly.

Make sure that **passenger entry doors** open, close and lock correctly, and that entry steps are clear. Make sure that treads are not loose or worn enough to trip a passenger.

Check that **passenger seats** are securely fastened to the bus and don't have broken frames.

Make sure that **baggage compartment** doors are secure.

Truck tractor items: Check **air and electric lines** connected to trailer. Make sure the lines are not cut, cracked, chafed, worn, spliced, taped, tangled, crimped, pinched, frayed, or dragging against vehicle parts.

Check that the **catwalk** is secure.

Make sure to check the fifth wheel—**mounting** (look for loose or missing mounting brackets, clamps, bolts, nuts); **safety latch** (locked, to hold fifth wheel jaws shut); no cracks or breaks in the **platform structure; release arm** or device is in "engaged" position; **kingpin** appears undamaged and properly clasped by the fifth wheel locking jaws, with no space between upper (i.e., apron) and lower halves of the fifth wheel. Locking pins of sliding fifth wheel (if truck has one) must be present and locked in place.

Check to make sure that **lights and reflectors** on rear of tractor are present, intact, secure, clean, and working. Make sure **splash guards** or mudflaps are securely mounted.

Trailer front: Check that **air and electric lines** are not cut, cracked, chafed, worn, spliced, taped, tangled, crimped, pinched, or dragging against vehicle parts.

Make sure that a **header board** (front end structure), which protects the driver from forward movement of the cargo, is present, securely mounted, and undamaged.

Lights and reflectors on the front end of the trailer must be present, intact, secure, clean, and working.

Side of trailer: Check that all landing gear are fully raised and that the crank handle is present and secured. All landing gear frame parts must be present, secure, and not bent or damaged.

Check that the **lights and reflectors** on the side are present, intact, secure, clean, and working.

Check that the van body **doors** are securely shut and that cargo is properly tied down.

Make sure that the trailer **frame** has no cracks or bends in longitudinal members and that there are no loose, cracked, bent, broken, or missing cross members. There should be no signs of breaks or significant holes in the flooring or van body.

Rear: Check that the taillights, stop lights, turn signals, flashers, identification lights, clearance lights, and reflectors are present, intact, secure, clean, and working. Make sure that all cargo is tied or otherwise secured, as necessary, and that the van doors (if any) are securely shut.

10.2 BASIC CONTROL SKILLS TEST

This test is an informal procedure that is taken on a driving course, which will be marked off by boundary lines and traffic cones. The driving course may be an off-road site, or a road with very little traffic. To prepare for this test, you should keep in mind these objectives:

- Know and observe safety rules.
- Be familiar with the Basic Control Skills (BCS) performance criteria (encroachment, pullups, final position).
- Recognize the layout of each of the six BCS maneuvers:
    1. Right turn.
    2. Stopline.
    3. Straight line backing.
    4. Alley dock.
    5. Parallel park (sight and right side).
    6. Backward serpentine.

NOTE: This test may be comprised of seven exercises: one from each of the areas above, including one for each type of parallel parking.

GUIDE TO BASIC CONTROL SKILLS

Safety Rules

Follow these safety rules:

1. Make sure you keep the examiner in sight.
2. Make sure you signal "final position" with the horn. Always assume that the vehicle may move. Position yourself so you won't be hurt if it does.

Basic Control Skills Performance Criteria

Encroachment: Driving over boundary lines, traffic cones, or any other type of marker.

Pull-ups: Any time you stop your vehicle and move in reverse to better position the vehicle, or to correct a mistake.

Final Position: The point at which you have completed the test exercise. At this point, you signal completion with your horn.

Basic Control Skills Maneuvers

Right Turn: During the test, the examiner will ask you to drive forward and make a right turn around a traffic cone or some other type of marker. At the completion of the turn, signal your final position with your horn. The examiner will record the distance your truck came within the traffic cone/marker and whether or not you hit the cone/marker. He will also record the number, if any, of pull-ups that were made to complete the turn.

NOTE: You will fail this test if you drive over a traffic cone or marker.

Stop Line: The examiner will have you drive forward and then stop at a stop line. You must stop as close as possible to the stop line as you can, without going over it. Signal with your horn when you have completed the stop. When you have completed this exercise, the examiner will measure how close your bumper is to the stop line.

NOTE: You will fail this test if you go over the stop line.

Straight Line Backing: You will be tested on your ability to back in a straight line. You will be asked to back down an alley (an alley being the lane marked off by boundary lines and traffic cones) approximately 100 feet in length and 12 feet in width. You must back down the alley without driving over the sides of the alley. When you have finished this exercise, use your horn to signal final position. The examiner will record whether or not you touched any of the boundary lines and the number, if any, of pull-ups that were made to complete this exercise.

NOTE: You will fail this test if you cannot properly back-up, if you fail to use your mirrors, and/or if you need to move forward to straighten the vehicle three or more times.

Alley Dock: During this exercise, you will be asked to back into an alley, with the object being to get as close as you can to the left side and rear of the alley. You should not back past the end of the alley, or drive over any boundary lines or markers. When you have reached your final position, signal with your horn. The examiner will then record whether or not you touched or crossed any of the boundary lines or markers. He will also measure the distance between the stop line and the rear of your vehicle.

NOTE: You will fail this test if you back over a traffic cone, marker, or curb; if you fail to perform a complete alley dock; or if you must perform four or more pull-ups to complete the alley dock.

Parallel Park: There are two types of parallel parking that you will be asked to perform: parallel parking from the sight side and parallel parking from the right side.

Sight side parallel parking will require you to parallel park in a parking space that is on your **left** side. The parking space you will be parking in will be 10 feet longer than the length of your vehicle. You will have to drive past the parking space and then back into it. You must park your vehicle as close to the curbside and rear of the parking space as you can, with your vehicle completely in the space. You should signal with your horn upon completing this exercise.

The examiner will record the number, if any, of pull-ups that were made to complete this exercise. He will also record if you hit any cones, or touched or crossed any boundary lines. The last thing the examiner will do will be to measure the distance your vehicle is from the front, back, and curbside lines of the parking space.

Right side parallel parking will require you to parallel park in a parking space that is on your **right** side. You will follow the same procedure as in sight side parallel parking to perform this exercise; however, you will be approaching from the opposite direction. The parking space you will be parking in will be 10 feet longer than the length of your vehicle. You will have to drive past the parking space and then back into it. You must park your vehicle as close to the curbside and rear of the parking space as you can, with your vehicle completely in the space. Again, you should signal with your horn upon completing this exercise.

As with sight side parallel parking, the examiner will record the number, if any, of pull-ups that were made to complete this exercise. He will also record if you hit any cones, or touched or crossed any boundary lines. The last thing the examiner will do will be to measure the distance your vehicle is from the front, back, and curbside lines of the parking space.

NOTE: You will fail this test if you drive/back over a traffic cone, marker, or boundary line; if you cannot parallel park successfully; or if you perform three or more pull-ups to complete each exercise.

Serpentine: There are two types of serpentine that you may be asked to perform: forward and backward.

Forward serpentine is an exercise for which a row of three cones will be set up. You will have to drive through this course, weaving in and out of the cones, in a serpentine manner. You must not hit any of the traffic cones or markers. One pull-up may be allowed during this exercise, and some examiners may allow you to get out of your vehicle to check its position. You should stop when you move past the last cone and then signal final position with your horn. The examiner will record how well you drive through the course, if you hit any cones, and the number, if any, of pull-ups made to perform this exercise.

NOTE: You will fail this test if you drive over a traffic cone, boundary line, or marker; or if you cannot successfully complete the exercise.

Backward serpentine is an exercise for which a row of three cones will be set up. You will have to back through this course, weaving in and out of the cones, in a serpentine manner. You must not hit any of the traffic cones or markers. One pull-up may be allowed during this exercise, and some examiners may allow you to get out of your vehicle to check its position. You should stop when you move past the last cone and then signal final position with your horn. The examiner will record how well you back through the course, if you hit any cones, and the number, if any, of pull-ups made to perform this exercise.

NOTE: You will fail this test if you back over a traffic cone, boundary line, or marker; if you cannot successfully complete the exercise; or if you need to perform five or more pull-ups to complete the exercise.

10.3 ROAD TEST

For the road test, you must be able to correctly perform the following maneuvers:
- Left turns.
- Right turns.
- Procedure to follow at a railroad crossing.
- A stop and start on a grade.
- Driving up a hill or grade.
- Stopping at and going through intersections.
- Driving on straight sections of urban/rural roads.

Range Diagram—Exercise 2
(Serpentine)

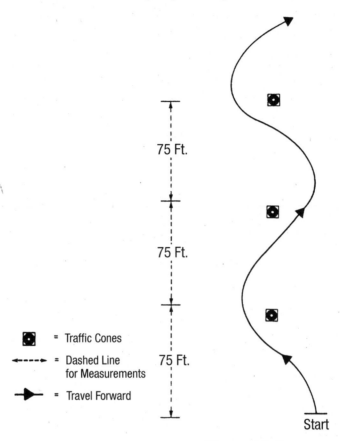

75 Ft.

75 Ft.

■ = Traffic Cones

◄----► = Dashed Line
for Measurements

►— = Travel Forward

75 Ft.

Start

Figure 10-3

- Driving around curves.
- Driving on an expressway.
- Backing in a straight line.
- Parallel parking.
- Forward stopping.

You will also be observed for your skill in:

- Using the clutch properly.
- Using gears properly.
- Using brakes properly.
- Obeying traffic signs.
- Operating the vehicle safely.

What the Examiner Will Be Looking for

Left/Right Turns: As you approach each turn, the examiner will check if you:

- Check traffic. You must look straight ahead, left, right, and to the rear using your mirrors.
- Signal. You must signal at least 100 feet before the turn.
- Slow down. Slow smoothly and change gears as needed to keep power. Do not coast with your foot on the clutch.
- Position your vehicle. Get into the correct lane and position your vehicle to make the turn.

You should time your arrival so stopping isn't necessary. If you must stop prior to the turn, the examiner will check if you:

- Maintain a gap. Stop far enough back so you can see the rear wheels of the vehicle in front.
- Stop in the correct place. Stop so your vehicle is:
  - Not in the intersection.
  - Not over the stop line.
  - Not past the sidewalk.
  - Not past the stop sign or other marker.
- Stop fully. You must not coast and must come to a full stop.
- Keep the wheels straight. You must keep your wheels straight ahead while stopped.

While turning, the examiner will check if you:

- Check traffic.
- Keep both hands on the wheel.
- Change gears. You must not change gears during the turn. Gear changing should only be done to get started from the stopped position.
- Maintain a smooth speed and turn smoothly without stops.
- Turn correctly. You must not turn too wide or short. Do not go over or touch the curb or cause other traffic to back up.

As you complete the turn, the examiner will check to see if you:

- Check traffic.
- Are in the correct lane. You must finish the turn in the correct lane. For a left turn, use the left lane; and for a right turn, use the right lane.
- Cancel the signal. You must turn off the turn signal.

- Accelerate for left turns and move right. You must accelerate smoothly and move into the right lane when traffic is clear.

Railroad Crossings: When crossing railroad tracks, the examiner will check that you:

- Check traffic. You should look left and right, roll down the window (or, if driving a bus, open the door) to listen.
- Do not change gears while on the tracks.
- Do not stop or brake on the tracks and do not make lane changes or pass on the tracks.
- Keep to posted speed limits.

Stop on Grades: The examiner may have you stop and start on a grade. When stopping on a grade, the examiner will check that you:

- Check traffic prior to stopping.
- Turn signals on.
- Position the vehicle on the right side of the roadway.
- Slow down smoothly, changing gears to keep power, and that you do not coast.

Once stopped, the examiner will check that you:

- Have positioned the vehicle parallel to the curb.
- Do not let the vehicle roll forward or backward.
- Cancel the turn signal and turn on the four-way flashers.
- Put on the parking brake, put the gear shift in neutral, release the foot brake, and take your foot off the clutch.

Start on Grades: The examiner will tell you to continue and check that you:

- Check traffic.
- Turn your four-way flashers off and your left turn signal on.
- Release the parking break, put vehicle in gear, and do not turn the steering wheel before the vehicle moves.
- Do not stall the engine when starting, or roll backward.
- Continue to check traffic.
- Accelerate smoothly and blend with traffic.

Driving up Grades: As you drive up a grade, the examiner will check that you:

- Select the proper gear, change gears to maintain speed, and do not lug the engine.

- Stay in the right-most lane.
- Keep hands on the steering wheel.
- Use four-way flashers if you are moving too slow for traffic.
- Check traffic, especially to the left and rear (use mirrors).

Driving Down Grades: As you drive down a grade, the examiner will check that you:

- Select the proper gear (lower gear) before the grade. Only gentle to moderate braking should be needed to control speed and engine RPM.
- Do not ride the clutch.
- Check the brakes by applying them before the grade.
- Maintain a steady speed and do not ride or fan the brakes.
- Stay in the right-most lane and maintain the correct following distance.
- Check traffic especially to the left and rear using your mirrors.

Intersections: If you must stop at the intersection, the examiner will check the same items as when you stop for a turn. As you drive through an intersection, the examiner will check that you:

- Check traffic.
- Yield to pedestrians and other traffic, as required.
- Do not change lanes in the intersection.
- Do not change gears in the intersection.
- Do not lug or rev engine.
- Smoothly drive through the intersection without disrupting traffic.

Straight Roads: As you drive down a straight city or county road, the examiner will check that you:

- Regularly check traffic, watch for hazards, and look far enough ahead (7 to 15 seconds).
- Select the proper lane and stay to the center of the lane without wandering back and forth.
- Maintain the correct speed and avoid continual slowing up, stopping, and accelerating.
- Maintain the correct following distance. One second per 10 feet of vehicle length plus one additional second for speeds over 40 MPH.

Changing Lanes: When you must change lanes, the examiner will check that you:

- Check the traffic to the front and the rear, especially the blind spot.

- Signal the lane change.
- Do not tailgate while waiting to change lanes.
- Make a smooth lane change and maintain your speed, allowing for correct distance between all vehicles.
- Cancel the signal.

Curves: In curves, the examiner will check that you:
- Reduce your speed before the curve.
- Do not brake while in the curve.
- Maintain your speed during the curve without a strong pull to the side.
- Keep all vehicle wheels in your lane.
- Continually check traffic and use your mirrors to watch the tracking of your vehicle.

Underpasses/Bridges: As you go under an underpass or over a bridge, the examiner may ask you:
- The posted height of the underpass.
- The weight limit of the bridge.

Expressway Driving: As you merge onto the expressway, the examiner will check that you:
- Check traffic.
- Check the blind spot.
- Signal at least soon enough that expressway traffic can see the signal.
- Merge without stopping.
- Use acceleration lane to accelerate to speed of traffic flow.
- Merge smoothly while maintaining following distance.
- Move to the center of the driving lane and cancel the signal.

When changing lanes on the expressway, the examiner will check that you:
- Check traffic to front and rear, especially in blind spots.
- Signal the lane change.
- Do not tailgate while waiting to change lanes.
- Make a smooth lane change, maintain your speed, and allow for the correct distance between all vehicles.
- Cancel the signal.

As you exit the expressway, the examiner will check that you:

- Check traffic in front and rear, especially to the right and in blind spots.
- Signal the exit.
- Smoothly enter the exit lane at the start of the exit lane.
- Slow down in the deceleration lane.
- Do not exceed the ramp speed and have no noticeable pull to the side on the ramp curve.
- Do not tailgate on the ramp.
- Cancel the signal.

Backing/Parallel Parking: During the test, the examiner will have you back up your vehicle. The examiner will check you as you back in a straight line and as you parallel park. Make sure you:

- Check your backing area.
- Sound your horn as a warning.
- Turn on your four-way flashers.
- Control your vehicle while backing.
- Do not run over curbs or course markings.
- Stop when directed by the examiner.

Forward Stopping: The examiner will have you forward stop your vehicle at a given point. Make sure you stop in one smooth braking action.

General Driving Skills: The examiner will check your general driving skills throughout the test. Make sure you:

- Use your clutch properly. Don't coast with the clutch in, don't ride the clutch, don't snap the clutch, and don't lug or over-rev the engine.
- Use gears correctly. Select the correct gear and don't grind or clash gears.
- Use brakes correctly. Brake smoothly with steady pressure.
- Don't ride the brakes and don't brake hard or fan air brakes.
- Steer correctly, keep both hands on the wheel, and don't under- or over-control the steering.
- Obey all traffic signs and laws.
- Drive safely without an accident. Do not run over curbs or sidewalks. Stay in your traffic lane. Drive so you are never forced to take evasive action.
- Wear your seat belt at all times.

Once again, for the road test, you will need to know how to make a left and right turn, and you must know what to do when you reach a railroad crossing. You may want to practice stopping and starting your truck on a grade, and driving up a hill or grade. Although you probably are familiar with driving on straight sections of urban and rural roads, and what the proper procedure is for stopping at and going through intersections, you may want to review these points carefully because you will be required to know how to do these correctly. Driving on curves and expressway driving will also be tested. If you have trouble backing in a straight line and parallel parking, you should brush-up on these skills before taking the test. Finally, you should make sure you can bring your truck to a smooth stop.

SCORING THE ROAD TEST

Each state develops its own tests and scoring systems. During your road test, the test route may offer many different types of traffic situations, which may require you to call upon all of your knowledge and driving skills. Although you may perform any of the driving maneuvers listed (in the beginning of this section) at many different times during your road test, your performance of a certain maneuver will not be graded each time it is performed. You may be graded on the maneuver more than once; however, this depends on the scoring system of the state.

When you take your road test, the examiner will have preplanned scoring rules that he will follow in determining when a certain maneuver will be graded. Before your test, it will be decided when and where each maneuver will be graded. For example, you may make seven left turns, but you may only be graded on three of them. The three graded turns will have been performed at certain locations that were decided upon before the test. This may work to your benefit, if you happen to make a mistake while performing a maneuver that is not being graded.

At each predetermined scoring location, the examiner may not only grade the maneuver you are performing as a whole, but may also grade you on:

- How often you check your mirrors.
- Your lane positioning.
- Your speed and how well you control it.
- Whether or not you use your signal.
- If you cancel the signal.
- Whether or not you begin or end in the wrong lane.
- Whether or not you swing your truck too wide or too short.
- Whether or not you search for hazards.
- How you perform gear shifts.
- If you check the traffic around you.
- Whether or not you notice and/or follow all traffic signs.
- Other skills.

Although you may not be penalized for making certain mistakes during a maneuver that is not being graded, you may be penalized for other, more serious offenses. The following offenses are very serious and are counted as **grounds for automatic failure:**

- Inability to correctly use your vehicle equipment.
- Refusing to perform or complete any part of the road test.
- Not yielding to a pedestrian who is in the process of crossing at a crosswalk and/or passing a vehicle that has yielded to a pedestrian crossing in a crosswalk.
- Passing a school bus that is in the process of unloading and/or loading students, while the bus is flashing its red lights.
- Running a stop sign, stop line, or red light.
- Turning from a wrong lane (turning left from the right lane of a street with four lanes), especially if this creates a traffic hazard.
- Driving the wrong way on a one-way street and driving the wrong way on a two-way street.
- Stopping your vehicle in a busy intersection.
- If you are involved in an accident in which someone was injured or in which there is any amount of damage to property.
- If other drivers are forced to take action to avoid an accident with you.
- If the examiner must help you to avoid an accident.
- Driving on sidewalks or up curbs, especially if this causes a hazard to pedestrians.

Although each state develops its own scoring systems, there are federal regulations, which state that "to achieve a passing score on the skills test, the driver applicant must demonstrate that he/she can successfully perform all of the skills listed." State scoring systems define in their own terms what it means to "successfully perform all of the skills listed."

There are different types of scoring systems used to score the road test. Some systems:

- Rank the performance of a maneuver as good, fair, poor, or failing.
- Only score imperfect performances of maneuvers.
- Assign fixed values to each maneuver.
- Give the final score in terms of a percentage.
- Credit you for each maneuver performed correctly.

Before taking the road test, be sure to find out how your state scores the test, the passing score, offenses for automatic failure, and how to go about taking the test over if you do fail.

The Commercial
Driver License Exam

General
Knowledge
Test

PART IV – PRACTICE KNOWLEDGE TESTS
General Knowledge Test

DIRECTIONS FOR ALL KNOWLEDGE TESTS: After reading each question carefully, decide which answer is best. There is only **one** correct answer for each question. Using a No. 2 pencil, mark the answer you choose on the answer sheets provided toward the back of this book by blackening the oval that corresponds to your answer. If you do not know the correct answer, guess. All questions should be answered. Do not leave any blank. Mark only one answer for each question. If more than one answer is marked, the question will be graded as incorrect.

1. To stop quickly and safely you can use the controlled braking method by which you

    (A) apply the brakes as hard as you can to lock the wheels.

    (B) apply the brakes as hard as you can without locking the wheels.

    (C) apply the brakes and make large steering adjustments.

    (D) apply the brakes but keep them released before and after you make steering adjustments.

2. Two possible causes of tire fires are

    (A) short circuits and duals that touch.

    (B) under-inflated tires and duals that touch.

    (C) improper fueling or loose fuel connections.

    (D) improperly loaded cargo and driver smoking.

3. Possession or use of drugs while on duty is prohibited by law except when

    (A) using amphetamines.

    (B) using over-the-counter drugs.

    (C) your doctor informs you that the certain drug prescribed will not affect safe driving abilities.

    (D) using alcohol.

4. Poor weight balance can make vehicle handling unsafe. Hard steering is caused by

    (A) underloaded front axles.

(B)   too little weight on the driving axles.

(C)   too much weight on the steering axle.

(D)   a high center of gravity.

5.   Which of the following statements about unbaffled or "smooth bore" liquid tankers is **not** true?

(A)   You must be extremely cautious, especially when starting and stopping.

(B)   There is nothing inside the tank to slow down the flow of liquid.

(C)   Food products will most likely be transported in an unbaffled liquid tank.

(D)   Forward and back liquid surge is reduced.

6.   You are driving a vehicle when two cars collide a short distance ahead of you. In order to safely avoid the accident, you should

(A)   always apply the brakes immediately.

(B)   make a sharp turn to clear the accident area.

(C)   turn quickly with one hand on the wheel and one hand on the horn.

(D)   grip the wheel firmly with both hands and turn only the amount of space needed to clear whatever is in your way.

7.   To correct a drive-wheel braking skid you should

(A)   brake harder.   (C)   countersteer.

(B)   turn slowly.   (D)   keep your foot off the clutch.

8.   If you are driving a long distance, you should

(A)   stop often and take short breaks before you feel really drowsy or tired.

(B)   take a short break once or twice during the trip when you are feeling tired or drowsy.

(C)   avoid short breaks, but keep the window open.

(D)   do some physical exercises after the trip.

9.   When transporting cargo, inspect the materials and securing devices

(A)   before the trip only.

(B)   before and after the trip.

(C)   within 25 miles after beginning the trip and during every driving break.

(D)   before the trip, within 25 miles after beginning the trip, after every 3 hours or 150 miles, and during every driving break.

10. Which of the following statements about tank vehicles is true?
    (A) Tank vehicles transport liquids only.
    (B) The term "tank vehicle" refers only to those vehicles having a permanently attached tank.
    (C) Special skills are required to haul liquid tanks.
    (D) All tank vehicles have some sort of bulkhead or baffle.

11. Dry bulk tanks and hanging meat
    (A) have low centers of gravity.
    (B) handle better than most cargo on sharp turns.
    (C) are unstable loads.
    (D) do not require special care.

12. To turn quickly and safely in the event of a traffic or vehicle emergency, you should be prepared to countersteer. This means you turn the wheel
    (A) the opposite direction of the obstacle.
    (B) away from the obstacle and then back in the other direction.
    (C) to the right of the obstacle.
    (D) to the left of the obstacle.

13. To prevent truck fires, you should inspect your vehicle and its gauges
    (A) before the trip only.   (C) before and after the trip.
    (B) after the trip.   (D) before and during the trip.

14. Which of the following is an effect of drinking and driving?
    (A) Driving in the wrong lane
    (B) Making quick, jerky movements
    (C) Running stop signs
    (D) All of the above.

15. Which of the following statements about a vehicle with a high center of gravity is true?
    (A) The vehicle is less likely to tip over.
    (B) The vehicle is less dangerous on curves.
    (C) The cargo is evenly distributed and as low as possible.
    (D) The cargo should be rearranged so that the heaviest parts of the cargo are under the lightest parts.

16. Outage is
    (A) a full liquid tanker.
    (B) the space allotted for expanding liquids.
    (C) the weight of the liquid in transit.
    (D) caused by liquid surge.

17. For cargo, blocking is
    (A) shaped to fit loosely over the cargo.
    (B) unattached to the cargo deck.
    (C) needed in the front of a piece of cargo only.
    (D) used in the front, back and/or sides of a piece of cargo.

18. In the event of an engine fire,
    (A) always open the hood to release the fire.
    (B) keep the engine running and use extinguishers.
    (C) try to keep the hood closed and shoot extinguishers through louvers or from the underside of the vehicle.
    (D) always open the hood and shoot extinguishers through louvers or from the underside of the vehicle.

19. The Federal Hazardous Materials Table names materials that are hazardous. If you are transporting any of these materials
    (A) only the shipper should know.
    (B) only the driver should know.
    (C) the shipper and the driver should know.
    (D) everyone who handles the material should know.

20. Which of the following should you **not** do in the event of hydraulic brake failure?
    (A) Pump the brakes   (C) Shift up
    (B) Find an escape route   (D) Use the parking or emergency brake

21. Which of the following statements about loading heavy or dense liquid is true?
    (A) Tanks carrying heavy liquids can sometimes be filled completely.
    (B) You must be aware of legal weight limits.
    (C) Heavy or dense liquids do not expand.
    (D) The weight of the actual liquid does not matter.

22. You have been driving for a long time and you are feeling tired. What should you do?
    (A) Take a half hour coffee stop.
    (B) Take an over-the-counter drug that will keep you awake.
    (C) Push on until your next stop and rest.
    (D) Make an early stop and sleep or pull off the road and nap.

23. In some emergencies, you may have to drive off the road and onto the shoulder in order to avoid collision with another vehicle. If possible, you should avoid
    (A) keeping one set of wheels on the pavement.
    (B) using the brake until your speed has dropped to about 20 mph.
    (C) coming to a complete stop before returning to the road.
    (D) All of the above.

24. When driving baffled liquid tanks,
    (A) bulkheads are included which stop side to side liquid surge.
    (B) there is no risk of rollover.
    (C) forward and backward liquid surge is controlled.
    (D) there is no risk involved in taking curves or making sharp turns at the posted limits.

25. The Gross Combination Weight Rating is
    (A) the maximum total weight of a single vehicle plus its load specified by the manufacturer.
    (B) the maximum total weight of a power unit plus trailer(s) plus the cargo as specified by the manufacturer.
    (C) the total weight of a single vehicle plus its load.
    (D) the total weight of a powered unit plus trailer(s) plus the cargo.

26. Which of the following statements about driving an over-length, over-width, and/or over-weight load is **not** true?
    (A) You do not need a special permit.
    (B) Driving is usually limited to certain times.
    (C) Special equipment may be necessary.
    (D) You may require a police escort.

27. Shippers must write the name of the hazard class of hazardous products
    (A) only on the shipping papers.

(B)   only on the diamond-shaped labels on the containers.

(C)   on the shipping papers and on the diamond-shaped labels or special tags on the container.

(D)   only on the special-fitting tags for the containers.

28.   A skid happens when tires lose their grip on the road. To prevent skidding, you should

(A)   turn the wheel sharply for all turns.

(B)   accelerate to give power to the drive wheels.

(C)   adjust to conditions while driving.

(D)   brake hard at all stops.

29.   Which of the following statements about tiedowns is true?

(A)   They go from the upper part of the cargo to the floor and/or walls of the cargo compartment.

(B)   The combined strength of all cargo tiedowns must be strong enough to lift one-and-a-half-times the weight of the piece of cargo tied down.

(C)   Tiedowns can be of any type or strength.

(D)   Cargo should have at least one tiedown for each 20 feet of cargo.

30.   If your vehicle is involved in an accident, try to

(A)   keep one empty lane between your vehicle and other traffic.

(B)   stop all traffic in other lanes.

(C)   honk your horn to warn other vehicles.

(D)   get it to the side of the road.

31.   A tank vehicle with a high center of gravity

(A)   should take highway curves or onramp/offramp curves well below the posted speeds.

(B)   should take highway curves or onramp/offramp curves at least five miles above the posted speed.

(C)   cannot turn over at the speed limit posted for curves.

(D)   is top-heavy, but not easy to rollover.

32.   What are placed on the outside of a vehicle to show the hazard class(es) of the transported product?

(A)   Shipping papers   (C)   Bills of loading

(B)   Placards   (D)   Hazardous waste manifests

33. Which of the following about covering cargo is **not** true?
    (A) You need to protect people from spilled cargo.
    (B) You should look at your cargo in the mirrors often while driving.
    (C) Flapping covers need not be tied down as long as the bulk of the cargo is covered.
    (D) You need to protect the cargo from the weather.

34. When a front-wheel skid occurs, the only way to stop the skid is to
    (A) brake hard.
    (B) turn sharply.
    (C) let the vehicle slow down.
    (D) increase acceleration.

35. In the event of a cargo fire in a van or box trailer, you should
    (A) keep the doors shut.
    (B) keep the doors open.
    (C) drive to the closest service station for assistance.
    (D) park close to the road so other vehicles can see the danger and call for assistance.

36. Liquid surge
    (A) increases steering ability.
    (B) is created by extreme pressure of liquid in completely filled tanks.
    (C) creates waves that can move the truck.
    (D) makes for better handling.

37. If an oncoming driver has suddenly drifted into your lane or if an obstacle suddenly blocks your path, you should
    (A) move to the right.
    (B) move to the left.
    (C) brake immediately.
    (D) apply brakes slowly and signal for a lane change.

38. Which of the following statements is **not** true about an overloaded vehicle?
    (A) The vehicle will have to go very slow on upgrades.
    (B) The vehicle may gain too much speed on downgrades.
    (C) The vehicle's stopping distance decreases.
    (D) All of the above.

39. Which of the following is true about drinking and driving?
    (A) Alcohol increases your ability to drive further.
    (B) Alcohol will reduce your ability to drive.
    (C) Coffee and a little fresh air will help sober up a driver who is about to drive.
    (D) A drink will wake up a sleepy driver.

40. For electrical fires and burning liquids, use
    (A) a B:C type fire extinguisher only.
    (B) an A:B:C or B:C type fire extinguisher.
    (C) water.
    (D) whatever means you can think of on the spot.

41. _____ protect you from your cargo in case of collision and should be inspected for good condition.
    (A) Tiedowns   (C) Blocking devices
    (B) Front-end header boards (D) Bracing devices

42. You see an accident on the road and wish to help. The steps you take to prevent further damage or injury are: protect the area, care for the injured, and
    (A) park your vehicle near the accident.
    (B) notify authorities.
    (C) always move the severely injured person(s) away from the accident.
    (D) keep the injured person(s) cool.

43. You must keep shipping papers for hazardous materials
    (A) in a pouch on the driver's door.
    (B) in the glove compartment.
    (C) under the passenger's seat.
    (D) with the hazardous materials.

44. When using an extinguisher on a truck fire
    (A) get as close to the fire as possible.
    (B) stay as far away from the fire as possible.
    (C) stop when you no longer see smoke or flames.
    (D) aim the contents of the extinguisher at the flames.

45. Since you cannot inspect sealed loads,
    (A) you can exceed gross weight and axle weight limits.
    (B) you must be lower than weight limits by 50 pounds.
    (C) you therefore need special tiedown devices.
    (D) you should therefore check that you do not exceed gross weight and axle weight limits.

46. A coupling device capacity is
    (A) the maximum safe weight a tire can carry at a specified pressure.
    (B) the maximum weight the device can pull and/or carry.
    (C) the manufacturer's weight capacity rating of the suspension system.
    (D) the weight transmitted to the ground by one axle or one set of axles.

47. Which of the following should you **not** do if you suspect that one of your vehicle's tires has blown out?
    (A) Keep driving until you are certain it was one of your vehicle's tires that blew.
    (B) Hold the steering wheel firmly.
    (C) Stay off the brake.
    (D) Check all tires after stopping.

48. If you do not have a Hazardous Materials Endorsement on your Commercial Driver License, you can
    (A) drive a vehicle that carries hazardous materials if it does not require placards.
    (B) not transport any type of hazardous material.
    (C) transport hazardous materials if your employer lets you.
    (D) only transport liquid hazardous materials.

49. Which of the following contains more alcohol?
    (A) A 12-ounce mug of 5% beer
    (B) A 5-ounce glass of 12% wine
    (C) A 1 1/2-ounce shot of 80 proof liquor
    (D) All three contain the same amount of alcohol.

50. If you are transporting livestock,
    (A) give livestock enough room to roam freely.
    (B) rollover is less likely.

(C)   there is always a high center of gravity.

(D)   use false bulkheads with less than a full load.

51.   No placard is required on a transport vehicle or freight container when the gross weight of _____ is less than 1,000 pounds.

(A)   a flammable solid

(B)   a radioactive material

(C)   class 1.3 explosives

(D)   a flammable gas

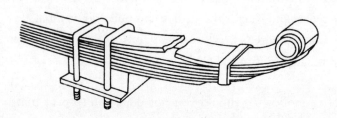

52.   If one-fourth of a multi-leaf spring is missing, which of the following is most likely to happen?

(A)   It will cause a pop-pop-pop sound.

(B)   It will put the vehicle out of service.

(C)   It will make it hard to steer.

(D)   It will have no effect.

53.   An indicator of a hydraulic leak is when

(A)   the drive wheels skid.

(B)   the vehicle jerks.

(C)   the brake pedal travels further than normal.

(D)   the air-conditioner fails.

54.   You are driving on a rainy day and the drive wheels begin to spin. To keep control of the vehicle, which of the following is the best action to take?

(A)   Brake hard.

(B)   Take your foot off the accelerator.

(C)   Steer to the left or right.

(D)   Accelerate slightly.

55. To extinguish an electrical fire,
    (A) use a lot of water.
    (B) use the A:B:C extinguisher on the flames of the fire.
    (C) use the B:C extinguisher on the base of the fire.
    (D) pull into a service station and wait for qualified firefighters.

56. What is the correct placement of warning devices when parked on the shoulder of a one-way or divided highway?
    (A) At 10 feet, 100 feet, and 200 feet from the front of the vehicle
    (B) At 100 feet and 500 feet from the front of the vehicle
    (C) At 100 feet and 500 feet from the rear of the vehicle
    (D) At 10 feet, 100 feet, and 200 feet from the rear of the vehicle

57. What is the total stopping distance when driving a heavy vehicle on dry pavement at 55 mph?
    (A) 4 1/2 seconds   (C) 6 seconds
    (B) 5 seconds   (D) 7 1/2 seconds

58. To go down a long, steep hill you should
    (A) shift to a low gear before starting down the grade.
    (B) shift to a high gear before starting down the grade.
    (C) shift to a low gear after starting down the grade.
    (D) apply your brakes hard.

59. Which of the following is the best way to slow the vehicle when driving down a hill?
    (A) Shift to a higher gear.
    (B) Keep light, continuous pressure on the brakes.
    (C) Apply heavy pressure on the brakes from time to time.
    (D) Shift gears to neutral.

60. A broken coolant hose while driving
    (A) causes the air-conditioner to fail.
    (B) can cause a fire.
    (C) increases the chances of tire failure.
    (D) causes the heater to fail.

61. How much tread depth should you have on your front tires when driving in the winter?

    (A) Minimum of 4/32 inch   (C) Minimum of 2/32 inch

    (B) Under 4/32 inch   (D) Maximum of 2/32 inch

62. You wish to turn left from one multi-lane two-way street into another multi-lane two-way street. Which of the figures below shows how the turn should be made?

    (A) Figure A   (C) Figure C

    (B) Figure B   (D) Figure D

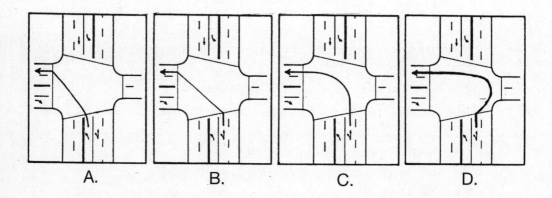

A.   B.   C.   D.

63. How often must drivers of trucks and truck tractors conduct a safety inspection?

    (A) Before driving

    (B) Before driving and every 3 hours during driving

    (C) Every 5 hours and after driving

    (D) After driving

64. When backing a trailer,

    (A) turn the steering wheel toward the direction you want to go.

    (B) turn the steering wheel in the opposite direction you want to go.

    (C) turn and back toward the right side.

    (D) use the highest reverse gear.

65. You are stopped on an incline. How do you keep from rolling back?

    (A) Engage the clutch.   (C) Put on the parking brake.

    (B) Shift to neutral.   (D) Pump the accelerator hard.

66. You are driving on slippery ice. Your rear drive wheels lock and you begin to skid. Which of the following is the best action to take?
    (A) Take your foot off the accelerator and push the brake.
    (B) Take your foot off the accelerator and push in the clutch.
    (C) Brake hard and pull off the road.
    (D) Shift to neutral.

67. A tie rod is part of the _____ system.
    (A) suspension   (C) exhaust
    (B) brake   (D) steering

68. Controlled braking is
    (A) stab braking.   (C) braking so that the wheels lock.
    (B) jamming on the brakes.   (D) releasing the brakes slowly.

69. Which of the following statements is true about alcohol?
    (A) Alcohol increases your ability to drive.
    (B) If you eat a lot first, you will not get drunk.
    (C) Some people are not affected by alcohol.
    (D) A few beers are the same as a few shots of whiskey.

70. What is a tractor jackknife?
    (A) Another name for hard steering
    (B) A device used in the hydraulic system
    (C) A drive-wheel skid
    (D) A type of trailer truck

71. You are stopped on the shoulder of a curve that prevents approaching traffic from seeing your vehicle. How far back should you place your last warning device?
    (A) 10 feet   (C) 200 feet
    (B) 100 feet   (D) 500 feet

72. Empty trucks
    (A) have better traction.   (C) require greater stopping distance.
    (B) require less braking power. (D) are easier to steer.

73. Which of the following is true about overhead clearance?

    (A) Posted heights are always correct.

    (B) A loaded truck is higher than an empty one.

    (C) Repaving or packed snow increases the clearance height.

    (D) An empty van is higher than a loaded van.

74. What is the proper way to make a right turn when you are driving a long vehicle?

    (A) Keep the rear of the vehicle far away from the curb.

    (B) Turn wide to the left as you start the turn.

    (C) Turn wide as you complete the turn.

    (D) Turn quickly to stop other drivers from hitting you.

75. If the radiator shutters freeze shut when driving in the winter,

    (A) the brakes will freeze.

    (B) the engine may overheat and stop.

    (C) carbon monoxide will leak into your vehicle.

    (D) it will be harder to steer.

76. Why don't new trucks use the same gear for going down a hill as they would for going up a hill?

    (A) They have low friction parts.   (C) They have more air drag.

    (B) They take up more fuel.   (D) They have weaker engines.

77. Your brakes have failed on a downgrade. Using an escape ramp, downshifting and _____ are helpful in slowing the vehicle.

    (A) countersteering   (C) applying your parking brake

    (B) shifting to a higher gear   (D) using your horn

78. You are driving on a highway and your front tire has just blown out. You should

    (A) brake hard.

    (B) pump the brakes.

    (C) stay off the brake until you have slowed down.

    (D) keep driving until you find a service station.

79. If the steering feels heavy or hard, it is probably a sign of

(A)   battery failure.   (C)   worn brakes.

(B)   tire problems.   (D)   engine problems.

80.   What is black ice?

(A)   Oil   (C)   Clear ice

(B)   Freshly paved tar   (D)   Fog or mist

81.   The controlled braking method is used

(A)   when making large steering wheel movements.

(B)   to make the wheels lock.

(C)   by applying the brakes as hard as you can without locking the wheels.

(D)   by applying the brakes slowly.

82.   If you have to steer away from what's ahead in order to avoid a crash, which of the following is the best action to take?

(A)   Hit the brakes.

(B)   Turn, then countersteer once you have cleared the obstacle.

(C)   Apply the brakes while turning.

(D)   Turn very sharply to clear whatever is in your way.

83.   What causes brakes to fade?

(A)   Using the brakes too lightly when going downhill

(B)   Coasting

(C)   Frozen brake pads

(D)   Slowing down from high speeds too quickly

84.   The proper distance to use high beams is at least _____ away from an approaching vehicle.

(A)   25 feet   (C)   1,000 feet

(B)   500 feet   (D)   50 feet

85.   What are the three types of safety equipment that you **must** have before driving?

(A)   Spare fuses, tire chains and a fire extinguisher

(B)   An accident reporting kit, three red reflective triangles and tire changing equipment

(C)   Tire changing equipment, spare fuses and a fire extinguisher

(D)   Spare fuses, three red reflective triangles and a fire extinguisher

86. You are approaching a vehicle for a pre-trip inspection. What should be the first step?

   (A) Starting the engine

   (B) Fastening your seatbelt

   (C) Putting the vehicle key in your pocket

   (D) Writing a written report on the condition of the vehicle

87. Which of the following should you examine when inspecting the **front** of your vehicle?

   (A) Condition of brakes

   (B) Condition of shock absorbers

   (C) Condition of battery

   (D) Condition of steering system

88. One of the steps in shifting up is to

   (A) release the clutch and shift to neutral.

   (B) increase engine and gear speed to the RPM required.

   (C) press the accelerator and shift to neutral.

   (D) push in the clutch and shift to the higher gear at the same time.

89. Some vehicles have automatic transmissions. Why is it important to select a low range when going down grades?

   (A) To allow the transmission to shift up

   (B) To get greater engine braking

   (C) To prevent hydroplaning

   (D) To prevent a hydraulic brake failure

90. Where and when is it best to downshift?

   (A) After starting up a hill   (C) Before entering a curve

   (B) After starting down a hill   (D) Before speeding up

91. You are driving a 60-foot rig at 55 mph. How many seconds of space should you have between you and the vehicle ahead?

   (A) 5 seconds   (C) 7 seconds

   (B) 6 seconds   (D) 8 seconds

92. You are driving a large vehicle that cannot make a right turn without swinging into another lane. Which of the figures that follow shows the correct way to make the turn?

(A) Figure A   (C) Figure C
(B) Figure B   (D) Figure D

93. Which of the following is one of the best ways to deal with tailgaters in heavy traffic?

(A) Speed up to increase the distance between you and the tailgater.

(B) Increase your following distance.

(C) Turn on your tail lights.

(D) Brake quickly several times to flash your brake lights.

94. At speeds below 40 mph, you need at least _____ for each _____ _____ of vehicle length.

(A) one second; 10 feet   (C) two seconds; 10 feet
(B) one second; 20 feet   (D) two seconds; 30 feet

95. When driving down a steep curve in the snow, you should

(A) use the engine brake.   (C) brake hard.
(B) use the speed retarder.   (D) turn as gently as possible.

96. You should inspect the tires every _____ when driving in very hot weather.

(A) one hour or every 50 miles   (C) three hours or every 200 miles
(B) two hours or every 100 miles   (D) four hours or every 400 miles

97.   The best kind of driver is a(n) _____ one.
      (A) slow   (C) sober
      (B) offensive   (D) defensive

98.   If you must pull over to the shoulder on a major highway, you should
      (A) keep one set of wheels on pavement, if possible.
      (B) use the controlled braking method.
      (C) turn onto the shoulder without braking.
      (D) brake quickly several times to flash your brake lights.

99.   Which of the following is one of the potential causes of fire in the electrical system?
      (A) Poor ventilation
      (B) Flammable cargo
      (C) Short circuits due to damaged insulation
      (D) Duals that touch

100. Why must you tab or keep shipping papers related to hazardous materials in special places?
      (A) Because they must be delivered first
      (B) In case there are no placards
      (C) Because you must know what products you can load together, and which you cannot
      (D) If the driver is in an accident and cannot speak, people must know the hazards involved.

GENERAL KNOWLEDGE TEST

ANSWER KEY

1. (B)	26. (A)	51. (D)	76. (A)
2. (B)	27. (C)	52. (B)	77. (C)
3. (C)	28. (C)	53. (C)	78. (C)
4. (C)	29. (B)	54. (B)	79. (B)
5. (D)	30. (D)	55. (C)	80. (C)
6. (D)	31. (A)	56. (D)	81. (C)
7. (C)	32. (B)	57. (C)	82. (B)
8. (A)	33. (C)	58. (A)	83. (D)
9. (D)	34. (C)	59. (B)	84. (B)
10. (C)	35. (A)	60. (B)	85. (D)
11. (C)	36. (C)	61. (A)	86. (C)
12. (B)	37. (A)	62. (C)	87. (D)
13. (D)	38. (C)	63. (B)	88. (D)
14. (D)	39. (B)	64. (B)	89. (B)
15. (D)	40. (B)	65. (C)	90. (C)
16. (B)	41. (B)	66. (B)	91. (C)
17. (D)	42. (B)	67. (D)	92. (A)
18. (C)	43. (A)	68. (A)	93. (B)
19. (D)	44. (B)	69. (D)	94. (A)
20. (C)	45. (D)	70. (C)	95. (D)
21. (B)	46. (B)	71. (D)	96. (B)
22. (D)	47. (A)	72. (C)	97. (D)
23. (B)	48. (A)	73. (D)	98. (A)
24. (C)	49. (D)	74. (C)	99. (C)
25. (B)	50. (D)	75. (B)	100. (D)

DETAILED EXPLANATIONS OF ANSWERS
General Knowledge Test

1. **(B)**   You need to keep your wheels unlocked so that you can maintain driving control on the road. If you lock your wheels, you may skid and lose control of the vehicle. (A) is incorrect because the brakes are locked. If you need to make steering adjustments, you need to release the brakes, so (C) is incorrect. Once the brakes are released to make steering adjustments, you need to reapply the brakes as soon as you can. (D) is incorrect because the brakes are not reapplied.

2. **(B)**   If tires are loose and touching or if there is not enough air in the tires, tire fires may occur. Short circuits due to damaged or loose connections may create **electrical** fires, so (A) is incorrect. Improper fueling or loose fuel connections may cause **fuel** fires, so (C) is incorrect. Improperly sealed or locked cargo, especially flammable materials and spilled fuel from a recent accident, may result in **cargo** fires if a driver's smoking ignites the fuel. (D) is incorrect.

3. **(C)**   As long as your doctor tells you that the drug he or she prescribed for you will not interfere with safe driving abilities, you may possess and use the drug legally as a driver. Amphetamines (including pep pills) and narcotics are prohibited by law, so (A) is incorrect. Certain over-the-counter drugs (including some cold medicines) and prescribed drugs may make a driver drowsy or otherwise affect safe driving abilities, so (B) is incorrect. Alcohol is a drug and can impair safe driving abilities, so (D) is incorrect.

4. **(C)**   Too much weight on the steering axle can cause hard steering and damage to the steering axle and tires. Under-loaded front axles caused by shifting weight too far to the rear can make the steering axle weight too light to steer, so (A) is incorrect. Too little weight on the driving axles can result in poor traction and cause the drive wheels to spin easily, so (B) is incorrect. A high center of gravity may cause rollovers, so (D) is incorrect.

5. **(D)**   Because there is nothing inside an unbaffled liquid tanker to slow down the liquid flow, surge is increased. This increase of liquid surge means that you must be extremely cautious when starting and stopping, so (A) is an incorrect choice. The term "unbaffled" indicates that there is nothing inside the tank to slow down the flow of liquid, so (B) is an incorrect choice. As sanitation regulations forbid the use of baffles because of the difficulties in cleaning the inside of the tank, food products,

such as milk, are usually transported in unbaffled tanks. Therefore (C) is also an incorrect choice.

6.   **(D)**   To turn safely, both hands should be firmly on the wheel as you turn only the amount of space needed to clear the obstacle. This way, you may turn back into traffic easily and unharmed. For total control over steering, you must have a firm grip on the steering wheel with both hands, not just with one hand, so (C) in incorrect. Do not turn any more than needed to clear the obstacle or you will increase the chances of a skid or rollover, so (B) is incorrect. Do not apply the brake while turning or you may lock your wheels and skid out of control; therefore (A) is also incorrect.

7.   **(C)**   A drive-wheel braking skid turns the vehicle off course. As the vehicle turns back on course, it has a tendency to keep on turning. Therefore, you need to turn the steering wheel quickly the other way so that you don't skid in the opposite direction. You need to let the rear wheels roll again to keep them from sliding further. To do this you should stop breaking, so (A) is incorrect. Pressing on the clutch will also let the wheels turn freely, especially on icy roads, so (D) is incorrect. You must steer the vehicle quickly in the direction you want to go once the vehicle begins to slide sideways, as in a drive-wheel braking skid, so (B) is incorrect.

8.   **(A)**   Short breaks can keep you alert, and, to prevent yourself from getting tired, the time to take a break is **before** you feel drowsy. Because you should take short breaks often and before you are tired, (B) is incorrect. While keeping cool can keep you more alert than driving in a hot, poorly ventilated cab, you should still take short breaks, so (C) is incorrect. (D) is also incorrect. Physical exercises can help you stay awake, but they only help during the trip, not after.

9.   **(D)**   It is best to check cargo and securing devices often and whenever possible. You should always inspect your cargo before the trip, but inspection is also needed during the trip, so (A) and (B) are both incorrect. You also need to inspect your shipment for overloaded or insufficiently secured cargo before you leave, so (C) is incorrect.

10.   **(C)**   Hauling liquids in tanks requires special skills because of a high center of gravity and liquid movement. Since tank vehicles are used to transport **both** liquid and liquefied gaseous materials, (A) is incorrect. The term "Tank vehicle" can also refer to a vehicle with a portable tank that has a capacity of 1,000 gallons or more, so (B) is incorrect. Smooth bore or unbaffled tankers are often used to transport food products, so (D) is incorrect.

11.   **(C)**   Dry bulk tanks and hanging meats are unstable loads that can shift easily from movement. Both have high centers of gravity, so (A) is incorrect. Because

these loads can shift, particular caution is needed going around curves or making sharp turns, so both (B) and (D) are incorrect.

12. **(B)** Once you have steered past whatever was in your path, you may have to turn the wheel back in the other direction to avoid collisions or other obstacles. To do this you counter or go against the original turn you made. (A), (C), and (D) are all incorrect because none mention the action of turning the wheel back in the other direction.

13. **(D)** In addition to making a complete inspection of the electrical, fuel, and exhaust systems and the tires and cargo, both **before** departure and **during** the trip, you should check the instruments and gauges for signs of overheating and use the mirrors to look for signs of smoke from the tires or the vehicle at these times. (A) is incorrect because you are only making a pre-trip inspection and fires can occur while driving. (B) is incorrect because the initial safety of the vehicle is never checked. (C) is incorrect because the vehicle is never monitored during the trip when it is possible for fires to occur.

14. **(D)** Alcohol affects more and more of the brain as the blood alcohol concentration builds up. The parts of the brain most affected are those that control self-control, judgement, muscle control and coordination, and vision. Therefore, drinking alcohol could result in your driving in the wrong lane (A), making quick, jerky stops (B), **and** running stop signs (C).

15. **(D)** A high center of gravity is created by cargo piled up high, or heavy cargo piled on top. Put the heaviest parts of the cargo **under** the lightest parts. A truck with a high center of gravity can tip over very easily, especially on curves or when swerving to avoid a hazard, so (A) and (B) are incorrect. (C) is also incorrect. In a vehicle with a high center of gravity, the cargo is piled high and is not evenly distributed.

16. **(B)** Liquids expand as they warm, so you must leave room for expanding liquids when transporting them in a tank. The space allotted for expansion is called outage. Loading a cargo tank to full capacity leaves no outage, so (A) is incorrect. The weight of the liquid is only one factor in determining outage, so (C) is incorrect. Because outage requires a partially filled tank, outage can cause liquid surge if the tank is not handled correctly. However, liquid surge cannot cause outage. (D) also is incorrect.

17. **(D)** When an entire piece of cargo needs to be secured to keep it from sliding, blocking is used. Blocking is shaped to fit snugly against the cargo to keep it in place, so (A) is incorrect. Blocking is secured to the cargo deck to prevent cargo

movement, so (B) is incorrect. (C) is incorrect because only the front of the cargo is secured.

18. **(C)** Adding oxygen to a fire will make it burn faster, so try to keep the hood closed. To use an extinguisher when the hood is closed, shoot it from the underside of the vehicle or through louvers or the radiator, wherever the contents will penetrate. (A) and (D) are incorrect because the fire is exposed to air, causing it to burn faster. (B) is incorrect because you should turn off the engine as soon as possible in the event of a fire.

19. **(D)** Hazardous materials can kill or injure on contact. To protect the driver and others from contact, all who are involved in the shipping process should be aware of the risk to be prepared for emergencies. (A), (B), and (C) are all incorrect because not enough people who deal with the materials are told that the products are hazardous. Shippers, drivers, and dockworkers all need to be alerted to the risk in case of emergency.

20. **(C)** If your brakes have failed, shifting up will only cause the vehicle to go faster and be harder to stop. Since pumping the brakes, finding an escape route, and using the parking or emergency brake are all things you **should** do in the event of a hydraulic brake failure and the question asks what you should **not** do, answer choices (A), (B), and (D) are incorrect.

21. **(B)** Because of the high density and great expansion ability of some heavy liquids, the amount of liquid that can be loaded into a tank is regulated by legal weights limits. Since liquids do expand when warmed, you can never completely fill a tank. This makes both (A) and (C) incorrect. A full tank of dense liquid, such as some acids, may exceed legal weight limits even before expansion occurs. You must consider this when loading, so (D) is incorrect.

22. **(D)** Sleep is the only thing that can help a driver overcome fatigue. If you have to make a stop anyway, make it whenever you feel the first signs of sleepiness, even if it is earlier than you planned. Since a nap as short as half an hour will do more to overcome fatigue than any amount of coffee, (A) is incorrect. While some drugs may keep you awake for a while, they won't make you alert, so (B) is incorrect. Pushing on when sleepy is a major cause of fatal accidents, so (C) is incorrect.

23. **(B)** Try to let your vehicle slow down to about 20 mph before braking. Then brake very gently to avoid skidding on a loose surface. (A) is incorrect because keeping one set of wheels on the pavement is a good way to maintain control. (C) is incorrect because it is safer to come to a complete stop on the shoulder before returning to the road. Since (B) is the only right answer, (D) is an incorrect choice.

24. **(C)** Baffled liquid tanks have bulkheads in them with holes that let the liquid flow through. The baffles help to control forward and backward liquid surge. Side-to-side surge can still occur, however, so (A) is incorrect. Because side-to-side surge can occur, rollover is still a possibility, so (B) is incorrect. (D) is also incorrect. You should always be extremely cautious in taking curves or making sharp turns in a liquid tanker.

25. **(B)** The Gross Combination Weight Rating is the maximum total weight of a power unit plus trailer(s) plus the cargo as specified by the manufacturer. The maximum total weight of a single vehicle plus its load specified by the manufacturer is the Gross Vehicle Weight Rating, so (A) is incorrect. Total weight for a single vehicle is the Gross Vehicle Weight, so (C) is incorrect. The total weight of a powered unit plus trailer(s) plus cargo is the Gross Combination Weight, so (D) is incorrect.

26. **(A)** Special transit permits are required to drive over-length, over-width, or over-weight loads. Because it is true that driving is limited to certain times, (B) is incorrect. "Wide Load" signs, flashing lights, flags, and other special equipment may be necessary to transport the load, so (C) is incorrect. Such loads may also require a police escort or pilot vehicles bearing warning signs or flashing lights; therefore (D) is incorrect.

27. **(C)** The name of the hazard class for hazardous products should be written on the shipping papers and on labels or tags that appear on the product containers. (A) is incorrect because only the papers are marked. (B) is incorrect because only the containers are marked. If diamond-shaped labels won't fit on the containers, then tags are used, but the shipping papers are still marked. (D) is incorrect because it does not mention the papers.

28. **(C)** Drivers who adjust their driving to conditions don't find themselves suddenly driving too fast, braking too hard, or steering too sharply to keep control of the tires on the road. Turning the wheel more sharply than the vehicle can turn may result in a skid or rollover, so (A) is incorrect. Supplying too much power to the drive wheels can cause them to spin, so (B) is incorrect. Braking too hard locks up wheels, causing them to skid, so (D) is incorrect.

29. **(B)** The combined strength of all cargo tiedowns must be strong enough to lift one-and-one-half-times the weight of the piece of cargo tied down. A securing device that goes from the upper part of the cargo to the floor and/or walls of the cargo compartment is called "bracing," so (A) is incorrect. Since the strength of the tiedowns depends upon the cargo and the type of truck carrying it, (C) is incorrect.

Cargo should have at least one tiedown for each **10,** not 20, feet of cargo, so (D) is incorrect.

30. **(D)** The first thing to do at an accident scene is to keep another accident from happening at the same spot, so try to get your vehicle off the travelled road. (A) and (B) are incorrect because traffic surrounds the accident scene, increasing the chances of another accident and preventing emergency vehicles from accessing the area. The best way to communicate that there is a problem is by putting on your flashers. Not everyone may hear your horn; therefore (C) is incorrect.

31. **(A)** A high center of gravity means the load's weight is carried high up off the road, making it especially easy for liquid tankers to roll over. For this reason curves should be taken very slowly. (B) is incorrect because the tanker would be going faster than the speed limit, increasing the chance of rollover. Tankers can indeed turn over at the speed limits posted for curves, so (C) is incorrect. Any vehicle that is top-heavy has an increased risk of rollover, so (D) is incorrect.

32. **(B)** Placards are diamond-shaped signs placed on the outside of a vehicle to show the hazard class(es) of a product. Shipping papers include information regarding hazardous materials, but are kept inside the cab, so (A) is incorrect. (C) and (D) are incorrect because they are types of shipping papers, also kept inside the cab.

33. **(C)** A flapping cover can tear loose, uncovering the cargo and possibly blocking your view or someone else's. To protect people from spilled cargo and to protect the cargo from the weather are two of the basic reasons to cover cargo; therefore, (A) and (D) are incorrect choices. Because you should check the security of your cargo often so as not to create a hazard for others, (B) is an incorrect choice.

34. **(C)** Most front-wheel skids are caused by driving too fast for conditions; therefore you must let the vehicle slow down. (D) is incorrect because if you accelerate you add speed. (A) is incorrect because braking hard creates skidding. In a front-wheel skid, the front end tends to go in a straight line regardless of how much you turn the steering wheel, so (B) is incorrect.

35. **(A)** Before trying to put out a fire, make sure that it does not spread any further. Try to keep it contained behind closed doors. (B) is incorrect because opening the van doors will supply the fire with oxygen and can cause it to burn faster. (C) is incorrect because the fire could expand and infect the area where flammable materials are located, creating an explosion. Parking your vehicle in an open area, away from buildings, trees, brush, other vehicles or anything that might catch fire is safest; therefore (D) is incorrect.

36. **(C)** Liquid surge results from movement of liquid in a partially filled tank. When coming to a stop, a wave of liquid can form which will hit the end of a tank and push the truck in the direction the wave is moving. For this reason, steering ability and handling capacity decrease, so (A) and (D) are incorrect. The surge can only be created by movement in trucks partially filled. It is not created by pressure in a completely filled tank, so (B) is incorrect.

37. **(A)** It is most likely that no one will be driving on the shoulder, but someone may be passing you on the left. Therefore, a move to your right is safest because there is less of a chance of creating an accident. (B) is incorrect because you may force a vehicle into oncoming traffic, creating a head-on collision. (C) and (D) are incorrect because you may not have the time or space to brake or make a lane change. Remember, you can almost always turn to miss an obstacle more quickly than you can stop.

38. **(C)** Stopping distance is the distance required to stop your vehicle. Because an overloaded vehicle will be very heavy and (B) gain much speed on downgrades, the vehicle will require a greater distance to stop. Stopping distance **increases**, not decreases. The extra weight of the overload will also cause the vehicle to go very slowly on upgrades, so (A) is an incorrect answer choice.

39. **(B)** People who drink alcohol are involved in traffic accidents resulting in over 20,000 deaths every year. Alcohol is a drug that will make you less alert and it will reduce your ability to drive safely for any distance, so (A) and (D) are incorrect. Only time will help a drinker sober-up. No other methods will work, so (C) is incorrect.

40. **(B)** A:B:C and B:C type fire extinguishers are both designed to work on electrical fires and burning liquids. (A:B:C extinguishers are designed to work on burning wood, paper, and cloth as well.) (A) is incorrect because only B:C extinguishers are mentioned. Using water on an electrical fire can cause you to get shocked, so (C) is incorrect. (D) is also incorrect. If you are not sure what to use, especially on hazardous materials fires, you should wait for qualified firefighters to come.

41. **(B)** Front-end header boards or "headache racks" protect you from your cargo in case of collision by blocking the forward movement of any cargo you carry. Tiedowns, blocking, and bracing are all methods of keeping cargo in place while in transit, but none is especially designed to protect the driver. Therefore, (A), (C), and (D) are incorrect.

42. **(B)** The police, fire department, and ambulance squads should know where

the accident is in order to assist all those involved and to prevent any further trouble from affecting the accident scene and other vehicles on the road. The area immediately around the accident will be needed for these emergency vehicles, so park away from the accident; therefore (A) is incorrect. You should never move severely injured persons **unless** the danger of fire or passing traffic makes it necessary, so (C) is incorrect. Keep the injured person warm, not cool, to prevent shock; therefore (D) is incorrect.

43. **(A)** Shipping papers should be kept in clear view and within reach. The glove compartment is too far away or may be difficult to get open in case of an accident, so (B) is incorrect. Under the passenger's seat is also a difficult place to see or reach, so (C) is incorrect. If there is an accident where hazardous materials leak, any papers attached to the product will be destroyed, so (D) is incorrect.

44. **(B)** In case of a shift in the wind or a resurgence of the fire, it is safest to stay far away from a fire. (A) is incorrect because you are endangering your life by standing too close to unpredictable flames. Since absence of smoke or flame does not mean the fire is completely out or cannot restart, (C) is incorrect. (D) is incorrect because you should aim at the source or base of the fire, not up into the flames.

45. **(D)** Even if you cannot inspect your cargo, you should make sure that you do not exceed certain weights for the safety of everyone. Without special permission, you cannot exceed weight limits for sealed or unsealed loads, so (A) is incorrect. There is no range except the legal weight limit that you must obey, so (B) is incorrect. You do not need special tiedown devices for a sealed load, only tiedowns that will properly and safely keep the load secure, so (C) is incorrect.

46. **(B)** Coupling devices are rated for the maximum weight they can pull and/or carry. The maximum safe weight a tire can carry at a specified pressure is called tire load, so (A) is incorrect. Suspension systems are very different from coupling devices, so (C) is incorrect. (D) is also incorrect. The weight transmitted to the ground by one axle or one set of axles is called axle weight.

47. **(A)** Quickly knowing you have tire failure will give you more time to react, so any time you hear a tire blow it is safest to assume the tire was yours. Keeping a firm grip on the steering wheel, staying off the brake, and checking all tires for blowouts are all things you **should** do to ensure safety when a blowout is suspected. Therefore, answer choices (B), (C), and (D) are incorrect.

48. **(A)** Even if you do not have a Hazardous Materials Endorsement on your CDL, you **may** transport hazardous materials when placards are not required. Since this means you can transport some types of hazardous materials, (B) is incorrect.

However, if the vehicle hauling the hazardous materials requires placards and you do not have a Hazardous Materials Endorsement, you can not drive the vehicle. This rule stands even if your employer says you may drive the vehicle or if the material is a solid, liquid, or gas. Choices (C) and (D) are incorrect.

49. **(D)** One mug of beer, one glass of wine, and one shot of hard liquor all contain the same amount of alcohol. Therefore, choices (A), (B), and (C) are incorrect. Do not falsely believe that your driving abilities will be affected any less if you drink only beer.

50. **(D)** Livestock can move around in a trailer causing unsafe handling. Use false bulkheads with less than a full load to keep livestock bunched together. You need to keep the animals close together and unable to move very freely to keep the weight balanced, so (A) is incorrect. Livestock can lean on curves, even when bunched together, so that the center of gravity always shifts and rollovers can occur; therefore (B) and (C) are incorrect.

51. **(D)** The hazard class of flammable gas does not require a placard if it is under 1,000 pounds. Answers (A), (B), and (C) are incorrect because a flammable solid, a radioactive material, and Class 1.3 explosives are hazard classes that always require a placard.

52. **(B)** If one fourth or more of a leaf spring is missing, it will put the vehicle out of service. Missing or broken leaves in any leaf spring could be dangerous and the vehicle must be fixed before it is serviceable, so answer (D) is incorrect. Answer (A) is incorrect because a pop-pop-pop sound comes from a defective muffler in the exhaust system. Answer (C) is incorrect because the leaf spring is part of the suspension system and not the steering system.

53. **(C)** If there is a leak in the hydraulic system, the brake pedal will feel spongy and will travel further than usual. Answer (A) is incorrect because drive wheels begin to skid if you use too much power when pressing the accelerator. Answer (B) is incorrect because the vehicle jerks when you accelerate roughly. Answer (D) is incorrect because the air-conditioner is not connected to the hydraulic brake system.

54. **(B)** Taking your foot off the accelerator will cause the vehicle to slow down and regain traction. Answer (A) is incorrect because hard braking could cause the vehicle to skid. Answer (C) is incorrect because steering left or right could cause the vehicle to slide. Answer (D) is incorrect because accelerating more could cause you to lose control of the vehicle.

55. **(C)** Use the B:C extinguisher on the base of the fire. The B:C and A:B:C type fire extinguishers are both designed to work on electrical fires. However, answer (B) is incorrect because aiming at the flames may spread the fire. You should aim at the source or base of the fire to extinguish it. Answer (A) is incorrect because you could get shocked by using water on an electrical fire. Answer (D) is incorrect because you should always park in an open area, away from anything that might catch fire.

56. **(D)** Place warning devices 10 feet, 100 feet and 200 feet toward approaching traffic. You should place warning devices at 10 feet to mark the location of the vehicle, so answer (C) is incorrect. When parked on a one-way or divided highway, traffic only approaches you from the rear. There is no need to set up warning devices in front of your vehicle, so answers (A) and (B) are also incorrect.

57. **(C)** In this case, the total stopping distance or the sum of the perception, reaction and braking distances is six seconds. Answer (A) is incorrect because it will take you 4 1/2 seconds for braking only. Answers (B) and (D) are incorrect because the perception and reaction distance each take 3/4 of a second. The sum of four and a half seconds, three-fourths, and three-fourths of a second is six seconds, not five or seven and one half.

58. **(A)** Shift to a low gear before starting down a long, steep hill. Lower gears, not higher ones, allow engine compression and friction to help slow the vehicle, so answer (B) is incorrect. Answer (C) is incorrect because if you wait until you have started down the hill to shift gears, you might get hung up in neutral and cause the vehicle to coast. Answer (D) is incorrect because applying your brakes hard will cause them to get too hot. They may fade until you cannot slow down or stop at all.

59. **(B)** Keeping light, continuous pressure on the brakes is the best way to slow a vehicle. This will slow the vehicle without the brakes getting too hot. Answers (A) and (D) are incorrect because shifting while going down hill could cause you to coast. You should shift to a lower gear before going down a hill. Answer (C) is incorrect because heavy pressure from time to time builds up more heat than light continuous pressure does. This causes the brakes to fade until they are inoperative.

60. **(B)** A broken coolant hose can lead to engine failure and fire. Answers (A), (C), and (D) are incorrect because a coolant hose helps keep the engine temperature down to satisfactory operating levels.

61. **(A)** To reduce skidding, front tires need 4/32 inch tread depth or more in winter conditions. Answers (B), (C), and (D) are all incorrect.

62. **(C)** Figure C shows the correct turning procedure. Take the right-hand turn lane and make sure you have reached the center of the intersection before starting

the left turn. Answer (A) is incorrect because the vehicle is in the inside lane and will have to swing right to make the turn. Answer (B) is incorrect because the driver has turned too soon and may hit another vehicle because of offtracking. Answer (D) is incorrect because the driver has swung wide and has blocked or crashed into the right lane traffic.

63. **(B)** Safety inspections must be conducted before driving and every 3 hours during driving. Drivers of trucks and truck tractors must inspect within the first 25 miles of a trip and every 150 miles or 3 hours afterward, so answers (A), (C), and (D) are incorrect.

64. **(B)** Turn the steering wheel in the opposite direction you want to go when backing a trailer. Turning the vehicle toward the direction you want to go is the method used when backing a car, straight truck or bus, so answer (A) is incorrect. Answer (C) is incorrect because you cannot see as well when turning and backing toward the right side. Answer (D) is incorrect because the lowest reverse gear, not the highest, should be used to enable you to stop quickly and correct steering errors.

65. **(C)** Put on the parking brake to keep the vehicle from rolling back on an incline. Answers (A) and (B) are incorrect because engaging the clutch or shifting to neutral will not prevent you from rolling back. Answer (D) is incorrect because pumping the accelerator hard can cause mechanical damage.

66. **(B)** To correct a skid, take your foot off the accelerator and push in the clutch. This will allow the wheels to turn freely. Answers (A) and (C) are incorrect because braking or accelerating will not help the rear wheels regain traction and can cause them to slide further instead. Answer (D) is incorrect because shifting to neutral will not stop the vehicle from skidding.

67. **(D)** A tie rod is a long rod connected to the steering arms in the steering system. Answers (A), (B), and (C) are incorrect because a tie rod is not part of the suspension, brake or exhaust system.

68. **(A)** With the controlled or stab braking method you apply the brakes all the way without locking the wheels. Therefore, answer (C) is incorrect. You should release the brake when the wheels lock up. Answer (B) is incorrect because applying the brakes hard will keep the wheels locked up and cause a skid. Answer (D) is incorrect because you should release the brakes quickly and keep applying them until the vehicle slows down.

69. **(D)** A few beers are the same as a few shots of whiskey. A 12-ounce glass of 5 percent beer contains the same amount of alcohol as a 1 1/2-ounce shot of 80 proof

liquor. Answer (A) is incorrect because alcohol makes you less alert and reduces your ability to drive safely. Answers (B) and (C) are incorrect because everyone who drinks alcohol is affected and food will not keep you from getting drunk.

70. **(C)**   In vehicles towing trailers, a drive-wheel skid can make the trailer push the towing vehicle sideways, causing what is termed a jackknife. Answers (A), (B), and (D) are incorrect.

71. **(D)**   When stopped on a curve, place a warning device 500 feet behind you. Answer (A) is incorrect because 10 feet is the closest you should put a warning device. Answers (B) and (C) are incorrect because devices at 100 or 200 feet do not give other drivers enough warning.

72. **(C)**   Empty trucks require greater stopping distance. Answers (A) and (B) are incorrect because an empty vehicle has less traction. It may bounce and lock its wheels, which causes poorer braking. Answer (D) is incorrect because the poor traction of an empty vehicle makes the vehicle harder to steer.

73. **(D)**   Because the weight of a cargo vehicle changes its height, an empty van is higher than a loaded van. If a vehicle is empty it will be higher, so answer (B) is incorrect. Answers (A) and (C) are incorrect because repaving or packed snow may reduce the clearance height, and height changes may not be posted immediately on signs.

74. **(C)**   Turn wide as you complete the turn. Answers (A) and (B) are incorrect because vehicles behind you may think you are turning left and try to pass you on the right. You may crash into the other vehicle as you complete your turn. Answer (D) is incorrect because you should turn slowly to give yourself and others more time to avoid problems.

75. **(B)**   If the radiator shutters freeze shut, the engine may overheat and stop. Failure to remove ice from the radiator shutters or driving with a winterfront that is closed too tightly may cause the engine to overheat and stop, so answers (A), (C), and (D) are incorrect.

76. **(A)**   For fuel economy, new trucks have low friction parts and streamlined shapes. Answers (B), (C), and (D) are incorrect because new trucks may have more powerful engines, less friction, and less air drag to hold them back when going down hills.

77. **(C)**   Apply your parking brake to help slow a vehicle without brakes. Holding the release button down when applying your parking brake lets you control the

power of the brake. Answers (B) and (D) are incorrect because shifting to a higher gear or blowing your horn will not slow you down. Answer (A) is incorrect because countersteering could cause you to lose control of the vehicle.

78. **(C)**   In the event of a tire blowout, stay off the brake until you have slowed down. Braking at high speeds when a tire has failed could cause you to lose control of the vehicle, so answers (A) and (B) are incorrect. Answer (D) is incorrect because you should pull off the road and stop as soon as possible.

79. **(B)**   Heavy or hard steering is a sign of tire problems. If a tire has gone flat or is under-inflated, it will affect the steering, so answers (A), (C), and (D) are incorrect.

80. **(C)**   Black ice is a thin layer of ice that is clear enough to see the road underneath. It makes the road look wet and is very slippery. Answers (A), (B), and (D) are incorrect.

81. **(C)**   In controlled braking you apply the brakes as hard as you can without locking the wheels. Answers (A) and (B) are incorrect because if the wheels lock while braking hard and make large steering wheel movements, the vehicle may skid. Answer (D) is incorrect because controlled braking is used to stop quickly and safely.

82. **(B)**   Turn, then countersteer once you have cleared the obstacle. Answer (A) is incorrect because hitting the brakes will not clear the vehicle from the obstacle. Answer (C) is incorrect because applying the brakes while turning could cause the wheels to lock, making your vehicle skid and go out of control. Answer (D) is incorrect because the sharper you turn, the greater the chance of a skid or rollover.

83. **(D)**   Brakes are designed to take a lot of heat. However, they can fade from excessive heat if you slow down from very high speeds too quickly or too often. Answer (A) is incorrect because light brake pressure will not cause excessive heat. Answer (B) is incorrect because when you coast you do not use the brakes. Answer (C) is incorrect because brakes fade when the pads wear out from the extreme heat of rubbing against the brake drum. Frozen brake pads will not wear away.

84. **(B)**   Dim your lights within 500 feet of an oncoming vehicle before they cause glare for other drivers. Also, dim them when following another vehicle within 500 feet to avoid shining your lights in their rearview mirrors. Answers (A) and (D) are incorrect because at close distances other drivers may be blinded by your headlights. Answer (C) is incorrect because high beams will only light the area 350 to 500 feet in front of you.

85. **(D)** Spare fuses, three red reflective triangles and a fire extinguisher. Answers (A), (B), and (C) are incorrect because tire chains, an accident reporting kit and tire changing equipment are all optional items.

86. **(C)** A pre-trip inspection begins when you approach the vehicle. You must check the exterior for damage and see if the vehicle is leaning to one side. You must also inspect underneath the vehicle for leaks. You should put the key in your pocket to prevent someone from moving the vehicle while you are underneath it. Answers (A) and (B) are incorrect because these steps are done after checking underneath the vehicle. Answer (D) is incorrect because it is part of the after-trip inspection.

87. **(D)** Condition of steering system should be examined from the front of your vehicle. You must check for defective or missing parts and you must grab the steering mechanism to test for looseness. Answer (A) is incorrect because the brakes should be examined when inspecting the right rear or the left front side of the vehicle. Answer (B) is incorrect because the shock absorbers should be checked when inspecting the right rear of the vehicle. Answer (C) is incorrect because the battery is examined when inspecting the left side.

88. **(D)** In order to shift up, you must push in the clutch and shift to the higher gear at the same time. Answer (A) is incorrect because in order to shift gears, you must apply the clutch and shift at the same time. Answer (B) is incorrect because engine and gear speed are increased when shifting down. Answer (C) is incorrect because you should first release the accelerator, then push in the clutch and shift to neutral at the same time. If you press the accelerator or release the clutch while shifting, the vehicle could stall.

89. **(B)** To get greater engine braking select a low range when going down grades. The lower ranges of automatic transmissions prevent the transmission from shifting up beyond the gear you select (unless the RPM is exceeded), so answer (A) is incorrect. Answer (C) is incorrect because hydroplaning occurs when wheels slide on water. Answer (D) is incorrect because hydraulic brake failure is usually caused by loss of hydraulic pressure or brake fade on steep hills.

90. **(C)** Downshifting before entering a curve lets you use some power during the curve to help the vehicle be more stable while turning. It also allows you to speed up after the curve. Answers (A) and (B) are incorrect because you should downshift **before** both climbing up and going down hills. If you downshift after starting a climb or descent, you may get stuck in neutral and stall. Answer (D) is incorrect because you should shift up to accelerate, not shift down.

91. **(C)** You need at least one second for each 10 feet of vehicle length at speeds below 40 mph. At greater speeds, add one additional second. In a 60-foot rig, at 55

mph, you will need 6 seconds plus one more second for traveling over 40 mph. The total is 7 seconds, so answers (A), (B), and (D) are incorrect.

92. **(A)**   As Figure A depicts, turn wide as you complete the turn while keeping the rear of your vehicle close to the curb. Answers (B) and (C) are incorrect because the vehicle turns wide to the left. If you do this, a following driver may think your vehicle is turning left and may try to pass on the right. You could crash into that driver as you complete your turn. Answer (D) is incorrect because the vehicle is in the wrong lane at the start of the turn.

93. **(B)**   To safely handle a tailgater, increase your following distance. Having more room in front of you will help you avoid sudden speed changes. It also makes it easier for the tailgater to get in front of you. Answer (A) is incorrect because speeding up in traffic will only cause you to apply your brakes harder to slow down. This could make the tailgater crash into the back of your vehicle. Answers (C) and (D) are incorrect because using tricks like turning on your tail lights and pumping the brakes to flash your lights will not only distract the tailgater but will increase the chances of a crash.

94. **(A)**   When driving at 40 mph and under, you should keep **at least** one second of space in front of you for each 10 feet of vehicle length. Answers (B), (C), and (D) are incorrect.

95. **(D)**   Slow down and turn gently to avoid skids when going down a steep curve in the snow. Answers (A), (B), and (C) are incorrect because these actions can cause the driving wheels to lock and skid on slippery surfaces.

96. **(B)**   In very hot weather, you should check the tire mounting and air pressure every 2 hours or every 100 miles, whichever comes first. If a tire gets hot, the air pressure will increase. You should stop until the tire cools off or it may blow out or catch fire, so answers (A), (C), and (D) are incorrect.

97. **(D)**   The best kind of driver is one that is alert and prepared to avoid any hazard that may occur, so answer (B) is incorrect. Answers (A) and (C) are incorrect because even if you are sober and drive slowly, it does not prevent another vehicle from crashing into you. It is better to be a defensive driver who is prepared to act if hazards become emergencies.

98. **(A)**   When pulling onto the shoulder, keep one set of wheels on pavement, if possible, to help maintain control. You should avoid braking until your speed has decreased to about 20 mph. Answers (B) and (D) are incorrect because using the controlled braking method at high speeds or braking quickly to flash your lights may

cause a following driver to crash into your vehicle, or cause you to skid on the loose surface of the shoulder. Answer (C) is incorrect because you could skid and lose control of the vehicle if you turn onto the shoulder at high speeds without slowing down first.

99. **(C)** Short circuits due to damaged insulation may cause fires in the electrical system. Answers (A), (B), and (D) are incorrect because these problems cause fires in the cargo area or in the tires.

100. **(D)** In order to prevent more damage or injury, firefighters and police must know the hazards involved. The driver's life and the lives of others may depend on quickly finding the shipping papers of hazardous cargo. Answers (A) and (C) are incorrect because these are not the reasons for special placement of the shipping papers for hazardous cargo. Answer (B) is incorrect because even if placards are required, you will still need shipping papers for cargo.

The Commercial
Driver License Exam

Endorsement
Tests

- Passenger Transport Test
- Air Brakes Test
- Combination Vehicles Test
- Hazardous Materials Test
- Tanker Test
- Doubles/Triples Test

The Passenger Transport Test

See directions on page 195.

1. On a pre-trip inspection of your bus make sure that
   (A) both front wheels have been recapped for improved traction.
   (B) both front wheels have been regrooved for improved mileage.
   (C) all emergency exits are open for easy access.
   (D) all defects reported by the previous driver have been fixed.

2. A charter bus carrying agricultural workers may have a maximum of _____ temporary seats in the aisle.
   (A) 4
   (B) 8
   (C) 12
   (D) 16

3. A hazardous material is a material that poses a risk to
   (A) health.
   (B) safety.
   (C) property.
   (D) All of the above.

4. The proper size and shape of a hazard label is
   (A) a four-inch triangle.
   (B) a four-inch diamond.
   (C) a five-inch triangle.
   (D) a five-inch diamond.

5. Buses may carry which of the following hazardous materials?
   (A) Small-arms ammunition
   (B) Class A poison
   (C) Class B poison in liquid form
   (D) Tear gas

6. In which situation is it most likely that you will accidentally scrape off your mirror?
   (A) At intersections stop
   (B) On banked curves
   (C) When pulling away from a bus
   (D) At railroad crossings

7. Which of these statements about railroad crossings describes a safe practice?
   (A) Look left because trains only travel left to right.
   (B) Stop on the tracks to look up and down the track more easily.
   (C) Shift into a lower gear while crossing the tracks.
   (D) Open the forward door if it helps you see or hear an approaching train.

8. What distance must you stop your bus in front of railroad crossings?

    (A) Between 15 and 50 feet   (C) At least 100 feet

    (B) Between 50 and 100 feet   (D) At least 100 yards

9. You are approaching a drawbridge that has no lights or traffic control attendant. You must

    (A) avoid the drawbridge because it is unsafe.

    (B) park your vehicle and get out to check that the draw is closed.

    (C) stop at least 50 feet before the draw of the bridge.

    (D) stop at least 25 feet before the draw of the bridge.

10. When driving a busload of passengers, which of the following is a proper practice?

    (A) Engage in small conversations with the passengers to make the ride a better experience for all.

    (B) Refuel in a closed building in cold weather.

    (C) Have the passengers leave the vehicle while you refuel it.

    (D) Tow the disabled bus, with passengers, to its destination.

11. Which of these statements is true of the brake and accelerator interlock system?

    (A) The rear door can be opened when the bus is in motion.

    (B) The interlock applies the brakes and holds the throttle in idle position when rear door is open.

    (C) The interlock applies the brakes and holds the throttle in idle position when the rear door is closed.

    (D) This safety feature can be used in place of the parking brake.

12. When driving a bus around a banked curve you should

    (A) accelerate, so that you get through the curve as quickly as possible.

    (B) drive at the same speed as the car ahead of you.

    (C) drive at the posted speed.

    (D) slow down if the bus begins to lean toward the outside.

13. When you have a drunk and disorderly passenger on board you should

    (A) drop the person off anywhere the person wants.

    (B) keep the person on the bus until your shift is over.

    (C) drop the person off at the next well-lighted, scheduled stop.

    (D) let the person off immediately to teach that person a lesson.

14. When must you check the bus for safety and defects?
    (A) Before your shift only
    (B) Before and after each shift
    (C) After your shift only
    (D) Once a week

15. Every banked curve has a specific
    (A) water level.
    (B) safe design speed.
    (C) traction.
    (D) roll-over width.

16. When you arrive at a streetcar crossing, what should you do?
    (A) Come to a complete stop and carefully check for crossing traffic.
    (B) Keep moving at normal speed since you have the right of way.
    (C) Accelerate in order to get through the crossing as quickly as possible.
    (D) Slow down and check for other vehicles.

17. Federal regulations require each bus to have
    (A) a fire extinguisher and emergency reflectors.
    (B) a firefighter's hose and a safety ladder.
    (C) seat belts for all passengers.
    (D) circuit breakers.

18. Which of the following is legally permitted in the passenger area of a bus?
    (A) Labeled radioactive materials
    (B) Gasoline
    (C) Any explosives, as long as they are labeled
    (D) None of the above.

19. Before accepting a hazardous material for transportation, check that the container has which of the following?
    (A) A flowchart on how dangerous the materials are
    (B) ID number and hazard label
    (C) A chart showing the chemical breakdown of each substance
    (D) Material's name, hazard label, and ID number

20. While driving
    (A) focus only on the road ahead of you.
    (B) scan the road from left to right.
    (C) scan the road in all four directions, as well as the interior of the bus.
    (D) scan the road in front of you and behind you.

21. Riders should not stand
    (A) in the bus.
    (B) in front of the standee line.
    (C) behind the rear of the driver's seat.
    (D) within two feet of another rider.

22. Which of the following must you check during the pretrip inspection?
    (A) Horn, lights, reflectors, rims
    (B) Coupling devices, steering mechanism
    (C) All of the above.
    (D) None of the above.

23. When transporting passengers on a charter bus, never
    (A) drive with a closed emergency exit door or window.
    (B) allow riders on the bus until departure time.
    (C) close the restroom service access panel.
    (D) All of the above.

24. You should mention to passengers the rules about smoking, drinking, and the use of radios and tape players
    (A) before the start of the trip.
    (B) once you are on the road.
    (C) at the first instance of a passenger violating one of the rules.
    (D) It is not necessary to mention the rules, since signs will be posted throughout the bus.

25. When refueling your bus at a rest stop, which of these is the best practice?
    (A) Refueling at an enclosed structure, if available, before parking
    (B) Waiting until all passengers have reboarded before refueling
    (C) Refueling before passengers reboard the bus
    (D) Requiring the passengers to remain on the bus during refueling, since refueling will take all the time that was allotted for the rest stop

26. When a drawbridge has an attendant, which of the following should you do?
    (A) Stop and wait for the attendant's signal.
    (B) Maintain speed.
    (C) Slow down.
    (D) None of the above.

27. Which of the following is an acceptable load of hazardous material on a bus?
    (A) 100 pounds of solid Class A poison
    (B) 100 pounds of solid Class B poison
    (C) 100 pounds of liquid Class A poison
    (D) 100 pounds of liquid Class B poison

28. You do not have to stop, but must slow down and carefully check for other vehicles at
    (A) a drawbridge that does not have a signal light.
    (B) railroad crossings.
    (C) a site where a policeman is directing traffic.
    (D) a drawbridge that does not have an attendant.

29. When pulling out into traffic from a bus stop, you should
    (A) assume that other vehicles will stop and allow you to merge, since you have the right of way.
    (B) honk your horn, since other drivers will have to stop when you signal.
    (C) wait for a gap to open before leaving the stop.
    (D) None of the above.

30. Before driving, always check to make sure that
    (A) everyone is seated.
    (B) all extra carry-on baggage is forward of the standee line.
    (C) items left on the floor or aisle can fit through the emergency exits.
    (D) all doorways and aisles are free of all carry-on baggage.

THE PASSENGER TRANSPORT TEST

ANSWER KEY

1.	(D)	16.	(D)
2.	(B)	17.	(A)
3.	(D)	18.	(D)
4.	(B)	19.	(D)
5.	(A)	20.	(C)
6.	(C)	21.	(B)
7.	(D)	22.	(C)
8.	(A)	23.	(B)
9.	(C)	24.	(A)
10.	(C)	25.	(C)
11.	(B)	26.	(C)
12.	(D)	27.	(B)
13.	(C)	28.	(C)
14.	(B)	29.	(C)
15.	(B)	30.	(D)

DETAILED EXPLANATIONS OF ANSWERS
The Passenger Transport Test

1. **(D)** All previously reported defects should be fixed before you sign the previous driver's report and use a bus for passenger transport. In addition, the front tires should not have been recapped or regrooved, which means (A) and (B) are incorrect. All emergency exits must be closed, not open, before driving. Hence, (C) is incorrect.

2. **(B)** For safety, a charter bus cannot have more than eight temporary folding seats. Hence (C) and (D) are incorrect. While four seats are permitted, this is not the maximum allowed. Therefore, (A) is incorrect. All other seats must be securely fastened to the bus.

3. **(D)** All of the above. These materials are regulated by federal agencies to protect persons and property from exposure to substances that could harm them. You must not transport a hazardous material unless the rules allow it.

4. **(B)** According to federal regulations, the hazard label must be a four-inch diamond. Therefore, (A), (C), and (D) are incorrect.

5. **(A)** Buses may carry small-arms ammunition labeled ORM-D. They can also carry emergency hospital supplies and drugs. Buses must never carry any Class A poison, liquid Class B poison, or tear gas. (B), (C), and (D) are forbidden hazardous materials.

6. **(C)** If you do not allow the proper clearance when pulling away from a bus stop, you are likely to scrape off your mirror or hit a passing vehicle. Intersections, curves, and railroad crossings are also dangerous, but the hazards in those cases are different.

7. **(D)** Open the door if it helps you see or hear an approaching train. Looking in one direction only, stopping on the tracks to check for trains, and shifting gears while crossing the tracks are all dangerous. (A), (B), and (C) are incorrect.

8. **(A)** Federal regulations require you to stop the bus 15 to 50 feet before railroad crossings. Then listen and look in both directions.

9. **(C)**   Stop at least 50 feet before the draw of the bridge and make sure the draw is completely closed before crossing. (D) is incorrect because it is too close. The absence of a light or attendant does not mean the drawbridge is unsafe, only that you must determine for yourself that the draw is closed. Therefore, (A) is incorrect. Because you are not required to leave your vehicle to check the drawbridge, (B) is also incorrect.

10. **(C)**   For the safety of the passengers, have them leave the vehicle (if possible) when you are refueling. You should never refuel in a closed building with passengers aboard. Therefore, (B) is incorrect. It is unwise to talk to passengers while driving since being distracted, even for a few seconds, can lead to an accident. (A) is incorrect. Do not tow or push a disabled bus with riders on board either vehicle, unless getting off would be unsafe. Then only tow or push the bus to the nearest safe spot to discharge passengers. (D) is incorrect.

11. **(B)**   The purpose of the interlock system is to apply the brakes and hold the throttle in idle position when the rear door is open. The interlock then releases when the rear door is closed. This means (B) is correct and (C) is incorrect. Since the vehicle is prevented from moving when the rear door is open, (A) is incorrect. The interlock is not a substitute for the parking brake, but an added safety feature on some urban mass transit coaches. Therefore, (D) is incorrect.

12. **(D)**   You should never accelerate when going around curves. (A) is incorrect. (B) and (C) are incorrect because a safe speed for a car may not be safe for a bus. Your speed in a curve should not be determined by other vehicles, but by what is safe for your vehicle. If your bus begins to lean toward the outside, you are going too fast and should slow down.

13. **(C)**   You must ensure a drunk or disruptive passenger's safety just as you would that of any other passenger. You should not discharge passengers where it would be unsafe for them, so (A) and (D) are incorrect. Keeping a disruptive passenger aboard your bus longer than necessary may put you and your other passengers at risk. Therefore, (B) is incorrect.

14. **(B)**   You must check before and after each shift. Your pretrip inspection should cover defects reported by previous drivers as well as general safety precautions. Your after-trip inspection is important to note any damage that has occurred during your shift. Both inspections are necessary each shift you work. Answers (A), (C), and (D) are incorrect.

15. **(B)**   Each banked curve has a specific design speed that is safe for that particular type of curve. (A), (C), and (D) are incorrect because these are not specific features of a banked curve.

16. **(D)** You do not have to stop [(A) is incorrect], but you must slow down and check for other vehicles at streetcar crossings. Continuing at your normal speed (B) or accelerating (C) is not safe because you may need to stop quickly.

17. **(A)** Make sure your bus has the fire extinguisher and emergency reflectors required by law. (B) is incorrect because these items are required for a fire prevention vehicle. At this time, buses are required to provide a seat belt only for the driver. (C) is incorrect. A bus that does not have circuit breakers must carry spare electrical fuses, but circuit breakers are not required by law. (D) is incorrect.

18. **(D)** None of the above. Labeled radioactive materials and explosives other than small-arms ammunition labeled ORM-D are not permitted in the space occupied by people. In addition to regulated hazardous materials, common hazards such as gasoline and car batteries are also forbidden on board a bus.

19. **(D)** Each container must carry all pieces of information: the material's name, ID number, and hazard label. (B) is incorrect because it only lists two of the three required items. (A) and (C) do not contain information that is required to be placed on the container.

20. **(C)** Scan the interior of the bus, as well as the road ahead, to both sides, and to the rear. (A), (B), and (D) are incorrect because they are incomplete. The passengers' safety is your top priority. Ensuring their safety requires that you be alert to dangers from any direction, and to disruptions or unsafe actions within your bus.

21. **(B)** All riders must stand behind the standee line, which is either a two-inch line on the floor or some other means of showing riders where they can and cannot stand. Since this line prevents riders from standing forward of the rear of the driver's seat, (C) is incorrect. (A) and (D) are incorrect because riders may stand on a bus if there are no seats available. In fact, on a very crowded bus, riders may be required to stand close together.

22. **(C)** All items listed are part of the pre-trip inspection. Other items that must be checked are service brakes (including air hose couplings), parking brake, tires, windshield wipers, and rear-vision mirrors.

23. **(B)** Never allow riders on the bus until departure time. This is to prevent theft or vandalism while the bus is unattended. Emergency exit doors and windows and all service panels should be closed before you drive. You should not drive with these open; therefore, answers (A) and (C) are incorrect. Since only one of the choices is correct, answer (D), all of the above, is not correct.

24. **(A)** You should mention any rules passengers must know before you actually get under way. Answers (B) and (C) are too late, since the purpose of the rules is to prevent unsafe or inconsiderate practices before they occur. You must always mention the rules because there may not always be signs and some passengers may not be able to read them. (D) is incorrect.

25. **(C)** The best time to refuel at a rest stop would be while the passengers are not on the bus. Therefore, (A), (B), and (D) are not as good choices as (C). You should not refuel with passengers aboard unless it is absolutely necessary.

26. **(C)** When a drawbridge has an attendant, you do not need to stop, but you must slow down and make sure it is safe. (A) and (B) are incorrect. Since the correct choice is (C), answer (D), none of the above, is incorrect.

27. **(B)** You are not permitted to carry any form of Class A poison on a bus. Thus, both (A) and (C) are incorrect. Liquid Class B poison in any amount is also forbidden, so (D) is incorrect. You may carry a maximum of 100 pounds of solid Class B poison. (B) is correct.

28. **(C)** You do not have to stop at a site where a police officer is directing traffic. You must always stop at drawbridges that do not have signal lights and railroad crossings. (A) and (B) are incorrect. In addition, you must stop at a drawbridge unless it has an attendant controlling traffic or a traffic light that is green when you arrive at the bridge.

29. **(C)** Wait for a gap to open before leaving the stop, even if this means remaining at the stop for some time. Since this is a correct answer, (D) is incorrect. You should not assume that other drivers will stop or give you extra room to merge, even if you honk your horn or use your turn signal. (A) and (B) are incorrect answers.

30. **(D)** All doorways and aisles must be clear of carry-on baggage before driving. This means (C) is incorrect. Neither passengers nor excess baggage can remain in front of the standee line, so (B) is incorrect. (A) is incorrect because passengers may stand on buses if there are no seats remaining.

The Air Brakes Test

See directions on page 195.

1. Air brakes use
   - (A) hot air.
   - (B) cold air.
   - (C) compressed air.
   - (D) decompressed air.

2. Air brake systems are three braking systems combined. They are
   - (A) emergency, service, hand.
   - (B) emergency, parking, service.
   - (C) parking, service, hand.
   - (D) None of the above.

3. Which of the following pumps air into the air storage tanks?
   - (A) Safety valve
   - (B) Air compressor
   - (C) Governor
   - (D) Reservoir

4. The main purpose of the alcohol evaporator is to
   - (A) put alcohol in gas tanks.
   - (B) remove alcohol from the compressor.
   - (C) remove alcohol from the storage tank.
   - (D) put alcohol in the air system.

5. A safety relief valve is installed in the first tank the air compressor pumps air to. The valve is usually set to open at what psi level?
   - (A) 130
   - (B) 140
   - (C) 150
   - (D) 160

6. The most common foundation brake is the
   - (A) wedge brake.
   - (B) S-cam drum brake.
   - (C) disc brake.
   - (D) front brake.

7. Front wheel braking
   - (A) is known for causing skids.
   - (B) is good under all conditions.
   - (C) is the worst on ice.
   - (D) None of the above.

8. The low-air-pressure warning light must come on before the air pressure in the tanks falls below what psi level?
   - (A) 30
   - (B) 40
   - (C) 50
   - (D) 60

9. Spring brakes

   (A) use air pressure to stop the vehicle.

   (B) will not work if all the air leaks out of the air brake system.

   (C) are held by mechanical force.

   (D) will come on fully at 50 psi.

10. Which of the following tells you how much pressure there is in the air tanks?

    (A) Stop light switch

    (B) Application pressure gauge

    (C) Supply pressure gauge

    (D) Low-air-pressure warning signal

11. A front brake limiting valve does which of the following?

    (A) Cuts normal air pressure to the front brakes in half

    (B) Increases the stopping power of the vehicle

    (C) Automatically switches from slippery to normal

    (D) Improves the stopping ability of the rear brakes

12. The braking power of spring brakes depends on

    (A) proper adjustment.

    (B) how far the modulating control lever (if present) is moved.

    (C) traction.

    (D) All of the above.

13. Most newer heavy-duty vehicles use dual air brake systems for safety. A dual air brake system has

    (A) two separate air brake systems and two sets of brake controls.

    (B) two separate air brake systems and a single set of brake controls.

    (C) one air brake system and two sets of brake controls.

    (D) one air brake system and one brake control.

14. Foundation brakes are used

    (A) only in emergencies.   (C) at each wheel.

    (B) when parking.   (D) at each axle.

15. During walkaround inspections of your vehicle, which parts of the air brake system should be checked?

(A)   Manual slack adjusters on S-cam brakes

(B)   Brake drums or discs

(C)   Air hoses connected to brake chambers

(D)   All of the above.

16.   During the walkaround inspection, if a slack adjuster moves slightly more than an inch where the push rod attaches to it, then

(A)   it has the perfect amount of slack.

(B)   it probably needs adjustment.

(C)   the brakes will stop the vehicle very suddenly.

(D)   it will pass roadside inspection.

17.   You have a fully-charged air system (125 psi). After turning off the engine and releasing the service brake, what are the maximum leakage rates per minute for both single and combination vehicles?

(A)   2 psi for single, 3 psi for combination

(B)   3 psi for both

(C)   4 psi for both

(D)   4 psi for single, 5 psi for combination

18.   In checking that the spring brakes come on automatically you should not

(A)   pull the parking brake control knob.

(B)   chock the wheels.

(C)   step on and off the brake pedal.

(D)   shut the engine off.

19.   Which of the following is a proper technique in using controlled braking?

(A)   Putting the brakes on very hard to lock the wheels

(B)   Releasing the brakes if you need to make large steering adjustments

(C)   Pressing harder on the brakes when you feel the wheels sliding

(D)   Turning the steering wheel while braking

20.   Which of the following statements is true?

(A)   Air brakes work as quickly as hydraulic brakes.

(B)   Light and steady braking builds up less heat than on-and-off braking.

(C)   Heated brakes will enable the vehicle to stop more quickly.

(D)   Brake lag distance is not a significant factor on dry pavements.

21. You are driving a vehicle at 55 mph on dry pavement under good traction and brake conditions. What is the approximate total stopping distance needed to bring your vehicle to a complete stop?

    (A) Two-and-a-half-times the length of the vehicle

    (B) Half the length of a football field

    (C) Just over the length of a football field

    (D) The length of the vehicle plus 20 feet

22. If the low-air-pressure warning comes on

    (A) use stab braking until you stop.

    (B) drive to the nearest rest area.

    (C) the vehicle will stop automatically.

    (D) stop your vehicle as quickly as possible and safely park the vehicle.

23. What is another name for "squeeze" braking?

    (A) Stab braking　　　　　　(C) Controlled braking

    (B) Speed braking　　　　　 (D) Test braking

24. When braking on downgrades

    (A) go slow enough so that a light, steady use of brakes keeps you from speeding up.

    (B) brake hard, then let up to cool brakes.

    (C) coast downhill, then apply brakes hard.

    (D) use stab braking until wheels lock, then release.

25. How often should you drain your air tanks?

    (A) Once a week　　　　　　 (C) Twice a week

    (B) At the end of each workday　 (D) Biweekly

26. Which of the following statements is true?

    (A) If you are gone only a short time, you do not need to use the parking brakes or chock the wheels.

    (B) Never leave your vehicle unattended without applying the parking brakes or chocking the wheels.

    (C) It is not necessary to use the parking brake or chock your wheels if you are parked on a flat road surface.

    (D) If you park right after coming down a very steep grade, you should always use the parking brake.

27. When should you not use the parking brakes?
    (A) If the brakes are very hot
    (B) If the brakes are wet during freezing weather
    (C) When testing the spring brakes
    (D) All of the above.

28. What protects the tank and the rest of the air system from too much pressure?
    (A) Safety valve   (C) Treadle valve
    (B) Foot valve   (D) Draining valve

29. Before driving a vehicle with a dual air system, allow time for the air compressor to build up to 100 psi pressure in which of the following?
    (A) The primary system only
    (B) The secondary system only
    (C) Both the primary and secondary systems
    (D) It only has to build to 60 psi pressure in each system.

30. Pressing and releasing the brake pedal quickly and repeatedly
    (A) will stop your vehicle faster.
    (B) will help cool your brakes.
    (C) can let the air out faster than the compressor can replace it.
    (D) pumps air back into the air brake.

THE AIR BRAKES TEST

ANSWER KEY

1.	(C)	16.	(B)
2.	(B)	17.	(A)
3.	(B)	18.	(A)
4.	(D)	19.	(B)
5.	(C)	20.	(B)
6.	(B)	21.	(C)
7.	(B)	22.	(D)
8.	(D)	23.	(C)
9.	(C)	24.	(A)
10.	(C)	25.	(B)
11.	(A)	26.	(B)
12.	(D)	27.	(D)
13.	(B)	28.	(A)
14.	(C)	29.	(C)
15.	(D)	30.	(C)

DETAILED EXPLANATIONS OF ANSWERS
The Air Brakes Test

1. **(C)** Air brakes use compressed air to make the brakes work. This makes (A), (B), and (D) incorrect. Air brakes are a safe way of stopping large vehicles if the brakes are well maintained and used properly.

2. **(B)** The three braking systems in the air brake system are emergency, parking, and service. This makes (A), (C), and (D) incorrect. Some types of brakes are hand controlled, but this is not the name of a component of the air brake system.

3. **(B)** The air compressor pumps air into the air storage tanks. (A) is incorrect because the safety valve protects the tank and the rest of the system from too much pressure. (C) is incorrect because it determines when the air compressor will pump air into the air storage tanks. (D) is simply another name for an air storage tank.

4. **(D)** The main purpose of the alcohol evaporator is to put alcohol in the air system to reduce the risk of ice in the air brake valves. (A) is incorrect because the gas tank is not part of the air brake system. (B) and (C) are incorrect because alcohol removal is not the purpose of the evaporator.

5. **(C)** The psi level is set at 150. At this pressure, air must be released to protect the system from serious damage. Answers (A) and (B) are pressures too low to activate the safety relief valve. Answer (D), 160 psi, is too high for safety.

6. **(B)** The most common foundation brake is the S-cam drum brake. (A) and (C) are less common foundation brakes. (D) is incorrect because foundation brakes are located at each wheel.

7. **(B)** Front-wheel braking is good in all conditions. Tests have shown front-wheel skids from braking are not likely even on ice. This makes (A), (C), and (D) incorrect.

8. **(D)** The warning light must come on when the air pressure falls below 60 psi in the system. (A), (B), and (C) are incorrect because these psi levels are too low to enable you to stop your vehicle easily and safely.

9. **(C)** Spring brakes work by mechanical force. This is a safeguard, so that if the air pressure is too low or all the air leaks out of the system, there will still be a way

to stop the vehicle. Therefore, (A) and (B) are incorrect. (D) is incorrect because it is too high; the spring brakes will come on fully when the air pressure drops to a range of 20-45 psi.

10. **(C)** The supply pressure gauge tells you how much pressure is in the air tanks. (A) is incorrect because the stop light switch turns on your brake lights. (B) is incorrect because the application pressure gauge shows how much air pressure you are applying to the brakes. (D) is incorrect because the warning signal will only tell you when your pressure is below a certain level (usually 60 psi). Otherwise, it will not be activated.

11. **(A)** The front brake limiting valve cuts the air pressure to the front brakes in half. (B) is incorrect because the limiting valve decreases the stopping power of the vehicle. (C) is incorrect because you must switch the control from slippery to normal in order to have normal stopping power. (D) is incorrect because the front brake limiting valve has no effect on the rear brakes.

12. **(D)** All of the above. As with regular brakes, proper adjustment of spring brakes is important to achieving the maximum braking power. The modulating control lever enables you to control braking; the more you move the lever, the harder the brakes come on. Traction is always a factor when braking. On wet or icy roads, braking power will be reduced.

13. **(B)** A dual air brake system has two separate air brake systems, but only a single set of brake controls. This makes (A), (C), and (D) incorrect.

14. **(C)** Foundation brakes are the primary braking system and are used at each wheel to provide equal stopping power on all four wheels. Therefore, (C) is correct and (D) is incorrect. In addition to foundation brakes, trucks, truck tractors, and buses are required to have emergency brakes and parking brakes for use when foundation brakes fail and when parking. Therefore, (A) and (B) are incorrect.

15. **(D)** The walkaround inspection of your vehicle as part of a seven-step inspection procedure is the appropriate time to check items (A), (B), and (C) of the air brake system.

16. **(B)** The slack adjuster probably needs adjustment. This rules out (A). With too much slack, your vehicle will not stop easily and will not pass inspection. Therefore, (C) and (D) are incorrect.

17. **(A)** The maximum leakage rates for single vehicles is 2 psi. For combination vehicles, it is 3 psi. (B) is too high for single vehicles. (C) and (D) are too high for both vehicles.

18. **(A)** To check that the spring brakes will come on automatically, you should chock the wheels, release the parking brake, shut the engine off, and step on and off the brake pedal to reduce the air pressure. Therefore, (B), (C), and (D) are all things you should do as part of this checking procedure. The parking brake control knob should pop out automatically when the air pressure is very low. You should not have to pull it out. Therefore, (A) is correct.

19. **(B)** In controlled braking, you should not allow the wheels to lock by pressing hard on the brakes, so both (A) and (C) are incorrect. You should also turn the steering wheel while braking. If you need to turn the steering wheel, you should release the brakes. (B) is correct, and (D) is incorrect.

20. **(B)** Tests have shown that light, steady braking builds up less heat. This is important to know because heated brakes do not stop as quickly. Answer (C) is incorrect. Brake lag is a feature of air brakes, but not hydraulic brakes, so (A) is incorrect. Because brake lag is always a factor in stopping, (D) is incorrect.

21. **(C)** The approximate total stopping distance needed to bring your vehicle to a complete stop from 55 mph is just over 300 feet, or the length of a football field. Total stopping distance is a function of perception, reaction, brake lag, and effective braking distances.

22. **(D)** Stop your vehicle as quickly as possible and safely park your vehicle. If you keep driving, you may lose all brake power. (B) is incorrect. (A) is incorrect because you should use controlled braking. (C) is incorrect because your vehicle will not automatically stop; rather, the reverse is true. It will take longer to stop.

23. **(C)** Another name for "squeeze" braking is controlled braking. Hence, (A), (B), and (D) are incorrect.

24. **(A)** When braking on downgrades, go slow enough that a light, steady use of brakes keeps you from speeding up. (B) and (C) are incorrect because they will cause hot brakes and might cause brake failure. (D) is incorrect because stab braking locks wheels and should only be used as an emergency method.

25. **(B)** To prevent brake failure, you should drain your air tanks at the end of each workday, even if they are not full. Thus, (A), (C), and (D) are incorrect.

26. **(B)** When you leave your vehicle unattended, always apply parking brakes or chock the wheels. This makes (A) and (C) incorrect. (D) is incorrect because after coming down a steep grade, your brakes will be hot and could be damaged by the heat. It is best to chock the wheels in this case.

27. **(D)** All of the above. Parking brakes can be damaged by the heat. In freezing temperatures, wet brakes can freeze and the vehicle will not be able to move. When testing the spring brakes, you need to release the parking brake so that the knob can pop out when the air pressure drops. (A), (B), and (C) are all correct. In each of these cases, you should chock the wheels in order to prevent your vehicle from rolling.

28. **(A)** The safety relief valve is installed in the first tank the air compressor pumps air into. It protects the tank and the rest of the system from too much pressure. (B) and (C) are incorrect because the foot valve and treadle valve are other names for the brake pedal. (D) is incorrect because the draining valve drains oil and water from inside the air brake system.

29. **(C)** Allow pressure to build to 100 psi in both systems. Watch the air pressure gauges (or needles on a single gauge, if applicable). This makes (A), (B), and (D) incorrect. If you were to drive with 60 psi in either system, the warning light would come on. This pressure is too low to stop quickly.

30. **(C)** Pressing and releasing the brake pedal too much can let out the air faster than the compressor can replace it. It will actually take longer to stop your vehicle because there is less pressure, which makes (A) incorrect. (B) is incorrect because on-and-off braking heats your brakes more quickly than slow, steady braking. The brake pedal does not pump air back into the system; the air compressor does. Thus, (D) also is incorrect.

The Combination Vehicles Test

See directions on page 195.

1. On trailer air lines, the service line is connected to _____ on the trailer(s) to apply more or less pressure to the trailer brakes.
   - (A) the emergency air line
   - (B) relay valves
   - (C) glad hands
   - (D) the air supply control

2. Fully loaded rigs are ____ times more likely to rollover in a crash than empty rigs.
   - (A) 5
   - (B) 10
   - (C) 20
   - (D) 8

3. Failure to keep the _____ lubricated could cause steering problems because of friction between tractor and trailer.
   - (A) trailer protection valve
   - (B) fifth wheel plate
   - (C) glad hands
   - (D) air supply knob

4. If the service and emergency air lines are crossed when hooking up an old trailer, what will happen?
   - (A) You will be able to drive away, but you won't have trailer brakes.
   - (B) The trailer spring brake will release.
   - (C) Nothing will happen.
   - (D) Water and dirt will enter the air lines.

5. When lowering the landing gear of a loaded trailer
   - (A) lower the gear until it makes firm contact with ground.
   - (B) turn the crank in low gear a few extra turns after the landing gear makes firm contact with ground.
   - (C) lift the trailer off the fifth wheel.
   - (D) turn the crank in high gear a few extra turns after the landing gear makes firm contact with ground.

6. The standard following distance behind other vehicles is
   - (A) at least two seconds for each ten feet of vehicle length.
   - (B) at least one second for each twenty feet of vehicle length.

(C)   at least two seconds for each ten feet of vehicle length plus one second if going over 40 mph.

(D)   at least one second for each ten feet of vehicle length plus another second if going over 40 mph.

7.   After the tractor has coupled with the semitrailer, in what position should you put the front trailer supports, or landing gear, before driving away?

(A)   Part way up without the crank handle secured

(B)   Half way up

(C)   Fully raised with the crank handle safely secured

(D)   On the ground

8.   Before you back your tractor under a semitrailer, you should

(A)   lock the trailer brakes.

(B)   lower the air pressure.

(C)   push in the "air supply" knob.

(D)   move the tractor protection valve to "normal."

9.   You are coupling a tractor and semitrailer, and ready to back your trailer under a semitrailer. When is the trailer at the right height?

(A)   When the tractor and semitrailer are even

(B)   When the kingpin is lower than the fifth wheel

(C)   When the trailer is raised slightly by the tractor as the tractor is backed under it

(D)   When the trailer is raised high above the trailer as the tractor is backed under it

10.   Why should the trailer glad hands be locked together or attached to "dead end," or dummy, couplers when not in use?

(A)   To keep dirt out of the lines

(B)   To keep air pressure normal

(C)   To prevent air from escaping

(D)   To keep the service and emergency glad hands from getting mixed up

11.   When coupling a tractor and semitrailer, you must lock the kingpin into the fifth wheel. Which is the best way to check the connection?

(A)   Drive forward.

(B)   Lock the trailer brakes and pull the tractor gently forward.

    (C)   Lock the trailer brakes and pull the tractor quickly forward.

    (D)   Back up and unlock the trailer brake.

12.   When coupling with a semitrailer, back the tractor up
    (A)   at an angle to the trailer.
    (B)   directly in front of the trailer.
    (C)   in front of the right wheel.
    (D)   slightly off the center of the trailer.

13.   When the wheels of a trailer lock up and the trailer begins to swing around _____ is likely to occur.
    (A)   rollover   (C)   trailer jackknife
    (B)   offtracking   (D)   a rear wheel braking skid

14.   When coupling a tractor to a semitrailer, what should you hook up before backing under the trailer?
    (A)   The emergency and service air lines
    (B)   Nothing; you are ready to back up
    (C)   The trailer air supply control
    (D)   The tractor protection valve

15.   When coupling, the fifth wheel jaws should close around the _____ of the kingpin.
    (A)   head   (C)   middle
    (B)   bottom   (D)   shank

16.   Which of the following may happen if the tractor protection valve doesn't work right?
    (A)   An air hose or trailer brake lead could drain all the air from the trailer and possibly cause a loss of control in the vehicle.
    (B)   The pressure may rise in the trailer.
    (C)   Nothing will happen.
    (D)   The engine may shut off.

17.   The tractor protection valve will close automatically if air pressure is low or in the range of
    (A)   0-10 psi   (C)   20-45 psi
    (B)   46 psi or above   (D)   11-19 psi

18. In combination vehicles, the trailer service brake should be tested with the _____ , but controlled in normal operation with the _____ .
    (A) hand valve; foot brake
    (B) trailer air supply control; hand valve
    (C) foot brake; hand valve
    (D) trailer emergency valve; foot brake

19. When parking trailers without spring brakes, use _____ to safely secure the vehicle.
    (A) the emergency brakes   (C) wheel chocks
    (B) the trailer hand brake   (D) the parking brake

20. The earliest and best way to recognize that your trailer has started to skid is by
    (A) seeing it in your mirrors.
    (B) feeling the rig "pull" to the right or left.
    (C) carefully watching how other drivers are reacting to your vehicle.
    (D) periodically applying the brakes to check for traction.

21. How much space should be between the upper and lower fifth wheel after coupling?
    (A) 6 inches   (C) No space
    (B) 1 foot   (D) More than 1 foot

22. Which of the following is a coupling device used to connect the service and emergency air lines from the truck or tractor to the trailer?
    (A) The tractor protection valve   (C) The relay valve
    (B) The trailer air supply control   (D) Glad hands

23. Emergency lines on combination vehicles are often color coded to keep them from getting mixed up. The service lines are coded with the color _____ , and the emergency lines are coded with the color _____ .
    (A) blue ... red   (C) red ... blue
    (B) red ... black   (D) blue ... yellow

24. To supply air to the trailer air tanks in a combination vehicle, you must
    (A) pull out the trailer air supply control.
    (B) press the trailer hand brake.

(C)   open the relay valve.

(D)   push in the trailer supply control.

25.   What are the two purposes of the emergency air line on combination vehicles?

(A)   To supply air to the trailer air tanks and control the emergency brakes

(B)   To control the emergency brakes and carry air controlled by the foot brake

(C)   To carry air which is controlled by the foot brake only

(D)   To supply air to the trailer air tanks and to connect the trailer air tank to the trailer air brakes

26.   The "normal" position of the trailer air supply control is used for

(A)   shutting the air off.

(B)   putting on the trailer emergency brake.

(C)   pulling a trailer.

(D)   parking a trailer.

27.   When should the trailer hand valve be used?

(A)   To park the trailer   (C)   To test the trailer brake

(B)   To drive the trailer   (D)   Only in an emergency

28.   Which of the following is the correct definition of offtracking?

(A)   When a vehicle is turning the corner, the front wheels and rear wheels follow the same path.

(B)   When a vehicle is turning the corner, the front wheels lead the rear wheels around the turn.

(C)   Keeping the front of the rig as close to the curb as possible to avoid entering other lanes.

(D)   When a vehicle is turning the corner, the rear wheels follow a different path than the front wheels.

29.   Your trailer has begun to skid. You should

(A)   use the trailer hand brake to straighten out the rig.

(B)   apply the foot brake hard, and come to a full stop.

(C)   release the foot brake to get traction back.

(D)   turn hard in the direction of the skid.

30. Which of the following reduces the risk of rollover?
    (A) Loading the cargo on one side of the truck only
    (B) Keeping the cargo as close to the ground as possible
    (C) Changing lanes quickly
    (D) None of the above.

THE COMBINATION VEHICLES TEST

ANSWER KEY

1.	(B)		16.	(A)
2.	(B)		17.	(C)
3.	(B)		18.	(A)
4.	(A)		19.	(C)
5.	(B)		20.	(A)
6.	(D)		21.	(C)
7.	(C)		22.	(D)
8.	(A)		23.	(A)
9.	(C)		24.	(D)
10.	(A)		25.	(A)
11.	(B)		26.	(C)
12.	(B)		27.	(C)
13.	(C)		28.	(D)
14.	(A)		29.	(C)
15.	(D)		30.	(B)

DETAILED EXPLANATIONS
OF ANSWERS
The Combination Vehicles Test

1. **(B)** The service line is connected to relay valves on the trailer to apply more or less pressure to the trailer brakes. The relay valves connect the trailer air tanks to the trailer air brakes. (A) is incorrect because the emergency line is a separate line that runs between tractor and trailer. Glad hands connect tractor service and emergency lines to trailer service and emergency lines, so (C) is incorrect. (D) is also incorrect because the air supply control is a knob which controls the tractor protection valve.

2. **(B)** Due to their higher center of gravity, fully loaded rigs are **ten** times more likely to rollover in a crash than empty rigs.

3. **(B)** The **fifth wheel plate** must be greased as required or steering problems caused by friction may result. The trailer protection valve, glad hands, and the air supply knob are all parts of the air brake system. Any malfunction among them would not cause friction and/or steering problems, so answers (A), (C), and (D) are all incorrect.

4. **(A)** If the air lines are crossed when hooking up an old trailer, you will be able to drive away, but you won't have trailer brakes. Because of this, answer (C), nothing will happen, is incorrect. (B) is incorrect because if air lines are crossed, no air is available to release the trailer spring brake. (D) is also incorrect. Water and dirt can only enter the air lines when the lines are not hooked up.

5. **(B)** Turning the crank in low gear a few extra turns will lift some weight off the tractor, making it easier for you to unlatch the fifth wheel and couple the next time. (A) is only true for empty trailers, and therefore is an inappropriate answer choice for this question. Answers (C) and (D) are also incorrect because they list procedures which should specifically not be followed when lowering landing gear.

6. **(D)** The standard following distance behind other vehicles is at least one second for each ten feet of your vehicle length plus another second if you are going over 40 mph. Though safe following distances, (A) and (C) are incorrect choices because they are greater than the standard distance for which the question asks. (B) is also incorrect. One second must be allowed for every ten, not twenty, feet.

7. **(C)** The correct position is fully raised with the crank handle safely secured. Driving without landing gear fully raised may cause the vehicle to catch on railroad tracks or other obstacles, so (A), (B), and (D) are all incorrect.

8. **(A)** Before you back your tractor under a semitrailer, you should lock the trailer brakes. Since air pressure should be normal, not below normal, before coupling, (B) is incorrect. (C) and (D) are also incorrect because the "air supply" knob should be pulled out, and the tractor protection valve control should be in the "emergency" position.

9. **(C)** When coupling a tractor and a semitrailer, the trailer is at the right height when the trailer is raised slightly by the tractor as the tractor backs under it. If the trailer is too low, the tractor may strike and damage the nose of the trailer, so (A) and (B) are incorrect. (D) is incorrect because the trailer may not couple correctly if it is too high.

10. **(A)** Attaching glad hands to dummy couplers or to each other will prevent dirt from getting into the glad hands and the air lines. (B) and (C) are incorrect because glad hands have no bearing on air supply when not attached to air lines. (D) is also incorrect. Glad hands are either color-coded or tagged to keep them from getting mixed up.

11. **(B)** Lock the trailer brakes and pull the tractor gently forward to check that the trailer is locked onto the tractor. (A) is incorrect because the trailer brakes must be locked before you pull the tractor forward. Driving forward quickly is dangerous because if the coupling is not secure the tractor and trailer could become disconnected and damaged, so (C) is incorrect. (D) is incorrect also, because you must attempt to pull the tractor in order to test the coupling.

12. **(B)** To couple correctly, the tractor should be backed up directly in front of the trailer. Never back up under the trailer at an angle. This may push the trailer sideways and break the landing gear. (A), (C), and (D) are all incorrect.

13. **(C)** When the wheels of a trailer lock up and the trailer begins to swing around, **trailer jackknife** usually occurs. Answer (A) is incorrect because rollover results from turning too quickly in a vehicle with a high center of gravity. Offtracking refers to the path the rear wheels of a vehicle follow while going around a turn, so (B) is incorrect. (D) is also incorrect. Rear-wheel braking skids occur when the rear drive wheels, not the trailer wheels, lock.

14. **(A)** The emergency and service air lines must be connected in order to couple; thus, (B) is incorrect. (C) and (D) are also incorrect because both the trailer air supply control and the tractor protection valve do not require any hooking up.

15. **(D)**   The fifth wheel jaws should close around the **shank** of the kingpin. The trailer will not couple correctly otherwise, so (A), (B), and (C) are incorrect.

16. **(A)**   If the tractor protection valve doesn't work correctly, an air hose or trailer brake leak could drain all the air from the tractor, causing the emergency brakes to come on, with possible loss of control. Therefore, (C) is incorrect. The air pressure would fall, not rise, if all the air were drained from the tractor, so (B) is incorrect. (D) is incorrect because the malfunction would not result in the engine's shutting off.

17. **(C)**   The tractor protection valve closes if air pressure is low or within the range of 20 to 45 psi. Answers (A) and (B) are incorrect. Once the tractor protection valve closes, no more air can be lost from the tractor. Therefore, tractor air pressure will never drop below 20 psi. (D) is also incorrect. If air pressure is 46 psi or above, the tractor protection valve will not close.

18. **(A)**   The trailer service brake should be tested with the **hand valve** but operated with the **foot pedal**. (B) is incorrect because the trailer air supply control is not involved in testing the trailer service brake. (C) is incorrect because the responses are in the wrong order. (D) is also incorrect. The trailer emergency valve tests the trailer emergency brake.

19. **(C)**   For safety, you must use **wheel chocks** when you park trailers without spring brakes. Answer (A) is incorrect because the emergency brakes will hold only as long as there is air pressure in the trailer air tank. (B) is incorrect because the trailer hand valve should only be used to test the trailer brakes. (D) is incorrect as well. Those trailers without spring brakes also have no parking brake.

20. **(A)**   While pulling a trailer, check the mirrors often to make sure the trailer is staying where it should. This is the best way to recognize trailer skids because you will always be able to see trailer movement before you can feel it. Because of this, answer (B) is incorrect. (C) is incorrect because you should never rely on other drivers to give you information about your own vehicle. (D) is also incorrect. If your trailer has begun to skid, applying the brakes will only cause more traction to be lost.

21. **(C)**   There should be **no space** between the upper and lower fifth wheel after coupling. If there is any amount of space, the kingpin may be in the wrong place and the tractor could come loose very easily. Answers (A), (B), and (D) are all incorrect.

22. **(D)**   Glad hands connect the service and emergency air lines from the truck or tractor to the trailer. Since the tractor protection valve keeps air in the truck or tractor, (A) is incorrect. The trailer air supply control controls the tractor protec-

tion valve, so (B) is incorrect. (C) is incorrect because the relay valve connects the trailer air tanks to the trailer air brakes.

23. **(A)** Service lines are coded blue; emergency lines are coded red. Since these are the standard codes, all other color combinations are incorrect. Answers (B), (C), and (D) are incorrect.

24. **(D)** Because **pushing in** the trailer air supply control supplies air to the trailer air tanks, answer (A), pulling out the control, is incorrect. Pressing the trailer hand brake causes pressure in the service line to change, so (B) is incorrect. The relay valve sends air pressure from the trailer air tanks to the trailer brake chambers, thus (C) is incorrect.

25. **(A)** The emergency air line supplies air to the trailer air tanks and controls the emergency brake. Answers (B) and (C) are incorrect because the service air line carries the air which is controlled by the foot brake. (D) is incorrect because the relay valve connects the trailer air tank to the trailer air brakes.

26. **(C)** The "normal" position is used for pulling a trailer. The "emergency" position is used for shutting the air off and putting on the trailer emergency brakes, so (A) and (B) are incorrect. (D) is also incorrect. The air supply control has nothing to do with parking the trailer.

27. **(C)** The trailer hand valve should be used only to test the trailer brake. It should never be used for parking because all the air might leak out, unlocking the brakes in trailers that do not have spring brakes. Therefore, answer (A) is incorrect. Since using the trailer hand valve while driving may cause the trailer to skid, (B) is incorrect. (D) is incorrect because the valve should not be used except to test the trailer brake.

28. **(D)** When a vehicle goes around a corner, the rear wheels follow a different path than the front wheels. This action is called offtracking. Since offtracking causes the path followed by a tractor-semi to be wider than the rig itself, answers (A) and (B) are incorrect. Answer (C) is also incorrect. You must turn the front end of the vehicle wide when going around a corner so that the rear end does not go up on the curb.

29. **(C)** Releasing the foot brake allows the trailer wheels to grip the road and regain traction. The trailer will then start to follow the tractor and straighten out. Answer (A) is incorrect because the brakes on the trailer wheels caused the skid in the first place. A hard application of the foot brake will only cause the trailer to lose more traction, so (B) is incorrect. (D) is incorrect because you should maintain the

forward movement of the tractor while waiting for the trailer to regain traction and follow the tractor.

30. **(B)** To reduce the risk of rollover, keep the cargo as close to the ground as possible. This is done by spreading out the cargo so that its weight is centered on the vehicle and by loading heavy cargo under light cargo. Since loading the cargo on one side of the truck makes the trailer lean, thereby increasing the risk of rollover, (A) is incorrect. (C) is also incorrect. Changing lanes quickly causes a "crack-the-whip" effect and increases the risk of rollover. Since (B) is the correct answer, (D), none of the above, is an inappropriate choice.

The Hazardous Materials Test

See directions on page 195.

1. If a shipment contains hazardous materials requiring placards, who is responsible for placarding the vehicle?

   (A) The shipper

   (B) The carrier

   (C) The driver

   (D) A law enforcement officer

2. You have had an accident while transporting hazardous materials. In which of the following circumstances must you or your employer phone the National Response Center?

   (A) A person is killed as a result of the accident.

   (B) A person suffers a minor injury as a result of the accident and is treated at the scene.

   (C) Estimated property damage of $10,000 occurs as a result of the accident.

   (D) All of the above.

3. Besides the material's hazard class, what else determines which placards you must use?

   (A) The cost of the material

   (B) The distance you are traveling

   (C) The weight of your vehicle

   (D) The amount of material being shipped

4. You must carry with you a written route plan when transporting

   (A) Division 1.1 explosives.

   (B) Division 1.1, 1.2, or 1.3 explosives.

   (C) Division 1.4 explosives.

   (D) radioactive materials.

5. Your vehicle is involved in a collision while you are transporting explosives. Which of the following is a proper thing to do?

   (A) Separate the vehicles from each other, and then remove the explosives from your vehicle.

   (B) Place the explosives at least 100 feet from the vehicles and occupied buildings.

   (C) Get bystanders to assist you in emptying your vehicle.

   (D) None of the above.

6. The person watching someone load or unload a cargo tank must be within ____ feet of the tank.

(A) 10   (C) 25

(B) 20   (D) 50

7. With which division(s) of explosives must you use a floor lining?

(A) 4.1

(B) 1.1, 1.2, and 1.3

(C) 6.1

(D) 2.1, 2.2, and 2.3

8. Your load contains 10 pounds of radioactive material, 500 pounds of flammable gas, and 1,000 pounds of nonflammable gas. What placards do you need?

(A) RADIOACTIVE, NONFLAMMABLE GAS

(B) RADIOACTIVE, FLAMMABLE GAS

(C) RADIOACTIVE, FLAMMABLE GAS, NONFLAMMABLE GAS

(D) NONFLAMMABLE GAS

9. You should not smoke or carry a lighted cigarette, cigar, or pipe within 25 feet of any vehicle that contains

(A) explosives.   (C) flammables.

(B) oxidizers.   (D) All of the above.

10. Which three classes of hazardous materials should not be loaded in a cargo space that has a heater?

(A) Explosives, flammable gases, oxidizers

(B) Flammable gases, flammable liquids, flammable solids

(C) Explosives, flammable gases, flammable liquids

(D) Flammable gases, flammable liquids, oxidizers

11. A placarded vehicle must have ____ identical placards.

(A) 2   (C) 4

(B) 3   (D) 5

12. If you discover a cargo leak, what should you do?

(A) Try to find the source of the leak by smell.

(B) Identify the material by using shipping papers, labels, or package location.

(C) Stay in your vehicle until help comes.

(D) Park upwind of people and buildings.

13. You discover a fire in your vehicle while transporting hazardous materials. Which of the following is a proper procedure?

(A) Put the shipping papers in the driver's door and leave the vehicle.

(B) Run for help.

(C) Feel the cargo doors to see if they are hot.

(D) Use a fire extinguisher to fight a cargo fire.

14. You should not transport substances that are "Forbidden." In which column of the Hazardous Materials Table should you look to determine if a material you have been given by a shipper is forbidden?

(A) Column 1, "+/A/W"

(B) Column 3, "Hazard class"

(C) Column 3a, "Identification number"

(D) Column 4, "Label(s) required"

15. Under which of the following circumstances must you stop before crossing railroad tracks?

(A) Your vehicle has an OXYGEN placard.

(B) Your vehicle has empty cargo tanks.

(C) You are carrying chlorine.

(D) All of the above.

16. For any package labeled INHALATION HAZARD, the vehicle transporting that package must have _____ placards.

(A) POISON   (C) OXIDIZER

(B) DANGEROUS   (D) OXYGEN

17. What does the transport index on a package label tell you?

(A) How much the package weighs

(B) The degree of control needed during transport

(C) The reportable quantity for a spill

(D) How far the package can be transported safely

18. You are transporting Division 1.1 explosives and you need to park and leave your vehicle. You may let someone else watch your vehicle if your vehicle is

    (A) parked on a bridge.

    (B) carrying less than 100 pounds of Division 1.1 explosives.

    (C) parked for less than 20 minutes.

    (D) parked on the shipper's property.

19. What does a star after an entry in the List of Hazardous Substances and Reportable Quantities mean?

    (A) This substance is not hazardous.

    (B) This substance is extremely hazardous.

    (C) This substance also appears in the Hazardous Materials Table.

    (D) This substance is a poison.

20. Corrosive liquids should never be loaded next to or above

    (A) Class A explosives.   (C) oxidizing materials.

    (B) flammable solids.   (D) All of the above.

21. You cannot have overhang or tailgate loads of

    (A) explosives, flammable solids, or oxidizing materials.

    (B) explosives, flammable liquids, or oxidizing materials.

    (C) explosives, flammable solids, or flammable liquids.

    (D) flammable solids, flammable liquids, or oxidizing materials.

22. A package labeled _____ should not be loaded in the driver's cab or sleeper.

    (A) POISON, POISON GAS, or IRRITANT

    (B) POISON or POISON GAS

    (C) POISON GAS or IRRITANT

    (D) POISON or IRRITANT

23. If you are transporting hazardous cargo, what is an acceptable place to keep the shipping papers?

    (A) In a pouch in the driver's door

    (B) Anywhere within reach and within view

    (C) On the driver's seat when you are not in the vehicle

    (D) All of the above.

24. The _____ pays for the cleanup of contaminated parking lots, road-ways, and drainage ditches caused by cargo leakage.
    (A) shipper
    (B) carrier
    (C) driver
    (D) Department of Transportation

25. Which of the following combinations of materials in the same vehicle is al-lowed?
    (A) Poison A and organic peroxide
    (B) Division 1.1 (Class A) explosives and charged storage batteries
    (C) Silver cyanide and battery acid
    (D) None of the above.

26. You are transporting Class B explosives and your vehicle breaks down. What should you use to signal for help?
    (A) Fusees
    (B) Yellow electric lights
    (C) Reflective triangles
    (D) Flares

27. In order to determine which placards you must use for a particular hazard-ous material, which column of the Hazardous Materials Table should you check?
    (A) Column 2, "Hazard materials descriptions and proper shipping names"
    (B) Column 3, "Hazard class"
    (C) Column 3a, "Identification number"
    (D) Column 4, "Label(s) required"

28. A driver transporting _____ in cargo tanks must have an approved gas mask in the vehicle.
    (A) chlorine
    (B) carbon dioxide
    (C) oxygen
    (D) gasoline

29. If hazardous material is spilling from your vehicle, what should you do?
    (A) Drive to the nearest truck stop and get help.
    (B) Drive to the nearest phone booth and call for help.
    (C) Park your vehicle and go for help.
    (D) Park your vehicle and send someone else for help.

30. You are transporting hazardous materials in a vehicle with dual tires and have just checked your tires for proper inflation. How soon must you stop and check your tire pressure again?

(A) In 1 hour

(B) In 3 hours

(C) In 50 miles

(D) In 2 hours or 100 miles, whichever is less

THE HAZARDOUS MATERIALS TEST

ANSWER KEY

1.	(C)	16.	(A)
2.	(A)	17.	(B)
3.	(D)	18.	(D)
4.	(B)	19.	(C)
5.	(D)	20.	(D)
6.	(C)	21.	(A)
7.	(B)	22.	(A)
8.	(A)	23.	(D)
9.	(D)	24.	(B)
10.	(C)	25.	(D)
11.	(C)	26.	(C)
12.	(B)	27.	(B)
13.	(C)	28.	(A)
14.	(B)	29.	(D)
15.	(D)	30.	(D)

DETAILED EXPLANATIONS
OF ANSWERS
The Hazardous Materials Test

1. **(C)** The shipper, carrier, and driver each have different responsibilities when hazardous materials are involved. The shipper packages the material and supplies placards and the carrier verifies that packages are labeled correctly, but it is the responsibility of the driver to placard the vehicle properly. Therefore, answers (A) and (B) are incorrect, and answer (C) is correct. Law enforcement officers are not involved in the packaging process, though they may inspect your vehicle. Therefore, answer (D) is incorrect.

2. **(A)** The National Response Center helps coordinate emergency response to chemical hazards. When someone is killed in an accident involving hazardous materials, you or your employer must phone the National Response Center. Therefore, answer (A) is correct. Answer (B) is incorrect. If a person receives injuries that require hospitalization, the National Response Center must be phoned, but if injuries are minor and the person is only treated at the scene, this is not necessary. Answer (C) is also incorrect because unless estimated property damages exceed $50,000, it is not necessary to phone the National Response Center. Since answers (B) and (C) are incorrect, answer (D), all of the above, is also incorrect.

3. **(D)** Placarding is a safety measure intended to warn others of the hazards associated with a vehicle transporting certain materials. Since some substances are designated as hazardous only when large enough quantities are being carried, answer (D) is correct. The cost of the material does not make the material more hazardous and does not affect placarding, so answer (A) is incorrect. Placarding is determined only by properties of the material being shipped, not by factors of the vehicle such as the distance it is traveling or the vehicle's weight. Therefore, answers (B) and (C) are also incorrect.

4. **(B)** Because of the dangers associated with Division 1.1, 1.2, and 1.3 explosives, a written route plan is necessary so that the safest delivery route can be established and followed. Answer (A), Division 1.1 explosives, is incorrect because it is incomplete. Answer (C) refers to a class of explosives for which a written route plan is not necessary, so it is also incorrect. Although the carrier must choose the safest route for transporting radioactive materials and must show this route to the driver, a written route plan is not required and answer (D) is incorrect.

5. **(D)** Answers (A), (B), and (C) are all incorrect. Answer (A) is incorrect because you should remove the explosives from your vehicle before separating the vehicles from each other. Answer (B) is incorrect because explosives should be placed at least 200 feet from the vehicles and occupied buildings. Answer (C) is incorrect because you should keep bystanders **away** from the vehicles, not ask them to come closer and endanger their lives. Since none of the choices given here is correct, the proper answer is (D), none of the above.

6. **(C)** Regulations specify how close a person supervising loading must be in order to have an adequate view of the loading process. While an observer 10 or 20 feet away from the tank is within the limit, the maximum allowable distance is 25 feet. Any distance greater than this is too far to see clearly. Therefore, answer (C) is the best choice.

7. **(B)** Answer (B) is correct because these are class A and B explosives and therefore must be placed on a liner that is either non-metallic material or non-ferrous metal. Answer (A) is incorrect because a division 4.1 material is a flammable solid. Answer (C) is wrong because Division 6.1 material is a poison, and (D) is wrong because divisions 2.1, 2.2, and 2.3 are gasses. None of these requires a floor lining when being transported.

8. **(A)** Radioactive materials in any amount require placards. Therefore, answer (D) is not correct. Flammable and nonflammable gases require placarding only if your vehicle contains 1,000 pounds or more of that hazard class. Since your load of flammable gas is less than 1,000 pounds, you do not need a placard for this, and answers (B) and (C) are incorrect. You do have 1,000 pounds of nonflammable gas, which requires placarding, so answer (A) is correct.

9. **(D)** Because of the risk associated with having a lit cigarette, cigar, or pipe near materials that can ignite or explode easily, regulations require that you keep such items at least 25 feet away from materials classified as explosives, oxidizers, or flammables. Since all three of these hazard classes are given as choices for this question, answer (D), all of the above, is the best choice.

10. **(C)** Regulations specify that for explosives, flammable gases, and flammable liquids, you must not use cargo space that has a cargo heater, including automatic cargo heater/air conditioner units. Answer (C) lists these hazard classes and is correct. Answer (A) and answer (D) list oxidizers and answer (B) lists flammable solids. These are hazard classes that are not specified in the rules concerning cargo heaters, and therefore, these answers are incorrect.

11. **(C)** A placarded vehicle must have placards on the front, the rear, and each side of the vehicle so that someone approaching the vehicle from any direction

can tell what hazardous materials the vehicle contains. For this reason, the proper number of placards is 4. Answers (A) and (B) are insufficient. Since a fifth placard is not necessary, answer (D) is incorrect.

12. **(B)**   Some substances are hazardous or fatal when not safely packaged. For this reason, if you discover a cargo leak, you should not remain in your vehicle or attempt to find the source of the leak by smell. Answers (A) and (C) are incorrect. If you park upwind of people and buildings, any harmful gaseous substances will be carried to where they are. Therefore, you should park **downwind**, and answer (D) is incorrect. Identifying the leaking material by using shipping papers, labels, or package location is a safe and proper technique. Answer (B) is correct.

13. **(C)**   If there is a fire in your vehicle, you should stop your vehicle and get out, taking your shipping papers with you so that you can give them to emergency personnel. Therefore, answer (A) is incorrect. You should not leave your vehicle unattended but should stay and watch it and send someone else for help. Answer (B) is incorrect. Using a fire extinguisher is proper procedure for small fires that have not reached your cargo, but if your cargo is on fire, you should not try to put the fire out. Therefore, answer (D) is incorrect. To determine whether your cargo is on fire, you should feel the cargo doors. If they are hot, it is possible that your cargo is on fire, and you should not open the doors, as this will feed the fire. Answer (C) is a proper procedure when you discover a fire in your vehicle.

14. **(B)**   Column 3 contains the material's hazard class, which you should use to determine which placards you must place on your vehicle. If a hazard class is not given for the material, the word "Forbidden" will appear in this column. Therefore, answer (B) is correct. Column 1 is used to set the shipping name of the material and to note whether the material is regulated if shipped by air or water. Column 3a gives the identification number for the hazardous material. Column 4 tells the shipper which labels to place on the packaged materials. The word "Forbidden" will not appear in any of these columns, and therefore answers (A), (C), and (D) are incorrect.

15. **(D)**   You must stop before crossing railroad tracks if your vehicle has any placards, so answer (A) is correct. You must also stop if your vehicle has cargo tanks, whether they are empty or full. Answer (B) is also correct. Finally, whenever you are carrying chlorine, you must stop before crossing railroad tracks, so answer (C) is also correct. Since all three choices are correct, the answer is (D), all of the above.

16. **(A)**   Regulations specify that if a package is an inhalation hazard, a poison placard is required in addition to any other placards needed. Answer (A) is correct. The other placards required are determined by the material's hazard class and

amount. Since these may vary, answers (B), (C), and (D) are incorrect. The only placard **always** required for an inhalation hazard is a poison placard.

17. **(B)** The purpose of the transport index is to control the amount of certain substances (such as radioactive materials) that are contained in one location and to determine how close to people, animals, and unexposed film these packages can be placed. These are determined by the transport index, so answer (B) is correct. Answer (A), the package's weight, can also be found on the package label, but it is not the same as the transport index. Reportable quantities are given in the List of Hazardous Substances and Reportable Quantities, not on package labels, so answer (C) is incorrect. How far a package can be transported safely does not depend on the transport index, so answer (D) is incorrect.

18. **(D)** Because of the dangers associated with Division 1.1 explosives, it is only acceptable to allow someone else to watch your vehicle if your vehicle is on the shipper's, carrier's, or consignee's property. Parking on private property other than such sites is not allowed unless you warn the owner of the risk. Parking on a bridge, answer (A), is permitted only when your work requires it, but it is not a condition under which you can leave your vehicle attended by someone else. The amount of explosive, answer (B), and the amount of time you will be gone, answer (C), are not correct, because any amount of Division 1.1 explosive can be dangerous, and an accident can occur in any length of time, no matter how short.

19. **(C)** The list of Hazardous Substances and Reportable Quantities is distinct from the Hazardous Materials Table. Not every hazardous substance will appear in the Hazardous Materials Table, but those that do are identified by a star after the name. Therefore, answer (C) is correct. Only hazardous substances appear in the List of Hazardous Substances and Reportable Quantities, so answer (A) cannot be correct. Answer (B), a statement about the relative danger of a hazardous substance, can be determined approximately by noting the reportable quantity of the substance, but not by whether an entry is starred or not. Therefore, this answer is incorrect. The List of Hazardous Substances and Reportable Quantities does not provide information about hazard classes (such as poisons), so answer (D) is incorrect.

20. **(D)** All three of the hazard classes listed here are substances that should not be loaded next to or below corrosive materials due to the hazards that might occur if they came into contact. Since Class A explosives, flammable solids, and oxidizing materials are all correct, answer (D), all of the above, is the proper choice.

21. **(A)** Regulations specify that explosives, flammable solids, and oxidizing materials must be loaded in a closed cargo space unless the packages are fire- and

water-resistant or are covered with a fire- and water-resistant tarp. Since answer (A) lists these three hazard classes, it is correct. Answers (B), (C), and (D) list flammable liquids, which are not specified as substances that must be transported in a closed cargo space, so these answers are incorrect.

22. **(A)** A package labeled with any of these three labels should not be loaded in the driver's cab or sleeper due to the hazards associated with being in close contact with these substances. Although answers (B), (C), and (D) contain items that should not be loaded in the cab or sleeper, they are not inclusive. For this reason, these answers are all incorrect.

23. **(D)** While you are in the vehicle, the shipping papers must be either in a pouch in your door or in any place where you can reach them while wearing your seatbelt and where they are in clear view. Therefore, both answers (A) and (B) are correct. When you are not in your vehicle, your shipping papers should be left in the vehicle in a place where they can be seen easily. The driver's seat is a good location. Therefore, answer (C) is also correct. Since all three choices are acceptable, the proper answer is (D), all of the above.

24. **(B)** If decontamination is required after cargo has leaked from a vehicle, the carrier must pay the expenses, because once a carrier accepts a shipment from the shipper it is his responsibility until it reaches its destination. For this reason, answers (A), (C), and (D) are incorrect.

25. **(D)** Because certain combinations of substances are very dangerous, regulations forbid the placement of these substances in the same vehicle. Choices (A), (B), and (C) are all examples of forbidden combinations. Since none of these combinations is allowed, the correct answer is (D), none of the above.

26. **(C)** Since it is dangerous to have explosives near flame or heat, answers (A), fusees, and (D), flares, are incorrect. Red electric lights, not yellow ones, or reflective triangles are appropriate signals. Therefore, answer (B), yellow electric lights, is incorrect, and answer (C) is the proper choice.

27. **(B)** The placards required are determined by a material's hazard class, which is given in column 3. Column 2 gives the proper shipping name to be placed on the shipping paper, but this does not appear on the placard. Therefore, answer (A) is incorrect. Column 3a gives the identification number for the particular substance, but placards are associated with hazard classes, not particular substances, so this column is not the correct one to look at for this information, and answer (C) is incorrect. Column 4 gives information about labeling the package, not the vehicle, so answer (D) is also incorrect.

28. **(A)**   Because of the dangers associated with inhaling chlorine fumes, you must carry a gas mask with you in the vehicle when transporting chlorine. Carbon dioxide, oxygen, and gasoline do not require such precautions, so answers (B), (C), and (D) are incorrect.

29. **(D)**   If you have a leak of hazardous material, you should stop as soon as safety permits. Driving to a truck stop or a phone booth with a cargo leak will cause you to spread the hazard further than is necessary, so answers (A) and (B) are incorrect. When you park your vehicle, you should stay with it and send someone else for help. For this reason, answer (C) is incorrect and answer (D) is the best choice.

30. **(D)**   Answers (A), 1 hour, and (C), 50 miles, are too small. Answer (B), 3 hours, is too long to wait before rechecking. To ensure that your tires are properly inflated at all times, you must stop and check your tires every 2 hours or 100 miles, whichever is less. The correct answer is (D).

The Tanker Test

See directions on page 195.

1. Tankers carrying liquids can _____ more easily than other vehicles.
    (A) stop   (C) turn
    (B) ascend a hill   (D) roll over

2. Which of the following is an unbaffled liquid tanker most likely to be carry-ing?
    (A) Milk   (C) Liquid nitrogen
    (B) Gasoline   (D) Dry cement

3. A tank vehicle is a vehicle used to transport
    (A) hazardous liquids.
    (B) gasoline or other petroleum products.
    (C) any liquid or liquefied gaseous material.
    (D) military equipment.

4. What device divides a liquid tank into several smaller tanks?
    (A) A baffle   (C) A bulkhead
    (B) A smooth bore   (D) None of the above.

5. You need special skills if you are hauling liquids because of
    (A) the loaded tanker's low center of gravity.
    (B) the movement of liquid in the tank.
    (C) the weight of the vehicle.
    (D) the length of the vehicle.

6. Compared to a low-profile tank, a conventional tank is always
    (A) wider.   (C) heavier.
    (B) safer.   (D) more top-heavy.

7. What is outage?
    (A) The room to be allowed in a tank above the liquid load for expansion
    (B) Liquid that is travelling through a bulkhead between two small tanks
    (C) Liquid that is leaking from a liquid tanker
    (D) The horsepower required to haul a liquid tanker

8. Tests have shown that tankers can turn over
   (A) when taking a curve above the posted speed.
   (B) when taking a curve at the posted speed.
   (C) while driving on icy roads.
   (D) while being loaded.

9. Why do baffles make handling a liquid tank vehicle easier?
   (A) They lower the center of gravity.
   (B) They put more weight on the front and rear of the vehicle.
   (C) They help control side-to-side surge.
   (D) They help control forward and backward surge.

10. You are filling a liquid tanker. Besides the outage requirement, what else must you consider in determining the amount of liquid you can legally carry?
    (A) Whether the tanker is baffled or unbaffled
    (B) The speed you will be traveling
    (C) The distance you will be traveling
    (D) The weight of the liquid

For questions 11–14, refer to this figure.

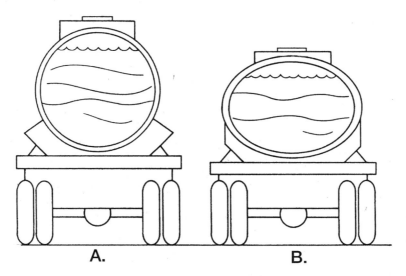

A.   B.

11. Tank B is called a
    (A) round-bodied tank.   (C) low-profile tank.
    (B) conventional tank.   (D) low-capacity tank.

12. Which of the following is a true statement?
    (A) Tank A has a lower center of gravity than Tank B.
    (B) Tank A is safer than Tank B.
    (C) Tank A will be less likely to roll over when taking curves.
    (D) None of the above.

13. Tank A was moving forward and has just stopped. The liquid surge will push the tank first in which direction?
    (A) Forward   (C) To the left
    (B) Backward   (D) To the right

14. Tank A and Tank B are the same length. Which of the following is true?
    (A) Tank A can carry more liquid than Tank B.
    (B) Tank B can carry more liquid than Tank A.
    (C) Tank A and Tank B can carry the same number of gallons.
    (D) Tank A will require more outage than Tank B.

15. An unbaffled tank is also called a
    (A) liquid tank.   (C) low-profile tank.
    (B) conventional tank.   (D) smoothbore tank.

16. When carrying liquids, you should take an off-ramp curve at a speed
    (A) well below the posted speed.   (C) at the posted speed.
    (B) slightly below the posted speed. (D) slightly above the posted speed.

17. A portable tank having a capacity of at least _____ is considered a tank vehicle.
    (A) 100 pounds   (C) 100 gallons
    (B) 1,000 pounds   (D) 1,000 gallons

18. The amount of liquid you can legally carry does **not** depend on
    (A) the amount the liquid will expand in transit.
    (B) legal weight limits.
    (C) the distance to be traveled.
    (D) the liquid's weight.

19. Which of the following is more dangerous when driving an unbaffled tank than when driving a baffled tank?
     (A) Changing lanes on a highway
     (B) Leaving the highway via a curved off-ramp
     (C) Going up a steep hill
     (D) Stopping suddenly

20. What is surge?
     (A) Acceleration of a truck caused by movement of its load
     (B) Movement of liquid in a partially filled tanker
     (C) The amount a liquid expands when heated
     (D) None of the above.

21. A tank vehicle's high center of gravity makes which of the following especially dangerous?
     (A) Driving on wet roads
     (B) Coming to a stop
     (C) Going uphill
     (D) Taking highway curves

22. Forward and backward surge is especially strong when a tanker is
     (A) baffled.   (C) turning a corner.
     (B) unbaffled.   (D) going up a hill.

23. When you are coming to a sudden stop, the liquid in a tanker will
     (A) splash up and down.   (C) surge backward and forward.
     (B) surge from side to side.   (D) stop moving suddenly.

24. Sanitation regulations forbid the use of baffles when transporting food products. Why?
     (A) Because baffles would increase the motion of the liquid.
     (B) Because an unbaffled tank can be driven at higher speeds and less time will be needed for transporting the load.
     (C) Because of the difficulty of cleaning the inside of a baffled tank.
     (D) None of the above.

25. When a tank vehicle comes to a stop, liquid will surge back and forth. When the wave hits one end of the tank, the truck will
    (A) be pushed in the direction the wave was moving.
    (B) be pushed in the direction opposite the direction the wave was moving.
    (C) roll over.
    (D) None of the above.

26. When loading a 5-compartment tank with different liquids, which of the following should you do?
    (A) Fill each compartment as full as possible.
    (B) Fill the first compartment highest.
    (C) Fill the last compartment highest.
    (D) Distribute the weight evenly.

For questions 27–30, refer to this figure.

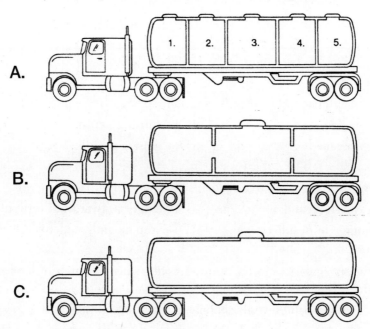

27. Which tank in the figure above is specially designed to reduce liquid surge?
    (A) Tank A   (C) Tank C
    (B) Tank B   (D) All of the above.

28. The design of Tank B will not affect handling in which circumstance?

    (A) Stopping (C) Turning

    (B) Starting (D) Accelerating

29. You are loading 3 different liquids that must not be mixed into Tank A. Which 3 compartments should you use?

    (A) Compartments 1, 3, and 5 (C) Compartments 1, 2, and 3

    (B) Compartments 2, 3, and 4 (D) Compartments 3, 4, and 5

30. Which of the following would Tank B be least likely to carry?

    (A) Liquid propane (C) Gasoline

    (B) Acid (D) Orange juice

THE TANKER TEST

ANSWER KEY

1.	(D)	16.	(A)
2.	(A)	17.	(D)
3.	(C)	18.	(C)
4.	(C)	19.	(D)
5.	(B)	20.	(B)
6.	(D)	21.	(D)
7.	(A)	22.	(B)
8.	(B)	23.	(C)
9.	(D)	24.	(C)
10.	(D)	25.	(A)
11.	(C)	26.	(D)
12.	(D)	27.	(B)
13.	(A)	28.	(C)
14.	(C)	29.	(A)
15.	(D)	30.	(D)

DETAILED EXPLANATIONS OF ANSWERS
The Tanker Test

1. **(D)** Tankers carrying liquids can roll over more easily than other vehicles. This is because of the tanker's higher center of gravity and because of liquid surge. Since liquid surge also makes it more difficult to stop or turn a liquid tanker, answers (A) and (B) are incorrect. Because of the tanker's weight, it is difficult for a tanker to climb a hill, so answer (C) is incorrect.

2. **(A)** Sanitation regulations do not permit the use of baffles because these make cleaning the tank more difficult. Therefore, of the choices given here, milk, a food product, would be the most likely load in an unbaffled tanker. Since baffles make a tanker easier to handle, other liquid products, such as gasoline [answer (B)] and liquid nitrogen [answer (C)], would be more likely to be transported in a tank with baffles. Since answer (D) is not a liquid, it is incorrect.

3. **(C)** This is a definition of a tank vehicle. Answer (A), hazardous liquids, and answer (B), gasoline or other petroleum products, are too specific, since a tank vehicle can be used to transport nonhazardous liquids and products other than petroleum. Answer (D), military equipment, is not correct, because it does not fit the definition of materials that can be transported in a tank vehicle.

4. **(C)** A baffle is a bulkhead with holes; it doesn't divide a tank into smaller tanks, but slows the flow of liquid within a single tank, so answer (A) is incorrect. A smoothbore is another name for an unbaffled tank. This means that a smoothbore liquid tank is undivided, so answer (B) is incorrect. Since answer (C), a bulkhead, is the correct answer, answer (D), none of the above, should not be chosen.

5. **(B)** Movement of liquid in the tank, called liquid surge, can make handling the vehicle difficult. A loaded tank has a high center of gravity, not a low one, so answer (A) is incorrect. Answers (C) and (D), the weight of the vehicle and the length of the vehicle, are true of **any** loaded vehicle, not only one transporting liquids. Since this question asks about special skills for carrying liquids, these answers are incorrect.

6. **(D)** Because a conventional tank is taller than a low-profile tank, it carries its load higher, and this makes it more top-heavy. Therefore, answer (D) is correct. A low-profile tank is wider than a conventional tank, so answer (A) is incorrect.

Since a conventional tank is more top-heavy, it will be harder to handle (and therefore less safe) in some situations than a less top-heavy one, so answer (B) is incorrect. Finally, although a conventional tank distributes weight differently than a low-profile tank, it is not necessarily heavier, so answer (C) is incorrect.

7. **(A)** Since liquids expand as they warm, space must be left above the liquid when it is loaded into a tank. This space is defined as outage. Liquid cannot travel through a bulkhead between two small tanks, so answer (B) cannot be correct. Answers (C) and (D) are not formally defined, so they are both incorrect.

8. **(B)** Since it is illegal to travel faster than posted speeds, it would not be necessary to test tanker handling under these conditions. Answer (A) is incorrect. Answer (B) is correct because under conditions that would be expected to be safe, tests showed that these conditions were not safe for tankers carrying liquids. No tests were reported for conditions (C) and (D) and these answers are incorrect.

9. **(D)** Baffles partially divide a tank from front to rear. Liquid movement backward and forward is slowed because the liquid has to pass through small openings. Answer (D) is correct. Baffles do not affect the center of gravity, so answer (A) is incorrect. Since baffles help minimize the movement of liquid to the front and rear of the vehicle, they do not put more weight in these areas, and answer (B) is incorrect. Baffles have no effect on side-to-side surge. This kind of movement is still dangerous when handling a baffled liquid tank vehicle, and answer (C) is incorrect.

10. **(D)** If you fill a tank with a very dense liquid, you may exceed legal weight limits, so you must know the weight of the liquid. Answer (D) is correct. Whether a tanker is baffled or unbaffled may affect your handling of the vehicle, but it does not determine the amount of liquid you can legally carry, so answer (A) is incorrect. The speed and distance you will be traveling are also not factors in determining how much liquid you can legally carry, so answers (B) and (C) are also incorrect.

11. **(C)** Tank B is called a low-profile tank because, compared to a conventional tank as depicted by Tank A, it is closer to the ground (it presents a low profile). Therefore, answer (C) is correct and answer (B) is incorrect. Since Tank B is much wider than it is tall, it is not a round-bodied tank and answer (A) is incorrect. The capacity of the tank is not affected by its shape as shown in these pictures, so it is not correct to call Tank B a low-capacity tank, and answer (D) is also incorrect.

12. **(D)** Because Tank A is taller than Tank B, its load is carried higher and it has a higher center of gravity than Tank B. Therefore, answer (A) is incorrect. This height and higher center of gravity makes Tank A more difficult to handle on curves and therefore less safe under these conditions than Tank B, so both answer (B) and

answer (C) are incorrect. Since none of the given statements are true, the proper answer is (D), none of the above.

13. **(A)**   Liquid surges first in the direction in which the vehicle has been moving. Since the vehicle has been traveling forward, the liquid will surge forward first, pushing the vehicle in this direction. Therefore, answer (A) is correct. Answer (B) is incorrect because the liquid will surge backward only after it has reached the front of the tank. Answers (C) and (D) are incorrect because side-to-side surge does not have a significant effect on the movement of the vehicle when stopping.

14. **(C)**   Although Tank A is taller than Tank B, Tank B is wider than Tank A. Since the shorter height of Tank B is offset by its greater width, it has the same capacity as Tank A. Thus, answer (C) is correct, and answers (A) and (B) are not. The amount of outage required is determined by the properties of the liquid (in particular, by how much the liquid expands when heated), not by the shape of the tank, so answer (D) is incorrect.

15. **(D)**   Answer (A) is incorrect because it is too general; a liquid tank can be baffled or unbaffled. Answers (B) and (C) refer to the shape of the tank as seen from the outside, not its internal construction. Both conventional tanks and low-profile tanks can be baffled or unbaffled, so these answers are also incorrect. "Smoothbore" refers to the fact that inside an unbaffled tank, there is nothing to slow down the flow of the liquid. Answer (D) is correct.

16. **(A)**   Because of liquid surge, curves are especially dangerous when carrying liquid. To be sure that your tank doesn't roll over, you should take on-ramp/off-ramp curves well below the posted speed. Since tests have shown that liquid tankers can overturn at the posted speed limit for a curve, turning at a speed slightly below [answer (B)] or at [answer (C)] the posted speed is risky, and these answers are incorrect. Traveling at a speed greater than the posted speed limit is not only dangerous but illegal. Answer (D) is also incorrect.

17. **(D)**   The capacity of a liquid tank is measured in gallons, not pounds, so answers (A) and (B) are incorrect. Answer (C), 100 gallons, is too small. A portable tank must be able to hold at least 1,000 gallons to be considered a tank vehicle. Answer (D) is correct.

18. **(C)**   The amount of liquid you can legally carry is determined by properties of the liquid (its weight and the amount it expands when heated) and by legal weight limits with which you must comply regardless of the particular material you are carrying. Answers (A), (B), and (D) refer to these factors. The amount of liquid you can legally carry is not affected by how far you are traveling, and so answer (C), the distance to be traveled, is the correct answer to this question.

19. **(D)** Baffles slow down forward and backward movement of liquid, so stopping suddenly is less dangerous for a baffled vehicle than an unbaffled vehicle. Answer (D) is correct. Answer (A), changing lanes on a highway, and answer (B), leaving the highway via a curved off-ramp, are not made easier by the presence of baffles; they are equally dangerous for all liquid tankers, and so these two answers are incorrect. Going up a steep hill is difficult for any loaded vehicle, whether carrying solids or liquids, so answer (C) is incorrect.

20. **(B)** In a partially filled liquid tanker, the liquid will move (surge) in different directions depending on the movement of the vehicle. Surge refers to the movement of the liquid, not the movement of the vehicle, so answer (A) is incorrect. Answer (C), the amount a liquid expands when heated, refers to the outage, or space above a liquid into which it will expand. This is not the same as surge, and this answer is incorrect. Since a correct definition of surge is given by answer (B), the choice of (D), none of the above, is incorrect.

21. **(D)** The tank vehicle's high center of gravity makes the vehicle top-heavy and increases the danger of the vehicle rolling over while taking a curve, especially at a high speed. Answer (A), driving on wet roads, and answer (B), coming to a stop, are more dangerous because of liquid surge, not because of the high center of gravity, so they are incorrect. Going uphill is difficult when driving a loaded vehicle, but the high center of gravity is not a factor here, and answer (C) is incorrect.

22. **(B)** Baffles slow the movement of liquid forward and backward, so an unbaffled vehicle will have greater surge in these directions than one with baffles. Therefore, answer (A) is incorrect and answer (B) is correct. Turning a corner causes side-to-side surge, not backward and forward surge, so answer (C) is incorrect. Going up a hill will tend to push liquid constantly toward the rear of the vehicle, so backward and forward surge is unlikely in this case, and answer (D) is incorrect.

23. **(C)** Liquid tends to move in the direction a vehicle has been moving, so when you stop suddenly the liquid will move forward; when it reaches the front end of the tank, it will be pushed backward. For this reason, answer (C) is correct and answer (D) is not. Up-and-down motion [answer (A)] is caused by up-and-down motion of the vehicle (when traveling over potholes, for example), so this answer is incorrect. Similarly, side-to-side motion [answer (B)] is caused by a sideways motion of the vehicle (when turning, for example), so this answer is incorrect.

24. **(C)** A baffled tank is harder to clean than one without baffles, and transporting liquid foods in a tank that has not been cleaned thoroughly is unsanitary. Therefore, answer (C) is correct. Baffles do not increase the motion of liquid; they slow it. Answer (A) is incorrect. An unbaffled tank is more difficult to handle than

a baffled tank, so it must be driven more slowly in certain situations and answer (B) is incorrect. Since answer (C) gives a proper explanation of the reason for the regulation, answer (D), none of the above, is incorrect.

25. **(A)**   The movement of liquid toward one end of the vehicle increases the weight at that end and acts as a push in that direction. Answer (A) is correct. Since answer (B) says exactly the opposite of this, it is incorrect. Answer (C) is incorrect because liquid moving backward and forward is not likely to cause a sideways motion as extreme as rolling over. Since the correct answer is (A), choice (D), none of the above, is not an appropriate answer.

26. **(D)**   Compartments should not be filled to the top because there must be room for liquid to expand when it becomes heated. Therefore, answer (A) is incorrect. Filling the first or last compartment highest will put more weight at one end of the vehicle and will tend to push the vehicle in that direction. This is unsafe, and answers (B) and (C) are incorrect. Distributing the weight evenly throughout all the compartments is the safest procedure because it allows the most control of the vehicle. Answer (D) is correct.

27. **(B)**   Tank B is designed with baffles. Baffles help control the forward and backward movement of liquids, thereby reducing surge. Answer (A) is incorrect. Tank A is designed with bulkheads which divide the tank into several smaller tanks. Answer (C) is incorrect because Tank C is an unbaffled smoothbore tank which has no means of reducing liquid surge. Because Tank B is the only tank specially designed to reduce liquid surge, answer (D), all of the above, is also incorrect.

28. **(C)**   The presence of baffles decreases forward and backward surge, so the design of Tank B will affect handling in all situations involving forward or backward motion, including starting, stopping, and accelerating. Therefore, answers (A), (B), and (D) are incorrect. Answer (C), turning, refers to sideways motion, and baffles will not affect handling in this situation. Therefore, this is the correct answer.

29. **(A)**   The safest way to load the compartments of a tank is to distribute the weight evenly among all of the compartments. Of the choices given here, answer (A) gives the most even distribution of the 3 liquids. Answer (B) places all of the weight in the middle of the vehicle, while answers (C) and (D) place all of the weight at one of the two ends. These unbalanced distributions give you less control over your vehicle than the distribution in answer (A), which is the best choice.

30. **(D)**   Tank B is a baffled tank. Because sanitation regulations do not allow baffled tanks to be used in the transportation of food products, answer (D), the only food product in this list, is the least likely item to be carried by Tank B.

The Doubles/Triples Test

See directions on page 195.

1. When doing a walkaround inspection of a double or triple trailer, the shut-off valves should be _____ at the rear(s) of the front trailer(s) and _____ at the rear of the last trailer.

    (A) open... closed   (C) closed... open

    (B) latched... open   (D) open... latched

2. Which of the following will probably happen if you are driving a double rig and a set of trailer wheels goes into a skid?

    (A) Nothing: the wheels will straighten themselves out quickly.

    (B) Your trailer will jackknife.

    (C) The entire vehicle will slide into the other lane.

    (D) Your brakes will fail.

3. During a jackknife, it is best to

    (A) jam on the brakes.

    (B) release the brakes to get traction back.

    (C) apply the trailer hand brake.

    (D) simply wait for the trailer to straighten out.

4. While inspecting your converter dolly coupling, you should make sure there is _____ between the upper and lower fifth wheel.

    (A) one inch of space   (C) no space

    (B) a little space   (D) 1/2 inch of space

5. Trucks with trailers have a dangerous "crack-the-whip" effect. Because of this, which of the following vehicle parts is most likely to tip over?

    (A) The rear trailer of a triple

    (B) The truck itself

    (C) The rear trailer of a double

    (D) The entire rig

6. When uncoupling, you should never unlock the _____ with the dolly still under the rear trailer.

    (A) landing gear   (C) service air line

    (B) emergency air line   (D) pintle hook

7.   When turning a double or triple at an intersection, the turn often cannot be completed without swinging wide. Which diagram shows the best way to turn?

(A)   Diagram A   (C)   Diagram C

(B)   Diagram B   (D)   Diagram D

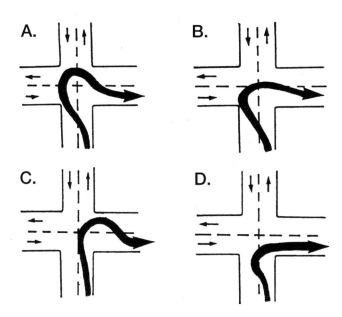

8.   You are driving a tractor with multiple trailers. Which of the following statements about offtracking is true?

(A)   Longer vehicles will offtrack more.

(B)   The rear wheels of a single trailer will offtrack more than the rear wheels of a double trailer.

(C)   The rear wheels of the last trailer follow the same path as the front wheels of the tractor.

(D)   The front wheels of the last trailer are most likely to offtrack.

9.   What is one function of the tractor protection valve?

(A)   To keep air in the tractor should the trailer develop a bad leak

(B)   To keep air in the trailer should the tractor develop a bad leak

(C)   To indicate that the parking brake is on

(D)   To stop any air from going out of the tractor if air pressure drops into the range of 50 to 65 psi

10. You open the emergency line shut-off valve at the rear of the last trailer and hear air escaping. This means
    (A) there is a leak somewhere in the service air line.
    (B) the entire emergency air line system is charged.
    (C) the entire service air line system is charged.
    (D) the shut-off valves on the other trailer(s) and dolly(ies) are in the closed position.

11. Trucks that are empty or lightly loaded
    (A) have poor traction, making it easy to lock up the wheels.
    (B) have a shorter stopping time.
    (C) have flexible suspension springs.
    (D) have little chance of jackknifing.

12. If you are driving a 200-foot triple at 35 mph, what is the minimum amount of space (in seconds) that you should keep ahead of you?
    (A) 10   (C) 25
    (B) 20   (D) 30

13. It is important to check the height of the trailer before connecting a converter dolly to a trailer. The trailer is at the correct height when
    (A) it is raised slightly by the converter dolly's backing under it.
    (B) the trailer and the converter dolly are lined up.
    (C) the trailer is raised high above the converter dolly.
    (D) the kingpin is above the fifth wheel.

14. You are driving with more than one trailer. Which trailer should come first behind the tractor?
    (A) The lightest trailer   (C) The heaviest trailer
    (B) The newest trailer   (D) The oldest trailer

15. Converter dollies often do not have
    (A) spring brakes.   (C) air tank drain valves.
    (B) one or more air tanks.   (D) All of the above.

16. In double and triple trailers, the trailer air supply control should pop or _____ _____ when air pressure drops into the range of 20 to 45 psi.
    (A) begin blinking
    (B) go from "normal" to "emergency" position
    (C) go from "emergency" to "normal" position
    (D) make a buzzing noise

17. When you are pulling trailers, which of the following statements is true about steering?
    (A) There is no difference between steering a straight truck and steering a double or triple.
    (B) The crack-the-whip effect does not apply to doubles and triples.
    (C) It is not dangerous to make quick lane changes.
    (D) If you make a sudden or large steering adjustment, you could tip over one or all of your trailers.

18. When checking the coupling system, make sure that the locking jaws are around the shank of the
    (A) fifth wheel.   (C) kingpin.
    (B) emergency air line.   (D) landing gear.

19. While doing a walkaround inspection of a double or triple, the converter dolly air tank drain valve should be _____, and the pintle hook should be _____ .
    (A) latched... open   (C) open... locked
    (B) closed... locked   (D) closed... open

20. In order to supply air to the air tanks of a second trailer, you must _____ the shut-off valves at the rear of the first trailer and _____ the shut-off valves at the rear of the second trailer.
    (A) close... open   (C) close... close
    (B) open... open   (D) open... close

21. The pintle hook plays a part in
    (A) coupling and uncoupling converter dollies and trailers.
    (B) uncoupling converter dollies and trailers only.
    (C) locking glad hands together.
    (D) locking shut-off valves at the rear of the last trailer.

22. When coupling twin trailers, you should _____ the pintle hook and secure the dolly support in the _____ position.

    (A) release... lowered   (C) disconnect... raised

    (B) lock... raised   (D) lock... coupled

23. _____ should be tested with the hand valve but controlled in normal operation with the foot pedal.

    (A) The parking brake   (C) The trailer brakes

    (B) The tractor brakes   (D) The tractor protection valve

24. When coupling twin trailers, a converter dolly is

    (A) needed between the first and second trailers.

    (B) not needed.

    (C) needed between the tractor and the first trailer.

    (D) needed between both the tractor and the first trailer and the first trailer and the second trailer.

25. What is most likely to happen if the trailer protection valve of a double or triple trailer does not function correctly?

    (A) Air pressure will rise.

    (B) An air hose or trailer brake leak could drain all the air from the tractor.

    (C) The emergency brakes will not work.

    (D) The truck will fill with air.

26. You are driving a triple trailer and there is a loss of air pressure in the emergency line. Which of the following will occur?

    (A) The emergency brakes of all three trailers will come on.

    (B) The emergency brakes of the first two trailers only will come on.

    (C) The tractor's emergency brakes will come on.

    (D) The vehicle will lose all braking power and it will be necessary to use an escape route to stop.

27. Which of the following must be connected when coupling tractor to trailer or trailer to trailer?

    (A) Safety chains   (C) Light cords

    (B) Air hoses   (D) All of the above.

28. Which of the following is true about loading cargo into double or triple trailers?

    (A) Cargo may be piled as high as possible in the first trailer.

    (B) Always pile the heavier cargo on top of the lighter cargo.

    (C) Keep the cargo as close to the ground as possible in every trailer.

    (D) It doesn't matter if the cargo in the first trailer is uncentered.

29. The braking systems of double and triple trailers are different than those of straight trucks because doubles and triples

    (A) never have spring brakes.

    (B) have two service lines.

    (C) have extra parts which control the trailer brakes.

    (D) have two emergency lines.

30. When driving a double or triple trailer, greater care must be given to

    (A) vehicle inspection.   (C) space management.

    (B) following distance.   (D) All of the above.

THE DOUBLES/TRIPLES TEST

ANSWER KEY

1.	(A)	16.	(B)
2.	(B)	17.	(D)
3.	(B)	18.	(C)
4.	(C)	19.	(B)
5.	(A)	20.	(D)
6.	(D)	21.	(A)
7.	(C)	22.	(B)
8.	(A)	23.	(C)
9.	(A)	24.	(A)
10.	(B)	25.	(B)
11.	(A)	26.	(A)
12.	(B)	27.	(D)
13.	(A)	28.	(C)
14.	(C)	29.	(C)
15.	(A)	30.	(D)

DETAILED EXPLANATIONS OF ANSWERS
The Doubles/Triples Test

1. **(A)** Make sure that the shut-off valves are **open** at the rear(s) of the front trailer(s) and **closed** at the rear of the last trailer. This will allow air to flow through the front trailer(s) to the rear trailer, but will not allow air to escape from the vehicle. Answers (B) and (D) are incorrect because shut-off valves have no "latched" position. (C) is an inappropriate choice because the order of positions is incorrect.

2. **(B)** The trailer will tend to swing around, or jackknife, if a set of trailer wheels goes into a skid. This makes (A) incorrect. In a jackknife, the trailer goes in a different direction than the tractor, so (C) is incorrect. (D) is also incorrect. The feeling that you have no trailer brakes is due to loss of traction, not brake failure.

3. **(B)** You must release the brakes to get traction back. (A) is incorrect because applying the brakes hard will only cause you to lose more traction. Since the brakes on the trailer wheels caused the skid in the first place, the trailer hand brake will not correct the jackknife, and therefore (C) is incorrect. (D) is incorrect because the trailer is not likely to straighten out unless you release the brakes.

4. **(C)** Make sure there is **no space** between the upper and lower fifth wheel. Any amount of space indicates improper coupling; therefore, answers (A), (B), and (D) are all incorrect.

5. **(A)** "Rearward amplification" causes the crack-the-whip effect and makes the rear trailer of a triple most likely to tip over. Answers (B), (C), and (D) are all incorrect.

6. **(D)** The **pintle hook** should never be unlocked when the dolly is still under the rear trailer because the dolly tow bar could fly up, possibly causing injury, and making it very difficult to recouple. Answers (A), (B), and (C) are all incorrect because the landing gear must be lowered and both air lines must be disconnected **before** the dolly is moved away.

7. **(C)** When turning a double or triple, you must steer the front end wide enough around a corner so that the rear end does not run over the curb, pedestrians, other vehicles, etc. At the same time you must keep the rear of the vehicle close to the curb to stop other drivers from passing you on the right. (A), (B), and (D) are

all incorrect turning procedures. Swinging wide to the left as you begin the curve may cause other drivers to try to pass you on the right. If you cannot make the turn without entering another lane of traffic, turn wide as you complete the turn.

8. **(A)**   Longer vehicles will always offtrack more than shorter vehicles. Since a single trailer is shorter than a double trailer, (B) is incorrect. (C) is incorrect because offtracking occurs when the rear wheels of the last trailer follow a **different** path than the front wheels of the tractor. Answer (D) is also incorrect. The very last set of wheels always offtracks the most.

9. **(A)**   The tractor protection valve keeps air in the tractor should the trailer develop a bad leak. Thus, answer (B) is incorrect. With a bad leak, air pressure will drop into the range of 20 to 45 psi, not 50 to 65 psi, so (D) is incorrect. (C) is incorrect as well. The tractor protection valve has no bearing on the parking brake.

10. **(B)**   Opening the emergency line shut-off valve at the rear of the last trailer is a way of checking that the entire emergency air line system is charged. Both (A) and (C) are incorrect because you must open the service line shut-off valve to check whether the service air line has any leaks or is fully charged. (D) is incorrect as well. If the other shut-off valves were closed, you would not hear air escaping because there would be no air in the last trailer.

11. **(A)**   Empty or lightly loaded vehicles have less traction than fully loaded vehicles, making it easy to lock up the wheels. (B) is incorrect because it takes longer to stop a vehicle when it is empty than when it is full. (C) is incorrect because the suspension springs on lighter vehicles are stiff, not flexible. Empty or lightly loaded vehicles also have a great jackknifing potential, so (D) is incorrect as well.

12. **(B)**   When driving a 200-foot vehicle at 35 mph, you should allow a following distance of at least twenty seconds. The amount of space can be easily figured out by this formula: allow at least one second for each ten feet of your vehicle length, plus another second if going over 40 mph. Since a following distance of 10 seconds is too few for a 200-foot vehicle, (A) is incorrect. While 25 and 30 seconds are safe following distances, they are greater than the minimum distance for which this question asks; therefore, answers (C) and (D) are incorrect.

13. **(A)**   The trailer should be low enough so that it is raised slightly by the converter dolly when the converter dolly is backed under it. Answers (B) and (C) are incorrect because if the trailer is too low, the converter dolly may strike and damage the nose of the trailer, and if the trailer is too high it may not couple correctly. (D) is also incorrect because the kingpin and the fifth wheel should be aligned.

14. **(C)** The heaviest trailer should always follow the tractor. Since the lighter trailer should be in the rear, (A) is incorrect. (B) and (D) are incorrect because the trailer's age has no bearing on its position.

15. **(A)** Converter dollies built before 1975 are not required to have spring brakes. Since each converter dolly has at least one air tank, (B) is incorrect. Every air tank, whether on a trailer or dolly, has a drain valve, so (C) is incorrect. Because (A) is the only correct answer, (D), all of the above, is not an appropriate choice.

16. **(B)** When air pressure drops into the range of 20 to 45 psi, the tractor protection valve closes, the trailer emergency brakes come on, and the trailer air supply control goes **from "normal" to "emergency."** Thus, (C) is incorrect. Only the movement of the air supply control indicates to you that the air pressure has dropped. The control does not blink or make a buzz. Therefore, both (A) and (D) are incorrect.

17. **(D)** When pulling trailers, you must be careful not to make sudden or large steering adjustments. Because you must be especially careful, (A) is incorrect. (B) is also incorrect because the crack-the-whip effect is a characteristic of trucks with multiple trailers. Since a quick lane change indicates a sudden and large steering adjustment, (C) is incorrect as well.

18. **(C)** The fifth wheel locking jaws should be firmly around the shank of the kingpin. Since the locking jaws are part of the fifth wheel, (A) is incorrect. (B) and (D) are also incorrect because neither the emergency air line nor the landing gear locks into the fifth wheel.

19. **(B)** The converter dolly air tank drain valves should be **closed** and the pintle hook should be **locked** for proper coupling. Answers (A), (C), and (D) all contain incorrect combinations, and are therefore inappropriate choices.

20. **(D)** In order for air to flow through the first trailer and into the second, you must **open** the shut-off valves of the first trailer. To keep the air from leaving the vehicle, however, you must **close** the shut-off valves of the second trailer. Both (A) and (C) are incorrect because if the shut-off valves of the first trailer are closed, air cannot flow into the second trailer. (B) is incorrect as well. If the shut-off valves are open at the rear of the second trailer, all the air flowing into the front of the second trailer will leak out the rear.

21. **(A)** The pintle hook must be locked in order to couple a converter dolly and a trailer properly and must be unlocked in order to disconnect the two. Since the pintle hook is involved in **both** coupling and uncoupling, (B) is incorrect. (C) and

(D) are both incorrect because the pintle hook does not affect the glad hands or the shut-off valves in any way.

22. **(B)** The pintle hook should be **locked**, and the dolly support should be secured in the **raised** position. Proper coupling will not occur otherwise; therefore, (A), (C), and (D) are all incorrect.

23. **(C)** Since the trailer hand valve only operates the trailer brakes, it cannot be used to test the parking brakes, tractor brakes, or tractor protection valve. Answers (A), (B), and (D) are all incorrect.

24. **(A)** In a twin trailer combination, a converter dolly is needed in between the two trailers. Without a converter dolly, the two trailers could not be coupled, so (B) is incorrect. Because the tractor already contains the devices needed to couple it with one trailer, a converter dolly is not used in between the tractor and the first trailer. Both (C) and (D) are incorrect.

25. **(B)** An air hose or trailer brake leak could drain all the air from the tractor. (A) and (D) are incorrect because air will leak out of the vehicle, not rise or fill the vehicle. This air leakage will cause the emergency brakes to come on, so (C) is incorrect as well.

26. **(A)** When there is a loss of air pressure in the emergency line of a triple trailer, the emergency brakes of **all three** trailers will come on. Thus, answer (B) is incorrect. Since the tractor protection valve closes when there is a loss of air pressure in the emergency line, air is stopped from going out of the tractor. Therefore, the tractor's emergency brakes will **not** come on, and answer (C) is incorrect. Answer (D) is also incorrect because both the tractor and the trailers retain some braking power.

27. **(D)** To secure trailers in case of a trailer breakaway, safety chains must be connected when coupling. Air hoses must be connected in order to supply air to the trailer(s). Additionally, unless the light cords are connected, the trailer lights will not operate. Since (A), (B), and (C) must all be connected, answer (D), all of the above, is the appropriate choice.

28. **(C)** No matter how many trailers you are pulling, you must insure a low center of gravity in **each** trailer and protect the rig from rollover. To lower the vehicle's center of gravity, keep the cargo as close to the ground as possible and pile heavy cargo under light cargo. Answers (A) and (B) are incorrect because they do not follow these guidelines. (D) is also incorrect because uncentered cargo in any trailer will cause the rig to lean and increase the risk of rollover.

29. **(C)** The extra parts of double and triple trailers cause them to differ from straight trucks. Answer (A) is incorrect because all trailers built after 1975 are required to have spring brakes. Answers (B) and (D) are incorrect as well. All trucks and trailer combinations, no matter what their size, have only two air lines: one service line and one emergency line.

30. **(D)** Because doubles and triples are larger vehicles, they contain more critical parts that must be inspected by the driver. The largeness of these vehicles also means that they will need more space in which to stop or turn. Following distance must be increased and space to the sides must be managed very carefully. Because (A), (B), and (C) are all important considerations when driving a double or triple trailer, answer (D), all of the above, is the correct choice.

The Commercial Driver License Exam

Answer Sheets

THE COMMERCIAL DRIVER LICENSE EXAM
General Knowledge Test
ANSWER SHEET

1. (A) (B) (C) (D)
2. (A) (B) (C) (D)
3. (A) (B) (C) (D)
4. (A) (B) (C) (D)
5. (A) (B) (C) (D)
6. (A) (B) (C) (D)
7. (A) (B) (C) (D)
8. (A) (B) (C) (D)
9. (A) (B) (C) (D)
10. (A) (B) (C) (D)
11. (A) (B) (C) (D)
12. (A) (B) (C) (D)
13. (A) (B) (C) (D)
14. (A) (B) (C) (D)
15. (A) (B) (C) (D)
16. (A) (B) (C) (D)
17. (A) (B) (C) (D)
18. (A) (B) (C) (D)
19. (A) (B) (C) (D)
20. (A) (B) (C) (D)
21. (A) (B) (C) (D)
22. (A) (B) (C) (D)
23. (A) (B) (C) (D)
24. (A) (B) (C) (D)
25. (A) (B) (C) (D)
26. (A) (B) (C) (D)
27. (A) (B) (C) (D)
28. (A) (B) (C) (D)
29. (A) (B) (C) (D)
30. (A) (B) (C) (D)
31. (A) (B) (C) (D)
32. (A) (B) (C) (D)
33. (A) (B) (C) (D)

34. (A) (B) (C) (D)
35. (A) (B) (C) (D)
36. (A) (B) (C) (D)
37. (A) (B) (C) (D)
38. (A) (B) (C) (D)
39. (A) (B) (C) (D)
40. (A) (B) (C) (D)
41. (A) (B) (C) (D)
42. (A) (B) (C) (D)
43. (A) (B) (C) (D)
44. (A) (B) (C) (D)
45. (A) (B) (C) (D)
46. (A) (B) (C) (D)
47. (A) (B) (C) (D)
48. (A) (B) (C) (D)
49. (A) (B) (C) (D)
50. (A) (B) (C) (D)
51. (A) (B) (C) (D)
52. (A) (B) (C) (D)
53. (A) (B) (C) (D)
54. (A) (B) (C) (D)
55. (A) (B) (C) (D)
56. (A) (B) (C) (D)
57. (A) (B) (C) (D)
58. (A) (B) (C) (D)
59. (A) (B) (C) (D)
60. (A) (B) (C) (D)
61. (A) (B) (C) (D)
62. (A) (B) (C) (D)
63. (A) (B) (C) (D)
64. (A) (B) (C) (D)
65. (A) (B) (C) (D)
66. (A) (B) (C) (D)
67. (A) (B) (C) (D)

68. (A) (B) (C) (D)
69. (A) (B) (C) (D)
70. (A) (B) (C) (D)
71. (A) (B) (C) (D)
72. (A) (B) (C) (D)
73. (A) (B) (C) (D)
74. (A) (B) (C) (D)
75. (A) (B) (C) (D)
76. (A) (B) (C) (D)
77. (A) (B) (C) (D)
78. (A) (B) (C) (D)
79. (A) (B) (C) (D)
80. (A) (B) (C) (D)
81. (A) (B) (C) (D)
82. (A) (B) (C) (D)
83. (A) (B) (C) (D)
84. (A) (B) (C) (D)
85. (A) (B) (C) (D)
86. (A) (B) (C) (D)
87. (A) (B) (C) (D)
88. (A) (B) (C) (D)
89. (A) (B) (C) (D)
90. (A) (B) (C) (D)
91. (A) (B) (C) (D)
92. (A) (B) (C) (D)
93. (A) (B) (C) (D)
94. (A) (B) (C) (D)
95. (A) (B) (C) (D)
96. (A) (B) (C) (D)
97. (A) (B) (C) (D)
98. (A) (B) (C) (D)
99. (A) (B) (C) (D)
100. (A) (B) (C) (D)

THE COMMERCIAL DRIVER LICENSE EXAM
Endorsement Tests
ANSWER SHEETS

Please use the following answer blanks for any of the Endorsement Tests.

1. (A) (B) (C) (D)	1. (A) (B) (C) (D)	1. (A) (B) (C) (D)
2. (A) (B) (C) (D)	2. (A) (B) (C) (D)	2. (A) (B) (C) (D)
3. (A) (B) (C) (D)	3. (A) (B) (C) (D)	3. (A) (B) (C) (D)
4. (A) (B) (C) (D)	4. (A) (B) (C) (D)	4. (A) (B) (C) (D)
5. (A) (B) (C) (D)	5. (A) (B) (C) (D)	5. (A) (B) (C) (D)
6. (A) (B) (C) (D)	6. (A) (B) (C) (D)	6. (A) (B) (C) (D)
7. (A) (B) (C) (D)	7. (A) (B) (C) (D)	7. (A) (B) (C) (D)
8. (A) (B) (C) (D)	8. (A) (B) (C) (D)	8. (A) (B) (C) (D)
9. (A) (B) (C) (D)	9. (A) (B) (C) (D)	9. (A) (B) (C) (D)
10. (A) (B) (C) (D)	10. (A) (B) (C) (D)	10. (A) (B) (C) (D)
11. (A) (B) (C) (D)	11. (A) (B) (C) (D)	11. (A) (B) (C) (D)
12. (A) (B) (C) (D)	12. (A) (B) (C) (D)	12. (A) (B) (C) (D)
13. (A) (B) (C) (D)	13. (A) (B) (C) (D)	13. (A) (B) (C) (D)
14. (A) (B) (C) (D)	14. (A) (B) (C) (D)	14. (A) (B) (C) (D)
15. (A) (B) (C) (D)	15. (A) (B) (C) (D)	15. (A) (B) (C) (D)
16. (A) (B) (C) (D)	16. (A) (B) (C) (D)	16. (A) (B) (C) (D)
17. (A) (B) (C) (D)	17. (A) (B) (C) (D)	17. (A) (B) (C) (D)
18. (A) (B) (C) (D)	18. (A) (B) (C) (D)	18. (A) (B) (C) (D)
19. (A) (B) (C) (D)	19. (A) (B) (C) (D)	19. (A) (B) (C) (D)
20. (A) (B) (C) (D)	20. (A) (B) (C) (D)	20. (A) (B) (C) (D)
21. (A) (B) (C) (D)	21. (A) (B) (C) (D)	21. (A) (B) (C) (D)
22. (A) (B) (C) (D)	22. (A) (B) (C) (D)	22. (A) (B) (C) (D)
23. (A) (B) (C) (D)	23. (A) (B) (C) (D)	23. (A) (B) (C) (D)
24. (A) (B) (C) (D)	24. (A) (B) (C) (D)	24. (A) (B) (C) (D)
25. (A) (B) (C) (D)	25. (A) (B) (C) (D)	25. (A) (B) (C) (D)
26. (A) (B) (C) (D)	26. (A) (B) (C) (D)	26. (A) (B) (C) (D)
27. (A) (B) (C) (D)	27. (A) (B) (C) (D)	27. (A) (B) (C) (D)
28. (A) (B) (C) (D)	28. (A) (B) (C) (D)	28. (A) (B) (C) (D)
29. (A) (B) (C) (D)	29. (A) (B) (C) (D)	29. (A) (B) (C) (D)
30. (A) (B) (C) (D)	30. (A) (B) (C) (D)	30. (A) (B) (C) (D)

1. Ⓐ Ⓑ Ⓒ Ⓓ	1. Ⓐ Ⓑ Ⓒ Ⓓ	1. Ⓐ Ⓑ Ⓒ Ⓓ
2. Ⓐ Ⓑ Ⓒ Ⓓ	2. Ⓐ Ⓑ Ⓒ Ⓓ	2. Ⓐ Ⓑ Ⓒ Ⓓ
3. Ⓐ Ⓑ Ⓒ Ⓓ	3. Ⓐ Ⓑ Ⓒ Ⓓ	3. Ⓐ Ⓑ Ⓒ Ⓓ
4. Ⓐ Ⓑ Ⓒ Ⓓ	4. Ⓐ Ⓑ Ⓒ Ⓓ	4. Ⓐ Ⓑ Ⓒ Ⓓ
5. Ⓐ Ⓑ Ⓒ Ⓓ	5. Ⓐ Ⓑ Ⓒ Ⓓ	5. Ⓐ Ⓑ Ⓒ Ⓓ
6. Ⓐ Ⓑ Ⓒ Ⓓ	6. Ⓐ Ⓑ Ⓒ Ⓓ	6. Ⓐ Ⓑ Ⓒ Ⓓ
7. Ⓐ Ⓑ Ⓒ Ⓓ	7. Ⓐ Ⓑ Ⓒ Ⓓ	7. Ⓐ Ⓑ Ⓒ Ⓓ
8. Ⓐ Ⓑ Ⓒ Ⓓ	8. Ⓐ Ⓑ Ⓒ Ⓓ	8. Ⓐ Ⓑ Ⓒ Ⓓ
9. Ⓐ Ⓑ Ⓒ Ⓓ	9. Ⓐ Ⓑ Ⓒ Ⓓ	9. Ⓐ Ⓑ Ⓒ Ⓓ
10. Ⓐ Ⓑ Ⓒ Ⓓ	10. Ⓐ Ⓑ Ⓒ Ⓓ	10. Ⓐ Ⓑ Ⓒ Ⓓ
11. Ⓐ Ⓑ Ⓒ Ⓓ	11. Ⓐ Ⓑ Ⓒ Ⓓ	11. Ⓐ Ⓑ Ⓒ Ⓓ
12. Ⓐ Ⓑ Ⓒ Ⓓ	12. Ⓐ Ⓑ Ⓒ Ⓓ	12. Ⓐ Ⓑ Ⓒ Ⓓ
13. Ⓐ Ⓑ Ⓒ Ⓓ	13. Ⓐ Ⓑ Ⓒ Ⓓ	13. Ⓐ Ⓑ Ⓒ Ⓓ
14. Ⓐ Ⓑ Ⓒ Ⓓ	14. Ⓐ Ⓑ Ⓒ Ⓓ	14. Ⓐ Ⓑ Ⓒ Ⓓ
15. Ⓐ Ⓑ Ⓒ Ⓓ	15. Ⓐ Ⓑ Ⓒ Ⓓ	15. Ⓐ Ⓑ Ⓒ Ⓓ
16. Ⓐ Ⓑ Ⓒ Ⓓ	16. Ⓐ Ⓑ Ⓒ Ⓓ	16. Ⓐ Ⓑ Ⓒ Ⓓ
17. Ⓐ Ⓑ Ⓒ Ⓓ	17. Ⓐ Ⓑ Ⓒ Ⓓ	17. Ⓐ Ⓑ Ⓒ Ⓓ
18. Ⓐ Ⓑ Ⓒ Ⓓ	18. Ⓐ Ⓑ Ⓒ Ⓓ	18. Ⓐ Ⓑ Ⓒ Ⓓ
19. Ⓐ Ⓑ Ⓒ Ⓓ	19. Ⓐ Ⓑ Ⓒ Ⓓ	19. Ⓐ Ⓑ Ⓒ Ⓓ
20. Ⓐ Ⓑ Ⓒ Ⓓ	20. Ⓐ Ⓑ Ⓒ Ⓓ	20. Ⓐ Ⓑ Ⓒ Ⓓ
21. Ⓐ Ⓑ Ⓒ Ⓓ	21. Ⓐ Ⓑ Ⓒ Ⓓ	21. Ⓐ Ⓑ Ⓒ Ⓓ
22. Ⓐ Ⓑ Ⓒ Ⓓ	22. Ⓐ Ⓑ Ⓒ Ⓓ	22. Ⓐ Ⓑ Ⓒ Ⓓ
23. Ⓐ Ⓑ Ⓒ Ⓓ	23. Ⓐ Ⓑ Ⓒ Ⓓ	23. Ⓐ Ⓑ Ⓒ Ⓓ
24. Ⓐ Ⓑ Ⓒ Ⓓ	24. Ⓐ Ⓑ Ⓒ Ⓓ	24. Ⓐ Ⓑ Ⓒ Ⓓ
25. Ⓐ Ⓑ Ⓒ Ⓓ	25. Ⓐ Ⓑ Ⓒ Ⓓ	25. Ⓐ Ⓑ Ⓒ Ⓓ
26. Ⓐ Ⓑ Ⓒ Ⓓ	26. Ⓐ Ⓑ Ⓒ Ⓓ	26. Ⓐ Ⓑ Ⓒ Ⓓ
27. Ⓐ Ⓑ Ⓒ Ⓓ	27. Ⓐ Ⓑ Ⓒ Ⓓ	27. Ⓐ Ⓑ Ⓒ Ⓓ
28. Ⓐ Ⓑ Ⓒ Ⓓ	28. Ⓐ Ⓑ Ⓒ Ⓓ	28. Ⓐ Ⓑ Ⓒ Ⓓ
29. Ⓐ Ⓑ Ⓒ Ⓓ	29. Ⓐ Ⓑ Ⓒ Ⓓ	29. Ⓐ Ⓑ Ⓒ Ⓓ
30. Ⓐ Ⓑ Ⓒ Ⓓ	30. Ⓐ Ⓑ Ⓒ Ⓓ	30. Ⓐ Ⓑ Ⓒ Ⓓ

The Commercial Driver License Exam

CDL
Directory

KEY COMMERCIAL DRIVER LICENSE CONTACTS*

ALABAMA
Department of Public Safety
Public Information/Driver License

Mailing Address:
P.O. Box 1471
Montgomery, AL 36102

Walk-In:
301 South Ripley St.
Montgomery, AL 36102

Phone: (334) 242-4400
Email: info@dps.state.al.us
Website: www.dps.state.al.us

ALASKA
Mailing Address / Walk-In:
Division of Motor Vehicles
1300 West Benson Boulevard,
Suite 200
Anchorage, AK 99503

Phone: (907) 269-5551
Email: dmv_webmaster@admin.
state.ak.us
Website: www.state.ak.us/dmv

ARIZONA
Department of Transportation
Motor Vehicle Division

Mailing Address:
PO Box 2100
Phoenix, AZ 85001-2100

Walk-In:
2739 E. Washington St.
Phoenix, AZ 85034

Phone: (602) 255-0072
Email: mvdinfo@azdot.gov
Website: www.azdot.gov/mvd

ARKANSAS
Office of Driver Services

Mailing Address:
P.O. Box 1272
Little Rock, AR 72203

Walk-In:
Ragland Building, Room 2067
1900 West Seventh Street
Little Rock, AR 72201

Phone: (501) 682-7060
Email: susan.sims@rev.state.ar.us
Website: www.arkansas.gov/dfa/
driver_services

* While Research & Education Association has made every effort to provide the most accurate, up-to-date information, readers should be aware that the information contained herein is subject to change at any time. Please consult your driving instructor.

CALIFORNIA
Department of Motor Vehicles

Mailing Address:
2415 1st Avenue Mail Station
F101
Sacramento, CA 95818

Walk-In:
4700 Broadway
Sacramento, CA 95820

Phone: (800) 777-0133
Email: The Automated E-mail
System is not available at this time.
Website: www.dmv.ca.gov

COLORADO
Motor Vehicle Division
Driver Services Division

Mailing Address:
Driver Services, Room 164
Denver, CO 80261-0016

Walk-In:
1881 Pierce Street
Lakewood, CO 80214

Phone: (303) 205-5613
Email: n/a
Website: www.revenue.state.co.us/
mv_dir

CONNECTICUT
Mailing Address / Walk-In:
Department of Motor Vehicles
60 State Street, Room 239
Wethersfield, CT 06161

Phone: (860) 263-5700
Email: mail@dmvct.org
Website: www.ct.gov/dmv

DELAWARE
Division of Motor Vehicles

Mailing Address:
P.O. Box 698
Dover, DE 19903

Walk-In:
303 Transportation Circle
Dover, DE 19903

Phone: (302) 744-2500
Email: dot-public-relations@state.de.us
Website: www.dmv.de.gov

DISTRICT OF COLUMBIA
DC Department of Motor Vehicles

Mailing Address / Walk-In:
301 C Street NW
Washington, DC 20001

Phone: (202) 727-5000
Email: use website response form
Website: dmv.washingtondc.gov

FLORIDA
Florida Department of Highway
Safety and Motor Vehicles
Division of Driver Licenses

Mailing Address / Walk-In:
Neil Kirkman Building
2900 Apalachee Parkway
Tallahassee, FL 32399-0500

Phone: (850) 922-9000
Email: DDL@hsmv.state.fl.us
Website: www.hsmv.state.fl.us

GEORGIA

Department of Motor
Vehicle Safety

Mailing Address:
P.O. Box 740381
Atlanta, GA 30374-0381

Walk-In:
2206 East View Parkway
Conyers, GA 30013

Phone: (678) 413-8400
Email: n/a
Website: www.dmvs.ga.gov

HAWAII

Mailing Address / Walk-In:
Division of Motor Vehicles
and Licensing
1199 Dillingham Blvd
Honolulu, HI 96817

Phone: (808) 532-7700
Email: n/a
Website: n/a

IDAHO

Idaho Transportation Department
Division of Motor Vehicles /
Driver Services Section

Mailing Address:
P.O. Box 7129
Boise, ID 83707-1129

Walk-In:
3311 W. State Street
Boise, ID 83707-1129

Phone: (208) 334-8735
Email: webmaster@itd.state.id.us
Website: itd.idaho.gov/dmv/

ILLINOIS

Mailing Address / Walk-In:
Department of Driver Services
2701 S. Dirksen Parkway
Springfield, IL 62723

Phone: (217) 782-6212
Email: use website response form
Website: www.sos.state.il.us/
departments/drivers

INDIANA

Mailing Address / Walk-In:
Indiana Bureau of Motor Vehicles
100 N. Senate Ave.
Indianapolis, IN 46204

Phone: (317) 233-6000
Email: use website response form
Website: www.in.gov/bmv

IOWA

Iowa Motor Vehicle Division

Mailing Address:
Park Fair Mall
P.O. Box 9204
Des Moines, IA 50306-9204

Walk-In:
Park Fair Mall
100 Euclid Ave.
Des Moines, IA 50306-9204

Phone: (800) 532-1121
Email: sonya.willis@dot.state.ia.us
Website: www.dot.state.ia.us/mvd

KANSAS

Department of Revenue
Division of Motor Vehicles

Mailing Address:
Driver's Licensing
Docking State Office Building
P.O. Box 2188
Topeka, KS 66601-2128

Walk-In:
Docking State Office Building
915 SW Harrison Street
1st Floor
Topeka, KS 66625

Phone: (785) 296-3963
Email: driver_license@kdor.state.ks.us
Website: www.ksrevenue.org/vehicle

KENTUCKY

Kentucky Transportation Cabinet
Division of Motor Vehicle Licensing

Mailing Address:
P.O. Box 2014
Frankfort, KY 40602-2014

Walk-In:
200 Mero Street
Frankfort, KY 40622

Phone: (502) 564-6800
Email: kytc.kyrenew@ky.gov
Website: www.kytc.state.ky.us/mvl

LOUISIANA

Office of Motor Vehicles

Mailing Address:
P.O. Box 64886
Baton Rouge, LA 70896

Walk-In:
7979 Independence Blvd.
Baton Rouge, LA 70806

Phone: (877) 368-5463
Email: Online email form
Website: omv.dps.state.la.us

MAINE

Bureau of Motor Vehicles

Mailing Address:
29 State House Station
Augusta, ME 04333

Walk-In:
101 Hospital Street
Augusta, ME 04333

Phone: (207) 624-9000
Email: n/a
Website: www.state.me.us/sos/bmv

MARYLAND

Department of Transportation
Motor Vehicle Administration

Mailing Address / Walk-In:
6601 Ritchie Highway NE
Glen Burnie, MD 21062

Phone: (800) 950-1682
Email: MVACS@mdot.state.md.us
Website: mva.state.md.us

MASSACHUSETTS

Registry of Motor Vehicles

Mailing Address / Walk-In:
630 Washington St.
Boston, MA 02114

Phone: (800) 858-3926
Email: Online email form
Website: www.mass.gov/rmv

MICHIGAN

Department of State
Treasury Building

Mailing Address:
Michigan Department of State
Lansing, MI 48918

Walk-In:
430 West Allegan St.
Lansing, MI 48922-0001

Phone: (517) 322-1460
Email: n/a
Website: www.michigan.gov/sos

MINNESOTA

Department of Public Safety
Driver and Vehicle Services

Mailing Address / Walk-In:
445 Minnesota St.
St Paul, MN 55101-5175

Phone: (651) 296-6911
Email: motor.vehicles@state.mn.us
Website: www.dps.state.mn.us/dvs

MISSISSIPPI

Highway Patrol – Driver Services
Commercial Driver License Services

Mailing Address:
P.O. Box 958
Jackson, NS 39205

Phone: (601) 987-1215
Email: gwhite@mdps.state.ms.us
Website: www.dps.state.ms.us

MISSOURI

Department of Revenue
Division of Motor Vehicle &
Driver Licensing

Mailing Address:
301 West High Street, Room 470
PO Box 200
Jefferson City, MO, 65105-0100

Walk-In:
Truman Office Building, Room 470
301 West High Street
Jefferson City, MO 65101

Phone: (573) 751-4600
Email: dlbmail@dor.mo.gov
Website: www.dor.mo.gov/mvdl

MONTANA
Motor Vehicle Division
Department of Justice

Mailing Address:
Scott Hart Building, Second Floor
303 North Roberts
Helena, MT 59620-1430

Walk-In:
Scott Hart Building, Second Floor
303 North Roberts
Helena, MT 59620-1430

Phone: (406) 444-1773
Email: mvd@mt.gov
Website: www.doj.state.mt.us/
department/motorvehicledivision

NEBRASKA
Nebraska Department of
Motor Vehicles Driver and
Vehicle Records Division

Mailing Address:
P.O. Box 94789
Lincoln, NE 68509-4789

Walk-In:
301 Centennial Mall South
Lincoln, NE 68509-4789

Phone: (402) 471-3918
Email: dvrweb@dmv.state.ne.us
Website: www.dmv.state.ne.us/dvr

NEVADA
Nevada Department of Motor
Vehicles

Mailing Address / Walk-In:
555 Wright Way
Carson City, NV 89711

Phone: (702) 486-4368
Email: info@dmv.state.nv.us
Website: www.dmvstat.com

NEW HAMPSHIRE
Department of Safety
Division of Motor Vehicles

Mailing Address / Walk-In:
23 Hazen Drive
Concord NH 03305

Phone: (603) 271-2371
Email: n/a
Website: www.nh.gov/safety/dmv

NEW JERSEY
Motor Vehicle Commission

Mailing Address:
P.O. Box 008
Trenton, NJ 08666-0008

Walk-In:
120 S. Stockton
Trenton, NJ 08611

Note: CDL *permits* are issued at all
NJ Motor Vehicle Agencies.

Phone: (888) 486-3339
Email: Use online form
Website: www.state.nj.us/mvc

NEW MEXICO
Motor Vehicle Division

Mailing Address:
P.O. Box 1028
Joseph Montoya Bldg
Santa Fe, NM 87504-1028

Walk-In:
Joseph Montoya Bldg
1100 S. St. Francis Dr.
Santa Fe, NM 87504-0630

Phone: (888) 683-4636
Email: GGarcia@state.nm.us
Website: www.state.nm.us/tax/ mvd/mvd_home

NEW YORK
Department of Motor Vehicles

Mailing Address:
Swan Street Building, Room 221
Empire State Plaza
Albany, NY 12228

Walk-In:
6 Empire State Plaza
Albany, NY 12228

Phone: (800) 342-5368
or (800) 225-5368
Email: Use online form
Website: www.nydmv.state.ny.us

NORTH CAROLINA
Division of Motor Vehicles

Mailing Address:
3148 Mail Service Center
Raleigh, NC 27699-3101

Walk-In:
1100 New Bern Ave.
Raleigh, NC 27697

Phone: (919) 715-7000
Email: use online form
Website: www.ncdot.org/DMV

NORTH DAKOTA
Department of Transportation
Drivers License and Traffic Safety

Mailing Address / Walk-In:
608 East Boulevard
Bismarck, ND 58505-0700

Phone: (701) 328-2600
Email: dot@state.nd.us
Website: www.state.nd.us/dot

OHIO
Department of Public Safety
Bureau of Motor Vehicles

Mailing Address:
P.O. Box 182081
Columbus, OH 43218-2081

Walk-In:
1970 West Broad Street
Columbus, OH 43218-2081

Phone: (614) 752-7500
Email: n/a
Website: bmv.ohio.gov/bmv

OKLAHOMA

Oklahoma Department of
Public Safety

Mailing Address:
Comment/Complaint Review
PO Box 11415
Oklahoma City, OK 73136-0415

Walk-In:
2501 Lincoln Blvd.
Oklahoma City, OK 73194

Phone: (405) 521-3101
Email: comment@dps.state.ok.us
Website: www.dps.state.ok.us

OREGON

Department of Transportation

Mailing Address / Walk-In:
DMV Headquarters
1905 Lana Ave NE
Salem, OR 97314

Phone: (888) 275-6368
Email: Use online form
Website: www.oregon.gov/ODOT

PENNSYLVANIA

Department of Transportation
Driver and Vehicle Services

Mailing Address / Walk-In:
1101 South Front Street
Harrisburg, PA 17104

Phone: (800) 932-4600
Email: Use online form
Website: www.dmv.state.pa.us

RHODE ISLAND

Division of Motor Vehicles

Mailing Address / Walk-In:
Apex Mall
(temporary location for 2005)
100 Main Street
Pawtucket, RI 02860

Phone: (401) 588-3020
Email: n/a
Website: www.dmv.state.ri.us

SOUTH CAROLINA

Department of Public Safety
Division of Motor Vehicles

Mailing Address:
Post Office Box 1498
Blythewood, SC 29016

Walk-In:
10311 Wilson Blvd., Building C
Blythewood, SC 29016

Phone: (803) 896-5000
Email: help@scdmvonline.com
Website: www.scdmvonline.com

SOUTH DAKOTA

Department of Revenue
Driver Licensing Division

Mailing Address / Walk-In:
118 W. Capitol Ave.
Pierre, SD 57501-2080

Phone: (800) 952-3696
Email: dps.sdlicensinginfo@state.
sd.us
Website: www.state.sd.us/dps/dl

TENNESSEE
Department of Safety

Mailing Address / Walk-In:
1150 Foster Avenue
Nashville, TN 37249

Phone: (615) 251-5310
Email: safety@state.tn.us
Website: www.tennessee.gov/safety

TEXAS
Department of Public Safety
Driver License Division

Mailing Address:
P O Box 4087
Austin, TX 78773-0001

Walk-In:
5805 North Lamar Blvd
Austin, TX 78752-4422

Phone: (512) 424-2000
Email: license.issuance@txdps.
state.tx.us
Website: www.txdps.state.tx.us/
administration/driver_licensing_
control

UTAH
Department of Public Safety
Driver License Division

Mailing Address:
PO Box 30560
Salt Lake City, UT 84130-0560

Phone: (801) 965-4437
Email: Use online form
Website: driverlicense.utah.gov

VERMONT
Division of Motor Vehicles

Mailing Address / Walk-In:
120 State St.
Montpelier, VT 05603-0001

Phone: (802) 828-2000
Email: bette.bailey@state.vt.us
Website: www.aot.state.vt.us/
dmv/dmvhp

VIRGINIA
Department of Motor Vehicles

Mailing Address:
P.O. Box 27412
Richmond, VA 23269

Walk-In:
2300 West Broad Street
Richmond, VA 23220

Phone: (866) 368-5463
Email: Use online form
Website: www.dmv.state.va.us

WASHINGTON
Department of Licensing
Driver Services

Mailing Address:
PO Box 9030
Olympia, WA 98507-9030

Phone: (360) 902-3900
Email: commercial@dol.wa.gov
Website: www.dol.wa.gov

WEST VIRGINIA

Department of Transportation
Division of Motor Vehicles

Mailing Address / Walk-In:
Building 3, Capitol Complex
1800 Kanawha Boulevard East
Charleston, WV 25317

Phone: (800) 642-9066
Email: dmvcommissioner@dot.
state.wv.us
Website: www.wvdot.com/6_
motorists/dmv

WISCONSIN

Department of Motor Vehicles
Department of Transportation
(WisDOT)

Mailing Address:
P.O. Box 7995
Madison, WI 53707-7995

Phone: (608) 266-2353
Email: driverrecords.dmv@dot.
state.wi.us
Website: www.dot.wisconsin.
gov/drivers

WYOMING

Department of Transportation

Mailing Address / Walk-In:
5300 Bishop Blvd
Cheyenne, WY 82009-3340

Phone: (307) 777-4375
Email: Use online form
Website: www.dot.state.wy.us

CANADA

Mailing Address / Walk-In:
1570 Walkley Rd.
Ottawa, ON K1V 5P6
Canada

Phone: (800) 387-3445
Email: Use online form
Website: www.mto.gov.on.ca

Available at your local bookstore or order directly from us by sending in coupon below.

The High School Tutors®

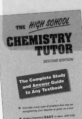

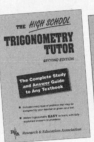
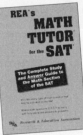

The **HIGH SCHOOL TUTOR** series is based on the same principle as the more comprehensive **PROBLEM SOLVERS**, but is specifically designed to meet the needs of high school students. REA has revised all the books in this series to include expanded review sections and new material. This makes the books even more effective in helping students to cope with these difficult high school subjects.

If you would like more information about any of these books,
complete the coupon below and return it to us or go to your local bookstore.

RESEARCH & EDUCATION ASSOCIATION
61 Ethel Road W. • Piscataway, New Jersey 08854
Phone: (732) 819-8880   **website: www.rea.com**

Please send me more information about your High School Tutor books.

Name _____

Address _____

City _____ State _____ Zip _____

REA's Test Preps
The Best in Test Preparation

- REA "Test Preps" are **far more** comprehensive than any other test preparation series
- Each book contains up to **eight** full-length practice tests based on the most recent exams
- **Every** type of question likely to be given on the exams is included
- Answers are accompanied by **full** and **detailed** explanations

REA publishes over 60 Test Preparation volumes in several series. They include:

Advanced Placement Exams(APs)
Biology
Calculus AB & Calculus BC
Chemistry
Computer Science
Economics
English Language & Composition
English Literature & Composition
European History
Government & Politics
Physics B & C
Psychology
Spanish Language
Statistics
United States History

College-Level Examination Program (CLEP)
Analyzing and Interpreting Literature
College Algebra
Freshman College Composition
General Examinations
General Examinations Review
History of the United States I
History of the United States II
Human Growth and Development
Introductory Sociology
Principles of Marketing
Spanish

SAT II: Subject Tests
Biology E/M
Chemistry
English Language Proficiency Test
French
German

SAT II: Subject Tests (cont'd)
Literature
Mathematics Level IC, IIC
Physics
Spanish
United States History
Writing

Graduate Record Exams (GREs)
Biology
Chemistry
Computer Science
General
Literature in English
Mathematics
Physics
Psychology

ACT - ACT Assessment

ASVAB - Armed Services Vocational Aptitude Battery

CBEST - California Basic Educational Skills Test

CDL - Commercial Driver License Exam

CLAST - College Level Academic Skills Test

COOP & HSPT - Catholic High School Admission Tests

ELM - California State University Entry Level Mathematics Exam

FE (EIT) - Fundamentals of Engineering Exams - For both AM & PM Exams

FTCE - Florida Teacher Certification Exam

GED - High School Equivalency Diploma Exam (U.S. & Canadian editions)

GMAT CAT - Graduate Management Admission Test

LSAT - Law School Admission Test

MAT- Miller Analogies Test

MCAT - Medical College Admission Test

MTEL - Massachusetts Tests for Educator Licensure

MSAT- Multiple Subjects Assessment for Teachers

NJ HSPA - New Jersey High School Proficiency Assessment

NYSTCE: LAST & ATS-W - New York State Teacher Certification

PLT - Principles of Learning & Teaching Tests

PPST- Pre-Professional Skills Tests

PSAT - Preliminary Scholastic Assessment Test

SAT

TExES - Texas Examinations of Educator Standards

THEA - Texas Higher Education Assessment

TOEFL - Test of English as a Foreign Language

TOEIC - Test of English for International Communication

USMLE Steps 1,2,3 - U.S. Medical Licensing Exams

U.S. Postal Exams 460 & 470
